D0341605

ALSO BY RACHEL COHEN

A Chance Meeting: Intertwined Lives of American Writers and Artists

Bernard Berenson: A Life in the Picture Trade

Austen Years

Austen Years

A

MEMOIR

IN

FIVE NOVELS

RACHEL COHEN

Farrar, Straus and Giroux
New York

Farrar, Straus and Giroux
120 Broadway, New York 10271

Copyright © 2020 by Rachel Cohen
All rights reserved
Printed in the United States of America
First edition, 2020

Library of Congress Cataloging-in-Publication Data
Names: Cohen, Rachel, 1973– author.
Title: Austen years : a memoir in five novels / Rachel Cohen.
Description: First edition. | New York : Farrar, Straus and Giroux, 2020. | Includes
    bibliographical references.
Identifiers: LCCN 2019056414 | ISBN 9780374107031 (hardcover)
Subjects: LCSH: Cohen, Rachel, 1973-—Books and reading. | Austen, Jane,
    1775–1817—Appreciation. | Austen, Jane, 1775–1817—Influence. | Books and
    reading—Psychological aspects. | Meaning (Philosophy) in literature. |
    Grief—Biography.
Classification: LCC PS3603.O374 Z46 2020 | DDC 814/.6 [B]—dc23
LC record available at https://lccn.loc.gov/2019056414

Designed by Abby Kagan

Our books may be purchased in bulk for promotional, educational, or business use.
Please contact your local bookseller or the Macmillan Corporate and Premium Sales
Department at 1-800-221-7945, extension 5442, or by e-mail at
MacmillanSpecialMarkets@macmillan.com.

www.fsgbooks.com
www.twitter.com/fsgbooks • www.facebook.com/fsgbooks

1   3   5   7   9   10   8   6   4   2

For Sylvia and Tobias,
for Matt,

and in memory of
Michael Cohen

In a small way having children learn to read is a warning of their growing up and leaving home.

—Michael Cohen, diary, September 28, 1981

She read it again. Widely different was the effect of a second perusal.

—Jane Austen, *Pride and Prejudice*

CONTENTS

One

THE BEGINNING

A READER

About seven years ago, not too long before our daughter was born, and a year before my father died, Jane Austen became my only author. I began to read her before sleep every night, and when I woke in the night; I read her at my desk when I couldn't make progress with the biography I was supposed to have finished writing, and on the slow bus that crossed the river to the ob-gyn. I would come to the end of a scene and turn the leaves back to read it again, almost without noticing. I was not sure what to make of my condition.

Was this a retreat, a seclusion? Life was running thin and fast across unfamiliar land. A baby was coming, a baby that M and I had wanted for a long time. We had known each other for twenty-one years and had been together for four. He and I are both slow to step forward. I had lived and taught in New York, but now we were where he taught, in Cambridge, Massachusetts. The rhythm of days altered.

My father was ill. His cancer had recurred two years before I got pregnant. We were going forward, and we were also waiting. Sometimes anticipation was joyful; at other moments, time held like that odd prolongation one may feel right before an accident.

The world careened. When I saw pictures in the news of people who had been hurt, or killed, I was newly aware of the mourners at the edges and beyond the edges of the pictures. Over every person I saw cross the street seemed to hover the anxious thought "That is a mother's child." I had stopped teaching and did not have a place to tend. The weather, the seasons, were unpredictable and strange. At night, I folded up the day, as I did the small clothes people were giving us, uneasily.

In the past, as I had worked on writing my first book, and on different series of essays, if anyone happened to ask me what I was reading, I was relieved. To say "I'm reading James Baldwin," or "I'm reading Russian poets," was to give the truthful answer one never does to the polite question "How are you?" I had meant, among other things, "I'm paying attention." Now I sat on the bus that went across the river, with a finger holding a place in *Persuasion*, and heard again in my mind the sound of the coming baby's heartbeat. On the pages, there was asperity, definiteness, endings known, bearable, even triumphant. Still, if you had told me that years were coming when I would hardly pick up another serious writer with any real concentration, that the doings of a few English families would come to define almost the entire territory of my reading imagination, and that I would reach a point of such familiarity that I would simply let Austen's books fall open and read a sentence or two as people in other times and places might use an almanac to soothe and predict, I would have been appalled.

The baby was born, in spring. Light and sound ran through her, every lamp, every shadow of a leaf. I would walk with her in the streets around our apartment, stepping softly because she would startle awake at any passing car. I tried to be with her, I was with her, in that hushed iridescence. This is still the atmosphere around S, quiet, intent.

In those first months, I would sometimes walk with her into one of two used bookstores, but the books seemed almost to repel me. I bought other copies of Jane Austen's novels, ones with abstract covers, or interesting prefaces. In the evenings, we would put S to sleep next to our bed, in the cradle that had been mine when I was a baby, and then my sister's, then, decades later, her daughter's, and now was ours. M and I had attached a mobile with soft turtles to it; the light from the streetlamp outside would shadow the turtles on the wall, and they would tremble as S moved a little in her sleep. Coming and going in the night, I would read a few lines from *Persuasion*, and then a few more.

There was repose near Anne Elliot, who was experienced, and thoughtful. She had fallen in love with Captain Wentworth at nineteen, and had been persuaded to give up her engagement, "forced into prudence in her youth, she learned romance as she grew older." It has happened gradually, "more than seven years were gone since this little history of sorrowful interest had reached its close." She meets him again at twenty-seven, an age when love and family would have begun to seem unlikely for a woman in Austen's day. I was thirty-nine, M was forty, we had had two decades of complicated friendship, missed chances, other relationships. It still seemed very near to me, the lives that might have been. I had been with women and men, relationships serious, deep, but I had not been able to promise permanence. Writing from within a household had made me territorial and secretive; I had followed the writing out of the relationships. It had been when I had learned, the first time, that my father had cancer, that I had gone through a year of loneliness and change that I could no longer postpone. Second chances may come when some chances are gone. Austen is always described as witty, stylish, but *Persuasion* is a melancholy book. Anne is still in mourning for her mother. I loved its odd mixture of sorrow and hope.

As month followed month, I sometimes said to friends, bookish friends, that Austen was all I read. They were usually somewhere between encouraging and tactful. "Austen is *domestic*," one said, looking around at our living room, which was littered with objects that I by then categorized as intended to be chewed on and not safe to chew on. The implication, one I couldn't entirely disagree with, was that my sphere of life had been constrained more or less to the walls of our house, and that naturally I would read something drawn to similar dimensions.

It was 2012 when S was born. Until I was pregnant and my father was ill, I had preserved my concentration and my apartness by avoiding having a cell phone, but I felt I should be more reachable and bought one. Now, wherever I was, there was elsewhereness. I had been afraid that this would change the shape of my mind, and it did.

I had been a copious keeper of journals. I began instead to take very brief notes, more often visual ones. I photographed my ever-different body in the mirror. Was this self-acceptance or bidding farewell? My mind went on playing over certain phrases from Austen, not the famous epigrams and ripostes, but ones that to me suggested depths. Elizabeth Bennet in *Pride and Prejudice* exclaims to herself, "Till this moment I never knew myself." In *Mansfield Park*, Fanny Price wonders aloud about memory: "Our powers of recollecting and of forgetting, do seem peculiarly past finding out." Emma's inner life moves "with all the wonderful velocity of thought." Anne Elliot in *Persuasion* speaks out loud to a friend of her experience "of loving longest, when existence or when hope is gone." I did not know why these little groups of words felt so clear and whole and inexhaustible, but they did.

MEMOIRS

Last thing at night, I almost always read Austen. But in the morning, I would read the news online. The pictures were of the worst refugee crisis since World War II; of mourning and protests in different American cities after a series of racist killings; of repeated acts of terrorism; and of calamitous forest fires, earthquakes, oil spills, the end of tigers, of frogs, of polar bears, of the migration of the monarchs. At the beginning of these years, I did not think that an even darker period of national and international life might be coming, but the world was full of foreboding signs. I began to read one other thing: memoirs.

In my reading life, I had, to this point, avoided memoirs. I had taught what is called creative nonfiction at universities and colleges for nearly ten years, and at first, I had been quite sharp in discouraging my students from writing about themselves. I wanted them to look outward. I taught them to write about history, rivers, art, but could not avoid noticing that many of their best pieces began from their own experiences. One of the students had grown up on the Navajo Nation in what is now called Arizona; another had grown up working on urban farms in abandoned lots in downtown Detroit; many had been through violence; several had survived cancer; most struggled bravely for money and time. My students were eighteen, and fifty-four, and eighty. Over years, I learned to see how their stories brought the world, and now that I had stopped teaching, their stories were often with me.

A few months after S was born, my friend Jessica gave me Anne Lamott's *Operating Instructions*, about Lamott's first year of being a single mother, and about the death of her best friend. I read that straight through, laughing and crying. A number of months later, I took the train for a rare overnight trip to New York. I didn't even bother to bring a book, I was reading so little. Missing Austen, I stood in the Penn Station bookstore, contemplating aspects of Austen devotion that I still thought were quite different from my own reading—P. D. James's *Pemberley* and also *Pride and Prejudice and Zombies*. I chose instead Es'kia Mphahlele's *Down Second Avenue*.

On the train home, I read Mphahlele's memoir, published in 1959—of growing up, first in the rural village of Maupaneng, and then in a condition of poverty and police brutality in the restricted township of Marabastad, Pretoria, in apartheid South Africa. The book made the constraint and motion of the train car indelible. Mphahlele worked to make sense of his own history, "beginning to put into their proper places the scattered experiences of my life in Pretoria." Reading, I saw the world assembled again, differently, with room for things I had seen and heard, this world in which S would grow up.

At home in Cambridge, I would sometimes sit at my desk and try to see what my students had been doing. I thought that my view of history and rivers and art was actually a lot like their ideas of memoir. I had always been interested in letters, and diaries, in what felt like private history. It was as if my students and I believed in a vast tapestry of the inner lives of all the people who had ever lived, and we were trying to weave every figure into it, our own and everyone else's.

As the Austen years went on, I accumulated shelves of memoirs. Most of the time, reading memoirs seemed contemporary, and like it might be the opposite of reading Austen. I had noticed, but not looked into, something Anne Elliot says in *Persuasion*. Anne recommends to a new friend that he should read "memoirs of characters of worth and suffering." Another phrase of Austen's that I put in my pocket like a stone.

The people I knew took it as a given that the domesticity of Austen was isolated from the wide world and its violence, and they were charitable about what they assumed was my impulse to hide away at the end of messy days. If they were women without children they said "That sounds delightful," or even "I want to do that," and the tone was like that of a well person saying to an invalid that we all deserve a little time at a spa. If they were men with grown children, they nodded in confirmation, and the gesture meant "You are in a woman's situation, and you must make the most of it." Sometimes they were couples with young children, bravely undertaking their new life by reading out loud together, and then I found that they were often reading Austen, too, but when they said "Delightful . . . like Mozart . . . no trouble . . . ," that didn't make me feel better.

In the first Austen years, I didn't even argue with my friends in my head, I just felt a dim detachment in my mind that was myself, not yet insisting that there was more to it, but feeling that insistence taking shape. Austen's subject, I would be able to say years later, is not women embroidering on sofas but life with other people, and, if you are reading again and again, she will not really let you forget this.

"Comfort reading," one intellectual said briskly when I, some springs ago, after a little hesitation, once again confessed that Austen was all I read. It is another kind of comfort, not, I think, the kind my friend meant, that the people who live in Austen's rooms know that much of the time will is all one has to work with, that there is often not going to be guidance, that one will wait a long time for understanding to come and will have acted, over and over and probably not for the best, before it arrives. These are repeated lessons of being a parent and of watching a parent sicken and die.

A DEATH

The summer after S was born, my father began to have trouble breathing. When his cancer had recurred, he had retired, precipitously, from the university where he had worked for his whole career, studying organizations, and the ways people work and play together. He had grown interested in how much you can understand about people and relationships by watching what they do habitually, and he was often drawing our attention to the things we do correctly without giving them much thought—driving without accidents, walking to work without getting lost, even explaining so that we make sense, listening so that other people do.

In the first couple of years after the cancer recurred, he had undertaken new research. And he and my mother, a professor of theater and a director, traveled together, as they loved to do. They were able to be with my sister in the fall and then with me in the spring, when our first children were born. The symptoms came on late that summer; he couldn't get his breath, his back was very painful, taking a walk became hard.

In what seemed a matter of months, my father's life tore from his hands. He died eight months after S was born. My father and I had been very close. I did not know what to do.

Grief runs through the whole of life and leaves nothing untouched. A voice on the car radio, a knife in the kitchen drawer, each carries a thought of the dead. The baby was so little, and I did not want her to feel the death, and the fear of death, that I knew I was imparting to the objects in our house. At the same time, I was also, sometimes, less afraid of death, and beginning to have ideas about how people continue in the world, and I wanted to be able to tell her about that, how it was that I would be with her when death comes, and after. I wished that I could talk to my father a little more, and that from this I would learn what to say.

When this feeling was strong, I turned to Austen, but it was not obvious why. She doesn't talk much about mortality, and she wasn't a writer my father particularly thought about. He read widely, but not novels, and I only remember one conversation with him in which I raised Jane Austen. It is my mother whom I dimly remember talking about Austen with, as I first rushed through all six novels in high school. Another woman important to me, the woman with whom I did psychoanalysis for five years, was also an avid Austen reader. Reading Austen was a way to stay near to writing women who had watched over me, as I now felt responsible to do for our child. Which also seemed peculiar in its way, since Austen hardly writes about children. She does, though, write about growth, and about death, rupture, and imagination. Even so, for a long time, I thought of her books as mere comedies, and all of the same kind.

On any given night, I would read any one of them—any one of five of them, really, for I only looked into *Northanger Abbey*. But, for each of the novels I read repeatedly, there were concentrated reasons within what seemed diffuseness. When I began to write about Austen's books, I saw some of what I had asked of each one.

Here is a woman, a reader, in winter, reading *Persuasion*. In the spring, she has a baby. She and her husband and the baby, her father and her mother, all go out to walk together. The next winter, her father is hospitalized. She and her husband and the baby go home for the last week of his illness. She brings *Mansfield Park*. For her, *Mansfield Park* is a book of constriction and breadth. Sometimes it seems a painfully muted book. Later, when she has thought more, she will see how, in its rooms, memory is accompanied by forgetting.

The reader's father dies. There is a memorial service, at which she and her sister both speak. She comes back to the life she has had. For the first year, she reads *Sense and Sensibility*, about two sisters, who are going through the first year after their father's death. She is struggling to think about her father's death, she and her sister both are; they are planning to have second children, whom their father knew nothing of. The reader wants to begin writing again.

She unfolds Jane Austen's novels like a map. She is pregnant a second time. And now it is *Pride and Prejudice*—a book about changing one's sense of time, and reading again—that goes with her to the hospital. When the second baby can sit up, and the weather is warm enough to take him for a walk, she thinks she is probably done with Jane Austen. She plans to write an essay about reading Jane Austen and mark the conclusion. But they move to a new city. There is an election and the world changes. Only now, two children growing up around them, does she begin to really read *Emma*, and then, again, *Mansfield Park*.

Emma and *Mansfield Park* are important to each other. She cannot shake the sense that between the two of them she will find it—whatever of the past she must retrieve, whatever of the future she must imagine. She will write until she finds it. She tries one way, another way. It will be done this season, next season, next year. Four years go by.

She is always, and still, reading *Persuasion*. She loves *Persuasion*. It is not the most brilliant or elegant or formally demanding, but it seems to know her, and all of them, so well. It has the depth of dreams, and like dreams it is incomplete, and she cannot really understand it.

WRITERS IN THE WORLD

Over time, I discovered that many writers I admired had written about reading Austen. I came upon a series of short essays that Ta-Nehisi Coates had posted in the midst of the experience. After some lines considering how Austen brings Mr. Darcy across, he remarks that it is "a portrait without a face, a portrait that, for me, needs no face." Something collaborative is at work. He is thinking of an artist, Teresa Jay, and a painting of hers called *Hide No Seek*. In the painting, "the girl's face is obscured by a tree, and that interruption is an appeal to, a place-holder for, our imagination. The picture seemingly ends, but just beyond the border is a place for me, a place where the thing becomes mine."

These odd spaces, in which the writer and reader both may be present, not necessarily mingled but each needing the other, in these thinner spaces behind, almost within, the pages, a reader may place her own memories, or a sense of the troubled world. Space that will open for a writer who lives in New York and is soon to begin making the case for reparations, and for another in Tehran, trying to decide whether to leave the Islamic Republic.

In *Reading Lolita in Tehran*, Azar Nafisi writes of having resigned from her last academic post, about her struggle with "the tyranny of time and politics." She formed a private seminar, later, wrote her "memoir in books." In their clandestine meetings, she and her students chose to read, among other books, *Pride and Prejudice*. "Every great book we read," Nafisi remembered, "became a challenge to the ruling ideology . . . Nowhere was this challenge more apparent than in the work of Jane Austen." Why was that—because, she says, Austen had sharp ideas of individual freedom, an incredibly fine sense of the relationship between the public and the private, and something else, something peculiar, to do with voices, and with memory. "If a sound can be preserved in the same manner as a leaf or a butterfly, I would say that within the pages of my *Pride and Prejudice*, that most polyphonic of all novels . . . is hidden like an autumn leaf the sound of the red siren."

Austen's novels offer strange friendship; in their company you may feel more yourself, look out at the world with clear sight.

Jane Austen was born in 1775, drafted her first three novels as a very young writer in the 1790s, went through a relatively quiet period until about 1809, and then, in a great stream of revision and creativity, between 1811 and 1815, published *Sense and Sensibility*, *Pride and Prejudice*, *Mansfield Park*, and *Emma*. She became ill, and died in 1817, leaving several manuscripts in varying states of completion. After her death, her family titled and published two novels—*Persuasion*, which, she had written in a letter that year, was "ready for publication," and *Northanger Abbey*, which she had written was not.

Austen lived, and wrote, and died, in a period that must have seemed to her almost as convulsive as ours does to us. For much of her adult life, England was under threat of invasion, was fighting the Napoleonic Wars, and was pouring its resources into building a maritime empire of rapacious and complex power. There were shortages of food and of basic necessities. Austen and her brothers and sister grew up in an England in which merchants were turning to more systematic exploitation of workers, and she observed in the aristocracy a kind of fever for enclosing what had been common green lands for their own use and profit. The trade in people who were enslaved, a trade in which the British were among the most greedy and merciless, was not abolished in Britain until 1807, and slavery itself not until 1833. Austen's own sympathies were firmly with the abolitionists. In the England she lived in, the position you took on enslavement was a moral question that every person had to answer.

Jane Austen and her family learned their times by living them—two of her brothers were naval officers—one, Frank, eventually reached the highest rank, admiral of the fleet, in the British navy. In 1805, Frank was on a ship sent by Lord Nelson to fetch supplies and so, to his lifelong regret, missed the Battle of Trafalgar. He sailed everywhere from Penang to Antigua. The other brother, Charles, also commanded ships, caught French vessels, received prize money, was stationed in the West Indies, married a young woman whose father had been attorney general of Bermuda, and died in 1852 in Burma in the Second Anglo-Burmese War. Frank and Charles were both active abolitionists and, after 1807, were employed in the suppression of the slave trade, sailing to catch illegal trade vessels. Austen wrote a voluminous correspondence with these brothers, and lived in Frank's household, not far from the shipping hub of Portsmouth, with his wife and children for more than two years. Another brother, Henry, who was her favorite brother, served in the militia, worked as a banker to the army, lived in London, and, when she stayed with him, went with her to the theater as much as they could. Henry was married to Eliza de Feuillide, a cousin of the Austens, whom they had grown up knowing, and who had first been married to a French nobleman. This first husband had been guillotined at the time of the revolution. A fourth brother was a clergyman, like their father. A fifth had severe disabilities and lived with a family in the countryside. A sixth was adopted by landed gentry, inherited wealth, and lived among the country aristocracy, at whose tables Austen herself sometimes dined. The events of the great world were intimately known to Austen through family life.

This knowledge was in the future for me. It took me four more years, of reading about Austen and her times, to get used to seeing that radical ideas about women and men and people and language, that extremities of brutality, subjection, and greed, were not absent from her books—I just had not known how to look for them. When, in *Sense and Sensibility*, the supremely selfish Mr. John Dashwood sits at a lavish dinner in London, describing how he is enclosing the village green, I had not seen hungry farmers. In *Persuasion*, the information that Anne's beloved, Captain Wentworth, had been rewarded for his bravery in "the action off St. Domingo" had not become a part of my thinking about him. Not having read Edward Said's famous interpretation of Fanny Price asking her rigid uncle Sir Thomas Bertram about his estate in Antigua and "the slave trade," I read the phrase in the novel with only the feeling of something misaligned. I thought the narrator of *Mansfield Park* was concerned with whether Fanny Price would get to live there, and I only later realized that I had also been taking up ideas about property and plantations, about the separation of families and forgetting. That the narrator of *Pride and Prejudice* might be laughing at the declarations of Thomas Jefferson and Edmund Burke: "It is a truth universally acknowledged, that a single man in possession of a good fortune must be in want of a wife." That the author might have read Mary Wollstonecraft's *Vindication of the Rights of Woman*, that the author had read, with passionate attention, Thomas Clarkson's abolitionist works on the slave trade, that she read the naval papers, delved into the worldly pages of historians and economists and travelers, and knew not only the works of Walter Scott and William Wordsworth and Madame de Staël but also the kinds of works that these worldly writers were themselves reading . . . well, for a long time it didn't occur to me to wonder. And, even once I did wonder, for an even longer time I didn't know how to put together the most interior experiences I had had reading Austen—going over the death of my father, the births of our children—with the world, hers and mine.

The very first thing Austen does in *Persuasion* is to mock Anne's father, Sir Walter Elliot, for reading only one book. It is the Baronetage: "there, if every other leaf were powerless, he could read his own history with an interest which never failed." Too self-interested, he resolutely misunderstands both history and his actual situation. Soon enough, the Elliots have to leave their ancestral estate, Kellynch. The tenants who are to take it over are the good Admiral and Mrs. Croft. Anne, who reads the naval papers, mentions that Admiral Croft was "in the Trafalgar action and has been in the East Indies since," and Sir William's only reply to this evidence of a life of action is to observe that Admiral Croft's face will then be "about as orange as the cuffs and cape of my livery," the uniform his servants wear. Later, Admiral Croft laughs to Anne Elliot that the one change he has had to make at Kellynch is to take away all the mirrors with which Sir Walter had filled his own rooms. Sir Walter will only read a book that reflects him flatteringly back to himself.

Austen herself did not put a mirror in place of a window. In phrases, here and there, pass militia companies and ships. Shawls are to be brought from India, gypsies camp beyond the edge of the village, some make sure there is food for those in need and others don't. The shapes of the world are impressed into the substance of the novels, holding the negative spaces among the characters, there to be sensed, the longer one lives in the pages.

Austen thought a lot about reading as education and as avoidance. The novel was emerging in Austen's era, and it was a form for new readers, ones without an aristocratic education—for women, and people who made money by working. Literary men and women had intense arguments about whether novels should uplift by extraordinariness, or depict something more like the everyday. And whose everyday was it to be? The Austen family itself, though well educated, had a fluctuating status, and their individual situations varied. Austen wrote hoping to earn a living. She was of a class of dependent women, shuffled about to different relatives' houses, where she might have to remain for months until someone could spare her a carriage. Reading, and writing, brought her some aspects of the world, and her allegiance to the new form was fierce. As Austen herself wrote to a friend of someone else's literary exclusiveness: "She might have spared this pretension to *our family*, who are *great novel-readers* . . ."

Unlike Sir Walter's comforting and unchanging family history in the Baronetage, the history of his family that appears in *Persuasion* shows many different people involved with many kinds of mourning, trying, and often failing, to be part of their own times. Sir Walter's problem is not only which book he reads, but how unexaminedly he reads it. Austen did believe that in reading, one may learn to be more oneself, or change the relationship between oneself and the world. There is depth in doing the same thing over, but differently. Novels were a place that could make you look again.

CERTAIN MEMORIES

My father died in winter, in a week of severe snowstorms. A few of our parents' neighbors, who had stood outside, heads lowered, to watch the ambulance take him to the hospital for the last time, argued over who would shovel their driveway. From the hospital windows, I looked down into institutional courtyards and watched people coming and going through the snow. Almost as soon as they had passed, their footprints would be erased. I stood, watching, at the end of a fluorescent corridor, and I called my friend Justin, whose mother had died of cancer, and I told him how the people were coming and going, and how even the trace of them was lost in the snow.

After my father's death, we found that he had put together two cardboard file boxes, the kind that hold a stack of magazines so that you can see the spines, one for my sister, one for me. Each contained copies of the papers he was proudest of, and of the two books he had coauthored: *Leadership and Ambiguity*, and *Harnessing Complexity*. He never wrote a book alone, although he had been starting out to. He had begun to write about ways that people, and whole organizations, have a steady character, and can make themselves again after ruptures and discontinuities. On each narrow box, there was a yellow sticky note, like a kind of dedication. *For Rachel*, mine said.

It's on a shelf next to my desk now, my box, a little bent by the wear and tear of three moves, still with the yellow note, his handwriting, near the family pictures, the small stone urn with some of his ashes. I have looked at the books but, with one exception, only glanced through the papers. The exception is a letter my father wrote for a colleague and sent to me while he was still alive, a letter about character, habits, and imagination. On the day he died, my father asked me to find a way for this letter to be published.

The letter turned out to be, in my mind, a kind of passageway. Into my father's thoughts, into Jane Austen's books, into the house my first family had lived in together, and to which there will be no return. I still find it hard to go back to his sentences, but as I began to write about reading, lines from his letter appeared in my thoughts again and again. Many of the ideas grew from literature, and shared language: "that radiant passage," he wrote, from Shakespeare, "And, as imagination bodies forth / The forms of things unknown, the poet's pen / Turns them to shapes, and gives to airy nothing / A local habitation and a name." He had been thinking, he said, about my mother's "deep interest in how playwrights imagine great characters . . . and in how actors develop the characters they inhabit on the stage." He had signed the letter: "In warm anticipation of conversations yet to come . . ."

In the last week of my father's life, while he was at home, before he returned to the hospital for the last time, we had a few moments of conversation that I remember in detail. These took place in my parents' bedroom, a space that had always been a bit separate from family life, but which was where the life of the house had begun, where it had been considered, and where it returned to, for those days. Two little bits of memory seem almost, and then again not quite, to bear on each other.

My father had already been in the hospital, initially for some tests and then in a prolonged and worsening way, and eventually I had insisted that we would come to Ann Arbor. He and my mother, distressed by what some doctors said and encouraged by others, decided to see whether he could manage at home with oxygen tanks. Their ambulance transport arrived at the house a few hours before we did. I knew the situation to be serious, but when we were standing in the kitchen with my mother, a person of great force and resolution, and she put her arms around me and leaned against me in relief, I began to feel the more profound terror of how serious it was.

The day before he returned to the hospital, my father and I attempted to say some last things. It was a bitter January day. He had gotten out of bed to sit in a chair, and I pulled one up next to him. We sat, shoulder to shoulder.

He knew he was close to death, although I think he still had intermittent hope that it would not be now. I thought there might be months, even a return to health, was encouraging him to write to close friends, to think about the papers he was at work on. He was trying to get me to understand something that he did not want to know. There were many barriers to speech. But we did speak. Because we did not look directly at each other, we had that freedom two people may have in a car, or taking a walk.

At one point, sitting there, I railed against my father's doctors. He answered, quickly, that modern medicine had not given him cancer, and then he added—and a little of his lightness broke into the room—that modern life might have. The firmness and good humor were like him. His decisive tone meant that blaming doctors was a path he had been down, and he was taking care to let me know that on that path you would go astray.

My father, I knew, had loved his modern life. At his bedside table when he died, he had, among other things, Wordsworth's poetry, and recent issues of *Scientific American* and *Sailing* magazine. He had the same kind of delight in advances in human understanding that he had in the movements of the wind and the stars. Once, when I was young, and had asked him about his religious beliefs, he said that he had a feeling not far from the pagan one that there were spirits that moved in the trees and the water. The sense was of a great continuity of life from which one came and to which one returned.

But in that conversation at home, something else happened. We came to the end of what we could say, and I stood and faced him. Something moved. It might have been that he reached to grab my arm, but I think it was just a look, like a mask across his face, that stayed for a prolonged moment. An expression I could not place, in the vicinity of anger, passion, and doubt. It had to do with the way he was leaving me, and us, and the world. It was as bleak and impassioned as I ever saw his face. It seemed that he had a feeling to which he could not put words, and which might have meant that, as he made his reckoning with the universe, the final abandonment was grim.

Here is the other memory, I think from the evening before: My father got out of bed with difficulty and dragged his oxygen pole across to a chair, and little S, who could sit up, played near us on the floor, and we talked with moments of ordinariness. I said that I was reading Jane Austen. I can't remember now if I mocked myself for only reading Austen, but I know I told my father a joke a friend of ours had recently told us, about the philosopher Gilbert Ryle. Someone had asked Ryle if he ever read novels in addition to philosophy. And Ryle replied, "Of course, I read all six every year." My father laughed.

My father laughed easily—he laughed with fondness for people's foibles, and with incredulity at the ways of the world; he could laugh with abandon, with delight, and with surprise. For years in my childhood I wanted to laugh like he did. I practiced a sound, a kind of rising hoo-hoo-hoo that I hoped had the quickness and soar of his beautiful laugh.

I did not then know that Ryle had written an essay on Jane Austen and her sense of proportion, but I did feel instinctively that my father and I had shared, in laughter, a sense of just proportion. Austen and Ryle are funny with a fine, deliberate miscalibration: that of suggesting that all literature is six novels, or that a single man of fortune is always in want of a wife. My father's laughter went together with his sense of time and of timelessness, of what mattered and how to live with that, and that was a kind of place I inhabited, like the parks of childhood, ready for a thoughtful walk. I suppose I kept reading Austen in part because, on a night when my father's death was becoming real to him, she and Gilbert Ryle had made him laugh.

A year—I read *Sense and Sensibility*, some *Mansfield Park*. Our daughter began to talk and to walk. I had finished writing the biography, about an art connoisseur, and about six women who had given his work structure, and endurance. I regretted that I had not sent a draft of the manuscript to my father. The book came out. I felt proud, and wistful, when S saw my picture on the book's back flap and said "Mama."

Our apartment was on the ground floor of what we called the Red House. We sat, in the living room, on the brown couch, to read to S. One of her first favorite books, which she would bring to us so that we could read it to her, was *Green Eggs and Ham*. The page she loved best came when, after pages and pages of telling Sam-I-Am that he will not, the central character is at last persuaded to try green eggs and ham, and hesitates. She loved the expression on his face, the uncertainty that, when you turn the page, will become surprise and delight. Her hands gripped and grabbed that page before the change. She tore off one corner, crumpled his face, and tried to plumb its depths. The book opens to that page, is built around it, the only one of three dimensions. I had read Austen like that, as an actor might memorize a part.

I was able to get pregnant again. We found a different house in Cambridge. Still close to the paths at Fresh Pond where I, growing larger, took

S, or walked alone in moments of solitude. I turned forty-one. Somewhere in there, I began with *Pride and Prejudice*. In November, our son, T, was born. We chose to give him, in the middle of his name, my father's. The winter after T's birth was one of the snowiest anyone in Boston could remember. There were pictures of people jumping from their second-floor windows into banks of snow. M shoveled. S went out, too, in her purple-and-turquoise snowsuit, and ran along the top of our four-foot fence on a ridge of snow. New snow would come, nearly every day, and cover her prints. T and I stayed inside. He was from the first an enthusiastic and clear-minded child. All we knew together was winter, in which, day after day, it was too cold to go outside even for a few minutes, and night after night, I would put him to sleep and then look out the window at the eerie moonlit heaps of snow that held fences and cars.

Spring did come. One morning, a little more than two years after my father had died, I carried T out onto the balcony, and he breathed the gentle air. A look came onto his face that I cannot exactly remember but will never forget having seen, a look that meant something like *There is this.*

A few days later, an early warm day, I buckled T into the stroller, and we set out for Fresh Pond. We went past the stand of large pines, past the smaller pond with the cattails where the dogs swim, and around even as far as the dry rise, enclosed by hornbeams and oaks, that would be covered in wildflowers later in the summer.

As we walked, I thought about writing. I felt the crossroads beneath my feet. S had started at a little nursery school. Our sitter, Shannel, skilled, loved by both children, could come take care of T three mornings each week. I had a study with a door that closed. For more than two years, I had been making sketches of different kinds, about paintings, about musicians, but they were broken pieces. A few friends would read them and say that something about them didn't make sense. I had always written from reading in large swaths. In a different life, I would read for six months to write one double portrait for a magazine. But now, what had I been reading? I might, I thought on this walk, write about reading Jane

Austen. By then I was standing in the driveway of our house. T was half asleep in the stroller. The sun shone on both of our faces. I thought I would write an essay, maybe a long one, that summer.

READING AGAIN

I had been reading Austen for about three and a half years. I sat down to write and discovered that I had hardly read her. I had missed huge parts of the plots, had noticed very little of the important differences between the novels, differences in tone and intention. I had not even thought to inquire about the sequence of the novels, or what the sequence might have meant to their author. I knew little of what other people had found in Austen. I had not worked at history, interpretation, biography. I had been too much alone.

I had, actually, also had a few conversations about reading Austen that were more encouraging, and now it emerged that I had a half dozen friends, all writers, who were glad to talk to me about Austen. I walked around Fresh Pond working at *Persuasion* with my friend Anna, a professor of literature, who told me critics to read; I wrote letters about the letters in Austen with Ben, a novelist; I talked about maritime trade and Napoleon with Maya, a historian; I stood in a gallery trying to figure out the nature of Austen's sentences with Vijay, a poet who has read all six many times; I visited Jessica, also a novelist, who has known me since before I could read, and we spoke of what is shared between memoirs and novels, and what isn't.

I went on reading Ryle, Coates, Nafisi, and I found other writers who had read Austen intently, and I began to have those conversations that you can have in your mind with people you do not know, who have written about a writer you both admire. (Notes on my reading, and information about quotations for each chapter, are at the back of this book.) More folders and shelves, of writings by critics—William Galperin, Edward Said, Frances Ferguson, Lionel Trilling, D. A. Miller, Margaret Doody, Stuart

Tave, Jocelyn Harris, and, above all, Virginia Woolf. So many critics had been able to say something that mattered to them more generally, by staying close to Austen's words.

Reading critics, I found myself looking for hidden memoirs, private experiences of Austen. Virginia Woolf wrote of Austen in every form, and at every stage of her writing life—in letters, diaries, essays, in her own first novel. Some nights she immersed herself in Austen, other times she read her in fragments, "two words at a time." As Woolf's own craft matured, there emerged for her a sense of Austen's revisions, and of where, in *Persuasion*, Austen might have been going.

Most readers have a few books that feel especially bound up with their own life and understanding. In these books, close reading and memoir are near neighbors. Austen lends herself to this kind of reading, about which D. A. Miller suggests a paradox: Austen seems to remove particularity, to speak with universal style and authority, but in such a way that the reader may preserve particularities of their own, may even need those and make use of them in order to read well. "My *Pride and Prejudice*," Ta-Nehisi Coates had written, "is truly *mine*." After I had learned more of what Austen had meant and meant to others, I saw more of who I had been, reading her pages.

If one were to attempt to locate Jane Austen among the elements in the periodic table of authors, there would be a difficult choice. On the one hand, she is, I think, like what are called the noble gases—unreacting, impervious, clear, and continuous in the air above. On the other, she seems like those most reactive metals that scarcely exist independently in nature, so fast are they to combine with other elements. Austen is always recognizably Austen, and yet different in every writer's hands. Even the few details we have of her life seem to shift with each biographer, each new era's perspective. Woolf wrote that "we have lives enough of Jane Austen," but I think she would have welcomed much of what we have come to know about Austen and her world in the last fifty years of efforts. At the time, I think Woolf worried that certain biographers had rendered Austen inert, and domesticated. Woolf wanted the reactive, various Austen, not staid lives of Austen, but lives *with* Austen. She knew, I think, that we would never run out of these, as we cannot run out of reading any writer willing to combine with us to make these rare shared substances. "For books continue each other," Woolf wrote in *A Room of One's Own*, "in spite of our habit of judging them separately." It does seem that so many are drawn to reading Austen again and again, and writing near her, because she, too, believed that books continue each other, and she was so peculiarly good at making clear her side of whatever that continuity is.

In the essay I tried to write, I thought that I would merely mention the death and births that had run under and through my reading. The more I wrote, the more it was obvious that what I had read in Austen was families and friendships and changing history, how we go back over what we have lived, and whether we can hand it on. My reading would make no sense without my father's ideas of imagining. And would it be right to think about my father without also thinking about what my sister said of my father? The essay became several. In our moment, we are very aware of how much each person's circumstances influence their reading and point of view, and it makes sense to be clear about the circumstances, in their many combinations of comfort and difficulty. Could I talk about reading Austen without saying that, for much of the time I was writing, M and I both worked, teaching inquiring students at a university with colleagues to talk with, and a library, at an institution itself interdependent with a landscape of businesses, laboratories, governments, within the political history of Chicago and the South Side, in years when, near the Great Lakes, it rained more and more? What I had made of Austen was not really separable from either my circumstances or the world's.

A written version of events has a way of becoming *the* story, and I did not want to write something that would overtake the stories others in our family—my sister, my mother, our children—were working out.

I decided to use initials to refer to the people in my family, in the hopes of suggesting places that were really openings in the pages, where there was not a character, but another possible author. Austen herself deliberately left unknowns, remarked different points of view, showed people talking to themselves in ways that changed as they looked back. All of which is of interest to readers and writers like me, who find themselves increasingly drawn to the uncertain, personal knowledge in memoirs. I have wanted to understand more about this—whether we are living in an age of memoir, whether I have reached some kind of age of memoir.

In recent years, it has become common practice to write fragments of memoir every day, to share pictures and written notes of experience with an audience of friends and strangers. We did not used to need to do this, but now we do. Writing personally is a way of making sense to and with other people that may express a belief in common language and common understanding. Of course, this is different from trying to be kind, or from trying to shelter one's family; sometimes it is neither kind nor sheltering, but it is its own imperative, to make sense.

A few weeks after I came back from Fresh Pond with T in his stroller, I started to read biographies. I was moved by Claire Tomalin's understanding of Austen, and exhilarated by what I learned from Paula Byrne. I read the memoir, restrained but insightful, written by Austen's nephew, and an old large brown volume of her collected letters that a perspicacious bookseller had once urged on me. Jane Austen began to take shape in my mind as a writing woman. I discovered an aspect of her biography of which I had been totally ignorant, but which came to seem part of the foundation of her work and of my immersion in it.

Austen grew up in the countryside, in a literary family that appreciated laughter. She was especially close to her father, and to her only sister, Cassandra. She walked, every day, weather permitting, in green places. She drafted three novels early on, when she was between twenty and twenty-three—these books, rewritten, would be published many years later as *Northanger Abbey*, *Sense and Sensibility*, and *Pride and Prejudice*. She read the early drafts of these books out loud to her family and delighted in their delight. She had become a practicing writer.

Then, one day, her father decided they should leave their home. The story was told by her nieces and nephews that Austen had been away on a visit, and had walked home. On returning, she was informed that they were to remove from the home she had always lived and written in, almost immediately, and go to town. She was said to have fainted to the floor.

When I read that, I could not take my eyes away from it. I felt it as a physical injury, and it was two or three days before I felt at home in my body. I am used to sympathizing with figures in history, but this was more like sharing physically in an experience of shock. It came not from thinking about the life, but because of reading the novels. I had been, slowly, minutely, prepared to know that this was behind the writing, and when I learned it, I knew it from within.

Austen's brothers by this time were grown and gone. With her father, her sister, and her mother, she moved around, quite a bit, and lived in Bath, which she hated. She drafted a piece of another novel and wrote less. Then her father died. She gave up the fragments. She probably wrote some underlayers of books that later became the published novels, and she made sketches, but there is no growing novel that we have a record of for the next four and a half years.

When Austen fell to the floor, she could not have said what it would mean to her that it would be eight and a half years before she would write continuously again, but by the time I learned this fact about her life, I had been reading the five major novels for a thousand nights. I thought I had been reading to find resolution, and I had, but it was a resolution that took form from its negative, from displacement. I had taken the imprint of rupture from every page.

After the years of wandering, she and her mother and her sister were offered a home by one of the Austen brothers, and the three women moved to Chawton Cottage. Jane Austen thought that habits were the inward structure of character, and this understanding continued in her family. Her nephew explains: "As soon as she was fixed in her second home, she resumed the habits of composition which had been formed in her first, and continued them to the end of her life."

The habits must have been very fine and flexible ones. So much had changed for her, and yet her every capacity had grown. Settled in the country, she revised and published *Sense and Sensibility* and *Pride and Prejudice*, and worked at *Northanger Abbey* but never solved it to her satisfaction, and she completed, in a year or two each, *Mansfield Park*, *Emma*, and *Persuasion*. When she died with *Persuasion* and a piece of the next novel still in her writing desk, she was forty-one.

I had been studying her life, and studying it in a particular way, one my father would have recognized, to see what she made of her regained habits of writing. I had been reading about going on being a writer, after a rupture and a loss. "Seven years," she wrote to her sister, when they were not yet resettled, and she was reflecting on how much had changed since they had left their first home, and their father had died. "Seven years, I suppose, are enough to change every pore of one's skin and every feeling of one's mind." But her father would have known her, if he had suddenly returned, and would have recognized the writer of her books. Even if its every feeling were different, it would still be her mind, writing itself; even though for a world without him, not forgetting him. I wonder if she also felt that she never would have written them as she did had he lived.

This time, of sitting in the evening by the bedside of first one child, and then another, and of talking about the day—how we went to the playground and went high on the swings—and then sitting with M after all is at last quiet, on the stiff, restuffed cushions of our brown couch, noticing together how S's drawings are changing, and telling each other again of T in hilarious mock battle with his toy crocodile . . . in this time, the capacity for creative thought has been as curtailed as it ever has been for me, and under the greatest demands and detractions from outside myself. A time of mourning that has also been the most joyous I have known.

Looking back at myself in earlier rooms, I think I would say that, in the evenings, studying the shards of meaning that remained after similar days, I was not primarily reading Austen either to accept, or to hide from, a new life, but because it gave me room for thought. Austen's rooms, like a stage set, are actually mostly empty—there are basic pieces of furniture, books, a plant or two. She does not describe clothes or carriages, but how her characters think about their things. Her characters are worried about money and time. In her rooms, as in ours, people live under great pressure. Time bears down upon us. The world is raging, and we have each of us but a tiny sphere of activity. We are subject to constant interruption, and we must nevertheless exert ourselves to make sense and to become coherent. One lives with one eye on the laundry and one eye on the reckoning.

The Tuesday before my father died, we were sitting in the same chairs, though I faced him from a different direction. I had cooked our meal, and my father was sorry that he could not really eat. S had been on the floor, watching us with her intent, luminous eyes. My father noticed again, as he often had, the absorbed way that she studies shadows, faces. And then he said, "Once you've been seen by those eyes, you'll never be forgotten."

I had been looking at him and I looked away.

Two

A WRITER

PERSUASION

Anne Elliot, I love. She is retiring, and people pain her, but she also finds them so funny. She is a mourner, and has two close friends, both also in mourning. Nearly everyone in her book is in mourning, in different ways.

I didn't know her at the time her mother died, when she was fourteen, and I didn't know her when she was first in love with Captain Wentworth, and she was nineteen, that summer of 1806, when he was briefly on land. I've only known her since after that, after one of her friends, Lady Russell, a widow, persuaded her to give him up, and he left and almost immediately made a reputation as a brave naval officer, and a fortune in prize money from taking enemy ships, but never wrote to her again. The "little history of sorrowful interest" seemed to come to a close. Seven years went by.

Those seven years have not been enough to change every feeling of her mind: "No one had ever come within the Kellynch circle, who could bear a comparison with Frederick Wentworth, as he stood in her memory." As I am watching, the Elliot family circumstances begin to alter. Anne's careless father and older sister have spent too much, and the whole family have to leave their estate, which is rented by Admiral and Mrs. Croft. Anne works to quiet her inner tumult; she alone remembers that Mrs. Croft is the older sister of Captain Wentworth. Their home gone, Anne goes to stay nearby with her other, married, sister in the family of the Musgroves. Captain Wentworth is again on land, and comes to the neighborhood.

Her feeling for him is perhaps even more powerful than it was before. But he is still angry with Anne for spurning him, as he sees it. He tries to attract the young Louisa Musgrove, and does. Anne cannot tell whether they will marry.

She says little, but her thoughts are often on her losses. When she speaks, it is more as if she is talking to herself. In truth, how could the people by whom she is surrounded—her father, the monstrously vain Sir Walter, her older sister, self-important and competitive Elizabeth, her married younger sister, Mary, always complaining of the afflictions of domesticity, a domesticity for which Anne herself is so gifted, and all the sundry others, with their degrees of good cheer and of selfishness—how could any of them really hear what Anne has to say, although they all rely on her, and some of them appreciate her? When she sits down to the piano, an instrument she plays well, she is accustomed to the fact that no one will notice. "Excepting one short period of her life, she had never, since the age of fourteen, never since the loss of her dear mother, known the happiness of being listened to, or encouraged by any just appreciation or real taste. In music she had been always used to feel alone in the world."

"The happiness of being listened to . . ." Jane Austen loved music. She sang, and it was lovely. She began every day by practicing the piano, pretty tunes, easy ones—she played early in the morning, one niece remembered, because no one else in the household much cared for music. Perhaps also because a day begun in music opens differently. Even before they came to their home at Chawton Cottage, in the first place where they had their own rooms, living with her brother Frank, she rented a pianoforte so that she could play. Music does seem like the one element in which one might hope to feel known, the universal beyond even language. To be unlistened to there, too—it is as if Anne lives behind a scrim.

Anne loses ground before she gains ground. This is as natural an order in a novel as it is in a story told from life. Acts of memory often precede those of imagination; you look backward before you can look out. When Captain

Wentworth talks with Louisa Musgrove, Anne is reduced to eavesdropping, no one hears her at all. She does have a little cheerful companionship at Uppercross; there come a few kinder exchanges with Captain Wentworth. He seems to actually see her, which is welcome and gives severe pain, the contrast with all that has been and will be. And she meets his close friends, warm people of integrity, perception, hospitality, and likes them immediately. "'These would have been all my friends,' was her thought; and she had to struggle against a great tendency to lowness."

Anne waits alone at Uppercross, expecting the news that Louisa and Captain Wentworth will marry. These rooms, she thinks, now "occupied but by her silent, pensive self," will soon be filled with "all that was glowing and bright in prosperous love, all that was most unlike Anne Elliot!"

I want to help, I know this place myself, I have been there, in the book, and outside the book:

> An hour's complete leisure for such reflections as these, on a dark November day, a small thick rain almost blotting out the very few objects ever to be discerned from the windows, was enough to make the sound of Lady Russell's carriage exceedingly welcome; and yet, though desirous to be gone, she could not quit the mansion-house, or look an adieu to the cottage, with its black, dripping and comfortless veranda, or even notice through the misty glasses the last humble tenements of the village, without a saddened heart.—Scenes had passed in Uppercross, which made it precious. It stood the record of many sensations of pain, once severe, but now softened; and of some instances of relenting feeling, some breathings of friendship and reconciliation, which could never be looked for again, and which could never cease to be dear. She left it all behind her; all but the recollection that such things had been.

It is complete. A small thick rain almost blotting out . . . dripping and comfortless . . . tenements of the village . . . once severe . . . some breathings of friendship . . . could never be looked for again . . . she left it all behind . . . This is the lowest point. She feels she can see to a dark, unchanging horizon.

She is silent. But she is going to speak. She walks from here to there, from this mournful rainy November day to being a writer of experience.

When I first knew Anne Elliot, I often thought of my own history. It seemed so recently that I had gained, after having repeatedly lost, the chance to be with M. We had known each other first in college, lived in neighboring dorms, taken similar classes. At nineteen, while I was out of the country, I had had the idea that we might be together, but for him there was someone else. "I will wait for him." I said it out loud, to myself, holding a letter. I didn't, though, not exactly. I was often in a hurry—I sped through books and cities. After college, every few years, each of us in and out of other relationships that could well have turned out to be the ones we would spend our lives in, one of us would visit the other—in Brooklyn, Pittsburgh, Berkeley—and things would be upset, we would be precipitated out of, and also into, these other relationships. He and I each held something in abeyance. Alone, at twenty-eight, I again told myself out loud that I would wait for him, on a gray day near the water. But nothing really changed. It was only that he figured in my journals; there were a few emails and letters, messages on answering machines. Some of the time, he was a counterpoint to men and women I loved. But now and again, it seemed they were counterpoints to him. I was thirty-four and living alone in Sunnyside, Queens, when I wrote to him again, and he wrote back, and came to visit.

The night before he arrived, I walked the few blocks to the YMCA where I used to swim a couple of days each week. The pool there was shallow, and people from all over the world made their way up and down the lanes, five or six in a lane, most of us slow swimmers. After I swam, I went to the small sauna in the locker room where women who had started out not far from the villages of my great-grandparents—in Ukraine, Poland, Ireland—sat together with others who had begun in the Andes and mainland China. We all had our own ways of being still in the heat. I lay on my back, looking up toward the wooden ceiling, and I thought, "If this goes right, this is the last night I will be solitary until one of us dies."

Four years later, reading *Persuasion* and waiting for the baby who was coming, sometimes I thought, simply, I was right, I am not solitary anymore. Sometimes I thought, what did that person even mean, perched there on that wooden plank, she didn't understand it at all. Anne Elliot was still solitary, but she seemed able to understand, even to anticipate, things about remembering and imagining another person that I, two years married, was bewildered by. Anne is not the only one. All of Austen's heroines are learning about living with other people and carrying on being themselves. The ways they begin—in the families they grew up in, with their friends and the strangers they meet—suggest how they will continue. Even in their continuity, they, too, are perpetually astonished by how much they didn't know when they look back.

Seven more years have gone by, and all my earlier selves, trying to make a life with M, seem haphazard and ignorant, as this self will soon enough. Though they noticed many of the same things about M that I notice now, they didn't have the same sense of proportion, which has grown together with his. I know that, from the first, I felt a kind of relief that he always had books nearby. In college, he had a duffel bag of them that went with him everywhere. I still breathe easier every time he packs twenty books for the children when we drive somewhere for a couple of days. Sometimes, even now, we think he has gathered his books to go out, but he is just taking them to the living room.

We move about the house in similar ways. I anticipate him, somewhat irritatingly; he points out that I am constantly standing where he is trying to go. Before we were together, I thought of him as about six feet tall, a couple of inches taller than I am, but by now he is completely various. Sometimes—when he is carefully carrying upstairs a child who is flailing in anger or illness—he seems tall, and broad, at others drawn in, smaller than I am. On the first trip we took as a couple, I, still nervous, apologized for having talked for too long, and he said, "Well, I definitely think we should keep count." He is reluctant to talk of his work in philosophy, but he longs to be heard. If you are walking next to him, and he is finally speaking about his own ideas, of how people are transparent to themselves, his steps will slow down.

It had begun, that next day. And we had, mostly, gone from being two intently independent people to being a married couple expecting a child. A year or so after he had come to visit, and though each of us has complicated feelings about marriage, we had gotten engaged. My father's cancer recurred. Two nights before our wedding, we worked out the service with our friend Matthias, who is also a philosopher, and who downloaded a license from the Universal Life Church to be able to marry us. M had taken on the task of reworking the vows in *The Book of Common Prayer*. We liked the old Elizabethan language, but the Christianity wasn't right for us; we had the modern problem of plighting—our Jewish mothers, some Irish Catholic in our fathers, M's respect for religion from outside it, my untethered belief. We kept "honor," took out "serve," we chose "as long as we both shall live." When we came to the remarks Matthias would make about the state of marriage we were to enter into, Matthias thought Hegel might be grounding. The two philosophers said, a little wryly, that according to Hegel, once married, we would become one substance. I said fuck that.

Sometimes it troubles me that the Austen I love most is the book where she seems, somehow, least Austen. D. A. Miller, in *Jane Austen, or The Secret of Style*, writes of the way Austen's fully formed style seems to slash away particulars, not "saying *I*," not "saying *you*," hardly any physical body, very little historical detail, it has an "impersonality" that gives it a great authority and "a beauty of expression," both "without equal." Austen style is, for him, fundamentally unmarried, outside the bonds of convention. Marriage finishes the books because it finishes their wild, clear, undetermined consciousness. Her style achieves itself by rigorously never indicating the experiences of the spinster she actually was. It is neither a man nor a woman writing, but a kind of abstraction, style itself, a No One, Miller says, above the page, never tempted to plunge into life and love below. I have felt this—freed by this style that is more general than any one person could be, the style that is doing the writing not quite a person in a body, not quite a desiring person. And I am sure that the most stylish Austen novels—*Pride and Prejudice, Emma*—have been not only a way to think over having myself arrived at marriage, but a kind of haven of unmarriedness for me.

Virginia Woolf, too, notes the absence of a tone of personal experience, thinks over how Austen's mind seemed, like Shakespeare's, to have "consumed all impediments." This puts Woolf in mind of a thought of Coleridge's, that a great mind is androgynous, might seem to encompass both genders, perhaps she would now say all kinds of genders, mixtures and absences and transformations of the idea of gender, but not one specific embodiment of it.

Until *Persuasion*, that is. In *Persuasion*, the style falters, and sounds like someone, a particular someone, a bit irritable, a bit wounded. It is not so witty anymore; Miller thinks *Persuasion* is "the great sentimental favorite." The readers, he writes, who favor it are really exulting over the stylish writer who has been made to admit that style is not enough compensation for loneliness. Loving *Persuasion*, I think it may be true that I am hoping that writing does not require loneliness I was long familiar with, or that I am nodding my head in too-eager agreement that no one escapes social life forever. There is, I think, also a glimmer of something else, which Miller, despite the sharp tone he takes with her for what he perceives as a "retraction" of her style, also remarks. In *Persuasion*, style begins to try out being a person, being, even, Anne. If the author of *Persuasion* is a bit less consummately a writer, the central character is more of one. Anne notices and interprets herself and the other characters in her book; she reads and studies language. She might wander out of the book and write a different one, maybe not quite as good.

Woolf says that there is "a peculiar beauty and a peculiar dullness in *Persuasion*." The dullness and beauty of going forward: "While we feel that Jane Austen has done this before, and done it better, we also feel that she is trying to do something which she has never yet attempted." That she is working to bring out aspects not only of her own observations but also of her own "experience." Not that she would have written autobiographically, but that her characters would have stretched toward inner depths. Some say the future Austen whom Woolf imagines is too much like Woolf herself; I think Woolf just sees writing from her own point of view. Woolf says Austen would have "trusted less . . . to dialogue and more to reflection . . . She would have devised a method, clear and composed as ever, but deeper and more suggestive, for conveying not only what people say, but what they leave unsaid; not only what they are, but what life is." She would have been "the forerunner of Henry James and of Proust—but enough. Vain are these speculations . . ."

We know that Austen went on to begin *Sanditon*, and to mortal illness, but only Austen, and perhaps her sister, glimpsed the book she might have been writing. Still, the writerly personage is there in *Persuasion*, proposing a kind of friendship for a reader who wants to make sense of what they have lived by putting words together. She has, in a way, been there all along in Austen. She turns to look back to *Sense and Sensibility*, and to the young Marianne, so full of feeling, one beginning of being a writer. This writerly personage is not that far away, but the day is hazy—I can almost, but not quite, make her out.

READING MEMOIRS

Part of *Persuasion* is about memoirs. Anne has traveled to Lyme with the Musgrove sisters and Captain Wentworth, and there they meet the Harvilles and the young Captain Benwick, who would have been "all my friends." Captain Benwick had been engaged to Captain Harville's young sister, who died suddenly of an illness. Captain Benwick is in mourning, and he tells Anne how he is struggling to recover from the death of his fiancée. She listens sympathetically.

After a little while, she tells him that he should read more broadly. He has lived on Romantic poetry. "She ventured to recommend a larger allowance of prose in his daily study." He is curious what she means, and it is then that she suggests, her stiff tone hiding years of effort, "such works of our best moralists, such collections of the finest letters, such memoirs of characters of worth and suffering, as occurred to her at the moment as calculated to rouse and fortify the mind by the highest precepts, and the strongest examples of moral and religious endurance." Anne sees that Captain Benwick has been too narrow, transfixed by his state of sorrow. She wants to offer him hard-won reading wisdom, and makes a gesture of friendship.

The small gesture has repercussions. Captain Benwick does begin to read what Anne has recommended, and to feel that, in her, he has a new friend. He comes out of the intense solitude of early grief, and he falls in love with Louisa, who falls in love with him. This liberates Anne's own captain, Captain Wentworth, from the obligation to Louisa that he had incurred, and would be in honor bound to. Anne has an effect on her own fate.

In Austen, we are often told what a character is reading, and how, and it always matters. Characters drawn to lurid or Gothic stories are unformed or unreliable, they want shoring up or reining in. Both lazy characters and rigid ones don't read; self-absorbed ones read too much, or with poor judgment. There is a balance in reading as in all things—to read in a desultory, uncommitted way shows a want of exertion, to live in books to the exclusion of one's real neighbors a want of compassion. Although we now think of reading as a generally solitary activity, in Austen's day people often read aloud to one another. Her family did this nearly every evening. They judged books by how they sounded on a second reading, a third. Austen's characters learn to read and to reread, and this, mysteriously, significantly, is a part of how they come to say what they mean and to live in the world together.

Here is a passage I look for at night. After Anne finishes her conversation with Captain Benwick, which for her has been stimulating and pleasant, she goes back to her hotel room. A hotel room. For me, and for a few other women I know, the liberty of a hotel room, since having children, is like nothing else. Really alone with my thoughts, and made aware by every unfamiliar impersonal bit of the surroundings that I am unto myself. Anne's days are usually a thicket of domestic obligation, but today she has had a conversation about books that she would never have with her sisters or her neighbors. I think I know a related feeling from teaching. A sigh of relief, to have spoken some of these inward reflections. Quickly followed by the uncertainty that I have said too much, too prescriptively. Often as I walk away from the classroom I am torn between the feeling of having offered something, and cringing, and laughing at myself for my presumption.

That night, in her hotel room, Anne "could not but be amused" to have come all the way to Lyme "to preach patience and resignation to a young man whom she had never seen before." Right away, she casts doubt on herself and on the memoirs she has recommended. She can't help noticing that "like many other great moralists and preachers, she had been eloquent on a point in which her own conduct would ill bear examination." In an old-fashioned memoir, one by a great moralist and preacher, Anne's conduct would ill bear examination, but in the novel I am reading, her self-examination is what makes her a kind of friend.

If Anne Elliot is almost a writer of her own experience, a memoirist with her own worth and suffering within the novel Jane Austen wrote about her, she becomes this almost-writer, or becomes her again, as she comes out of more absorbed grief and into a recognition of what that grief has been. It is she who describes herself, and her mournful love for both Captain Wentworth and her mother. Anne says to a friend that her experience has never been really understood or recorded in books. "If you please," she says, "no reference to examples in books. Men have had every advantage of us in telling their own story. Education has been theirs in so much higher a degree; the pen has been in their hands. I will not allow books to prove anything." She will instead speak of her own experience, never yet in a book. The speech is now a famous one, though it was quietly uttered. Anne makes a declaration that others may share in when she says that she is a woman, one of those "loving longest when existence or when hope is gone."

Jane Austen wrote in alternation, darker books and lighter ones, dimmer ones of sorrow and bewilderment next to brighter ones of comedy and clarity. In *Sense and Sensibility*, Elinor and Marianne struggle to grieve and to be known to each other; in *Pride and Prejudice*, Elizabeth is all resilience, rapidity, light. In *Mansfield Park*, the great hinge in Austen's writing, Fanny laboriously tries to join the forgotten past to the unknown future, and is frequently mute. Emma is alert, magnificent, often wrong, but her voice is absolutely clear. The heroines change their ways of living, and their names give the pattern of how. The brighter, more forceful characters, the E's—Elizabeth, Emma—already speak well for themselves. They will have to learn to read other characters. The more pensive and isolated characters, the anns—Fanny, Anne—are already attentive readers. They change the ways they speak and write.

It is in *Sense and Sensibility* that the patterns begin to emerge, but still confusedly. In that novel there are two heroines—an E, Elinor, and an ann, Marianne. Both sometimes speak well, but Elinor holds back, and Marianne says too much; Marianne reads a great deal, but it does not guide her. They are artificially separated and also tangled together. If you begin with *Sense and Sensibility*, as Jane Austen chose to when she returned to writing, it is a little easier to find the beautiful rhythm that comes in the rest of the books—working first at reading, then at self-expression, then at reading again—like the work of love, and friendship, and the work of writing itself.

Three

———————◆———————

MEMORIALS

A LETTER

It was about six weeks before he died that my father sent me the letter. He had not written it for me. It was a tribute for a colleague, and it was the beginning of the book my father wanted to write. The letter was about how when people work or live together, a kind of character grows among them, one other people can easily apprehend. A child who goes over to another household to play has a feel for what the life there is like; a person who gets a new job knows it will take a while to adjust to the culture. These characters of shared life have their own language and memory, they have ways of moving and rebuilding themselves out of the habits they have. My father's ideas about this were full of actors and lines from poems; his letter was as much influenced by literature as by social science. He was proud of the letter, and shy about it; in the note he sent with it he said, "on the off chance it's of interest." He knew it would feel incomplete to me, that I would be missing some necessary background and also that the ideas weren't entirely formed yet, but, he said, "you are good at filling in gaps."

I read it hurriedly. The baby needed something, or I did. I wanted to make sure I got to it, but I didn't really want to spend time with it. We had just been visiting at home for Christmas, and it was clear that my father was very ill, much more ill than I was able to allow myself to believe, and as I scanned his lines, there was a hovering pressure of time and ambition. I knew it was not going to be enough. I wanted the letter to break through and explain things that I had been finding vague in my conversations with him, and at the same time, I really didn't want it to. Familiarity was reassuring, whereas a sketch of new terrain that he might never reach would have been terrible to contemplate. I wrote back, briefly; I don't have my message anymore, but I said that it had been nice to think about what he said about Coleridge and imagination. I knew the letter was important, but I did not realize that my father was thinking this might be the best, and last, formulation of the ideas he had been at work on.

A month later, he was in the hospital. We went home, and he was able to leave the hospital for a few days, but then he went back. We stayed. My sister and her family came back from Berlin, and in the hospital room, he held on steadily for the evening of their return. The next day, he woke knowing that he would die.

My mother and my sister had gone to the hospital first, and he told them to call me to come in; there were things he wanted to say. Breathing and talking were so difficult by then, but my memory of what he said is all in his ordinary voice, the voice I've known since before I was born, gentle, playful, glad we were here in the world together. He had been thinking about what his death would mean to us. He said, "I know how much you all love me." I think he knew how we would wish we had said other things, called more, he didn't want us to worry. He spoke of continuities that my mother and my sister and I would turn over in the days and years that came after. It was something he could do for us, and he had prepared.

He decided that later in the day he would take morphine. He knew, and we knew, that that would at last bring relief from the pain he was in, and from the fear of not being able to breathe, but that it would also relax his breathing so that he would no longer get enough oxygen, and that he would die.

It was such a short day, and a long one. There were some stray minutes, when I tried to think of right things to say. I told him that I had admired the letter he had sent. I said, and I know I did, because I memorized my own phrase in the days after, that it was a beautiful expression of his thought. I think I said that I would go on thinking about it. He asked me, and there I do remember that the words came after long pauses for breath, to get in touch with the colleague he had written the letter for. He knew that the colleague had begun to write a response that was to be its own essay, and my father wanted the two documents, his letter and the colleague's reply, published together. I went to my computer; it happened that the colleague was at his. Within the hour, still, I think, before he took the morphine, I could tell him that this request would be honored. My father said, "Thank you, Rachel."

My mother and my sister and I were all there, around him. We were tender with one another and with him. I have the sense of us circling around him, and also the sense of us fading. I have sat at three deathbeds and I have noticed each time, as I try to be with the inner life of the person going out of the world, a faint inversion in the atmosphere. It is as if I and the other people around the bed are wraiths, our hands and voices but dimly perceivable. There is a tilt to the world—it slides toward the world of the spirits—and a sense that we are become the intangibles.

SENSE AND SENSIBILITY

Here are the Dashwoods. Openhearted Mrs. Dashwood is about to lose her husband, a loving man, and too trusting, who has not been able to secure much of his wealth for her and their daughters. The Dashwood daughters are Elinor, Marianne, and the young Margaret, who is but fourteen. Fatal illness comes upon Mr. Dashwood unexpectedly soon, and he asks his son, by his first marriage, who will inherit the whole fortune, to support these women he is leaving. There is an understanding that this support will amount to some thousands of pounds, and annual income. But, in the event, the son proves selfish, pliable to his intensely selfish wife. This wife is from the other family that figures large in the story, the Ferrars. There is a ferocious scene, in which the new master and mistress of the house decide that, for the widow and daughters, they need not after all add anything to a "valuable legacy" of some "china, plate, and linen." By this and other means, Mrs. Dashwood and her daughters are thrust into a condition Jane Austen knew well, of genteel, impoverished homelessness.

Elinor, steadfast and self-disciplined, begins to make a new attachment. While they remain in their old home, she has encountered another member of the Ferrars family, a brother of the selfish wife, and a liking has grown between her and Edward Ferrars, though something feels amiss in their relations.

A letter arrives. The Dashwoods are offered, by a kindhearted relation, a place to live in Devonshire, of modest rent, called Barton Cottage. (The name seems like that of Chawton Cottage, where Austen and her sister and mother found a home.) Eager for some small independence, the Dashwoods quickly accept the place, close by the much grander house at Barton Park, where their relatives live. They make the wrenching departure, travel to Barton Cottage, and stay there for a hundred pages, long enough to see many hopes come to nothing.

For a while, the novel keeps a secret, but eventually we learn that Edward is already clandestinely engaged to the manipulative Lucy Steele, and cannot extricate himself, nor can he bring himself to tell the truth to Elinor. Lucy's revelation of correspondence—she waves a letter from Edward in front of Elinor's face—the revelation that she has the power to write, from which Elinor is cut off, concludes Volume I.

The middle Dashwood sister, Marianne, is a romantic. She loves the poems of Byron and Scott, she plays the piano in a storm of feeling, she runs out of doors in the rain. *Sense and Sensibility* seems to take Elinor's point of view, but it is often surreptitiously putting in a word for Marianne. Marianne, literally, falls in love with Willoughby—a romantic like herself, though without her sincerity—by tumbling down a wet hill, spraining her ankle, and having him sweep her off her feet and carry her home. Willoughby is sensitive; he is also a man of expensive tastes. With an eye on wealth, he, too, is in the midst of acquiescing to a manipulative woman's demand, and he keeps this from Marianne. Suddenly, he has to go to London, and all communication ceases. Elinor watches anxiously for signs of the letters that would mean Marianne and Willoughby are actually engaged. The novel is interested in young women writing—whether and how they are able to write. It was then an inflexible rule that a woman was not allowed to write to a man to whom she was not engaged. The worlds of commerce, war, intellectual exchange were largely carried on in letters between men. Women wrote within their families, or their circle of women friends, but not to men, to strangers.

The sisters, without their mother so they are really alone and unguided, travel to London to wait for their fortunes to be determined. They stay in other people's households, and their fundamental dependence is acute. They are away from Barton Cottage for 160 pages. During this time, the two men who seem to have promised to give the sisters a home go back on the promise: Edward silently, Willoughby with the cruelty of disavowal. The cottage in the background hardly mitigates the sense that we are reading a history of their homelessness. Finally, they regain Barton Cottage, and this time it can be like coming home. Only there are they at last able to speak openly about their experience to each other. They have had to go over the death of their father and the loss of their first home by living it again, but with a different ending.

All my memories of reading *Sense and Sensibility* are at the house we call the Red House. Our apartment there was the ground floor. Our bedroom was small, an exact square around our square bed around the rectangular book. The windows of the bedroom looked over the driveway, where an old car that our landlady kept for her son was permanently parked. To the right, you could see part of a magnolia tree. Our landlady lived upstairs. She was an insomniac and sometimes when I was awake in the night, I could hear her pacing overhead.

If I think of the room now, it is summer, the magnolia is in leaf, and the neighborhood has ampleness and warmth. From this home, it was a simple matter to walk up the street and cross the Fresh Pond Parkway to take a walk around the Fresh Pond reservoir, and I often took S there. We loved to watch the dogs splashing in the smaller pond nearby, and she and I always took a drink from the water fountain with the frog and the turtle. But it was that first acute winter when I read *Sense and Sensibility* most, and then, if I went to walk, the trees were frozen and snow-laden, the pathways obstructed or slippery. I did not take S and walked, stumbling, by myself.

In the early weeks of grief, I had a squinting strain in my eyes. I remember telling M that even the branches of the trees did not look right, and I spoke harshly, bitter that he did not know my feeling. It was as if the trees backed away from my sight. Later, I thought about something my father had been interested in, descriptions Oliver Sacks made of the perceptions of people with unusual brain injuries. It can happen to people who have experienced such an injury that they are visited by a loved one and can identify the face, but denounce the visitor as some disturbing impostor. The face is right, but the feeling they should be having is gone, and without the feeling, instead of accustomed recognition comes a powerful alienation. This was how I felt about the trees—I knew them to be trees, but I had not realized that I always looked up to the trees with the sense that my father, too, was standing somewhere, looking up.

If, before, I had given any thought to *Sense and Sensibility*, it was as a romantic comedy, and one that didn't quite work. I had watched Emma Thompson's movie interpretation of *Sense and Sensibility* several times, with pleasure, and I would have said that, by contrast, there was something incoherent in the novel itself, where instead the romances are unsatisfying, and the wit is barbed. It is hard to imagine why Elinor falls in love with Edward. Thompson herself wrote new scenes so that the actor who played opposite her would actually have a speaking part in the first half of the story, which he, problematically, does not in the novel itself. In no other Austen novel does the world seem so dangerous or other people so unfathomable.

It is a part of the oddness of *Sense and Sensibility* that it is somehow easy for a reader, at least this reader, to forget that it begins with a death. The squabbling over the will and the departure are presented in such a satirical, amusing tone that death becomes a matter of petty economics, and one may neglect its metaphysical effects. As the novel unfolds, there is little to remind the reader that the sisters are in their first year of mourning. They do not speak of their father, and it is not clear whether he was a source of wise counsel during his life. The book is not usually described as a novel about grief.

Yet the Dashwood sisters are grieving as no other characters in Austen do, and their grief recurs in their experiences of being abandoned by the men they had thought were their suitors. Austen mentions tears twenty-three times in *Sense and Sensibility*; usually they belong to Marianne. And it is not only weeping and its repetition that give us the picture of these early, difficult months. The sisters' rudderlessness, Marianne's impulsive choices, her inability to believe in the reality of other people, the incredible force of will with which Elinor drags herself forward, and the fact that the spirits of all the main characters have the tendency to plunge suddenly and surprisingly low, speak to the absence that dizzies and unbalances them, unsettling the very ground beneath their feet.

Elinor and Marianne grieve both for their father and for their place in the world, and each judges the other's grief. Marianne, who often sees landscapes as an extension of her own feelings, remarks, as they take leave of their home, on the strangeness of the trees: "Ye well-known trees," she cries out, are "unconscious . . . and insensible," of we who "walk under your shade." It took me years to notice how similar this was to the strange bereft feeling I had tried to explain to M and felt angry that he did not share.

Marianne's grief is wound up with what the novel calls "sensibility":

Elinor saw, with concern, the excess of her sister's sensibility; but by Mrs. Dashwood it was valued and cherished. They encouraged each other now in the violence of their affliction. The agony of grief which overpowered them at first, was voluntarily renewed, was sought for, was created again and again. They gave themselves up wholly to their sorrow, seeking increase of wretchedness in every reflection that could afford it, and resolved against ever admitting consolation in future. Elinor, too, was deeply afflicted; but still she could struggle, she could exert herself.

Elinor is often described as exerting herself, and often herself uses the word "exertion." Early on, I read Stuart Tave's *Some Words of Jane Austen*, and his careful consideration of Elinor's exertions sent me back to etymologies and on toward my own understanding. "Exert" has a Latin basis, and is composed of "ex" and "sert." It is like "insert" and means to join an existing order, but by an outward movement. Beginning in the 1600s, "exert" was used particularly by biologists, so it had a scientific quality of organisms and their organization. For us now, "exert" and "exertion" have been completely overlaid with the meaning of vigorous effort, but this second meaning only came into use in the late 1770s, and was fairly new in Jane Austen's time. The word may carry a shade of religious conviction also. For Austen's first readers, these meanings would have been clearly present. Elinor is joining the order of the world, and she is responding to new circumstances with great, suppressive, internal effort, perhaps too great. When she loses Edward to Lucy, "the necessity of concealing" their secret engagement "obliged her to unceasing exertion." We are told that "no one would have supposed from the appearance of the sisters, that Elinor was mourning in secret."

Marianne's mourning, much to Elinor's alarm, is all in the open. When Marianne sees Willoughby with another woman at a ball, and he seems not even to recognize her, each sister responds precisely in character:

"Good heavens!" she exclaimed, "he is there—he is there—Oh! why does he not look at me? why cannot I speak to him?"

"Pray, pray be composed," cried Elinor, "and do not betray what you feel to every body present."

When the terrible callous letter, disavowing any mutual feeling, comes from Willoughby (a letter that has actually been dictated by his new fiancée, who can now write through him), Marianne collapses:

Elinor could no longer witness this torrent of unresisted grief in silence.

"Exert yourself, dear Marianne," she cried, "if you would not kill yourself and all who love you. Think of your mother; think of her misery while *you* suffer; for her sake you must exert yourself."

It does seem right that exertion—putting oneself into the order of the family and the world—may resist, mitigate, even transform grief. But if exertion means mourning in secret, that may make sincere feeling inaccessible, even to oneself. Marianne is not entirely wrong, even if what she says is funny, when she complains of Elinor to their mother. "Elinor," she says, "in quitting Norland and Edward, cried not as I did. Even now her self-command is invariable. When is she dejected or melancholy? When does she try to avoid society, or appear restless and dissatisfied in it?" Elinor may be taking too much responsibility for society and its orders, while Marianne, intemperate, cannot give true expression either. It is as if the capacity to live with grief has been divided between the two sisters, and they are both endangered by the division.

That winter, I almost always began from the place, fairly late in the book, where Marianne falls ill and recovers. Marianne's illness is like Marianne herself, dramatic and consuming. Elinor in tending to her is not, at first, worried, then she is very worried. The cold turns frighteningly feverish.

Marianne's life is in danger. The morbidity of her self-involvement, "if you would not kill yourself," has become real.

In the year following a death, all beds may seem close to deathbeds. Austen describes how Elinor "was almost hopeless" and how she went on "scarcely stirring from her sister's bed, her thoughts wandering from one image of grief, one suffering friend, to another." Reading, I felt I could imagine certain unbidden images that Elinor's mind wandered past. When Marianne is ill, both sisters play again the death of their father, but they do not speak of it to each other.

It did not occur to me that Marianne might be ill with the starkness of early, impacted grief, or that I wanted to see her get up from that bed and go on. I had an almost physical need to arrive at the road that ran in front of Barton Cottage where, at last, and for the first time in the novel, the two sisters take a walk that is really together. Over and over, even though I knew S would be up fresh in the morning, standing in her crib and calling, I stayed up until midnight and one and two to read every page, that whole last third of the book again.

REVEREND GEORGE AUSTEN

Jane Austen and her father were close. The Reverend George Austen was a genial clergyman who had been educated at Oxford, and he gave his precocious daughter the run of his library, which contained some five hundred well-chosen books. "Being not only a profound scholar, but possessing a most exquisite taste in every species of literature," wrote Henry Austen about their father, in a biographical notice of his sister, "it is not wonderful that his daughter Jane should, at a very early age, have become sensible to the charms of style, and enthusiastic in the cultivation of her own language." The Reverend Austen bought his daughter notebooks—at the time paper was expensive and rare, and these were not available to every daughter—and she filled them with stories and plays and mock histories that she dedicated to her father and brothers and her sister, Cassandra, who was her best friend, her first reader, and her lifetime companion. Their mother was busy, and perhaps not terribly interested in girls, or in children more generally before they could join an adult conversation. Cassandra began watching out for Jane before they could really remember.

The Austens lived in the village of Steventon, in Hampshire. Theirs was an exuberant family that also took religion seriously, and gave thought, on Sundays and other days, to virtue and to charity. In their own household, money was a consideration. In addition to Mr. Austen's duties as a clergyman, he and Mrs. Austen leased a substantial farm, and kept a school for boys who boarded in their home. Jane and Cassandra were two girls together among the boys. The mother and the brothers spent days writing things they could read aloud and laugh about in the evenings. Writing was, in its foundation, writing for the amusement of the family. When Jane Austen began to write her first novels, in the 1790s, her father would have heard his daughter read out early versions of both *Elinor and Marianne*, as *Sense and Sensibility* was called, and *First Impressions*, which was to become *Pride and Prejudice*. Austen's niece Caroline wrote in a remembrance, fifty years after her aunt's death, that Jane Austen "was considered to read aloud remarkably well." She continued: "I did not often hear her but *once* I knew her to take up a volume of Evelina and read a few pages of Mr. Smith and the Brangtons and I thought it was like a play."

Perhaps, listening to his daughter read of Elizabeth Bennet and her father, the Reverend Austen recognized something of their own shared, witty affection. In November of 1797, when Jane Austen was on the verge of turning twenty-two, her father was proud enough to send to a reputable publisher the completed manuscript of *First Impressions*. He even offered to help put up money toward its publication. It was declined by return of post, meaning the publisher had not opened the manuscript. Neither of those two early books was published until much later, in 1811 and 1813, by which point they had been reworked, and their author's thoughts and circumstances had changed. The Austens had left their family home, and, in 1805, the Reverend Austen had died.

Between the time that Austen first drafted the novels and the time they were published, the world had been through the Terror and many years of the Napoleonic Wars, and the close-knit Austen family had become far-flung. Jane and Cassandra Austen had watched their brothers find careers and households of their own. By 1801, only the mother, the father, and the two sisters remained together. It was in that year that the Reverend Austen took the sudden decision to leave the rectory at Steventon. James Edward Austen-Leigh's memoir describes this as a mortal loss:

> The loss of their first home is generally a great grief to young persons of strong feeling and lively imagination; and Jane was exceedingly unhappy when she was told that her father, now seventy years of age, had determined to resign his duties to his eldest son, who was to be his successor in the Rectory of Steventon, and to remove with his wife and daughters to Bath. Jane had been absent from home when this resolution was taken; and, as her father was always rapid both in forming his resolutions and in acting on them, she had little time to reconcile herself to the change.

Austen-Leigh wrote his memoir in careful consultation with his sisters, Anna Lefroy and Caroline Austen. Caroline Austen's letter to him about the moment of rupture had certain vivid details that he smoothed out:

> My Aunt was very sorry to leave her native home, as I have heard my Mother relate—My Aunts had been away a little while, and were met in the Hall on their return by their Mother who told them it was all settled, and they were going to live at Bath. My Mother who was present said my Aunt Jane was greatly distressed—All things were done in a hurry by Mr. Austen & of course this is *not a fact* to be written and printed—but you have authority for saying she *did* mind it—if you think it worth while—

They were discreet about matters that do not seem concerning, but rather of interest—I can picture it better, in the hall, their mother saying it was all settled, their father, who did all things in a hurry, her distress. And yet something is there in the less particular reflections that were published—not only measure or decorum, but a sense of general experience: "it is not wonderful that his daughter" should have been "enthusiastic in the cultivation of her own language." Or, "the loss of their first home is generally a great grief to young persons of strong feeling and lively imagination." Jane Austen's brother and her nieces and nephews all thought that she was incomparable, yet it was a part of their family language, and their social language, to think of even people one deemed radically unusual in general terms. A part of the reason, I think, that the characters in her novels, with all their specificity, still seem like open places to many readers.

When they were little, the nieces and nephews had loved and admired their aunt—it had been one of their greatest pleasures to visit her at Chawton: she made up such stories for them, which sometimes went on for two or three days, every fairy with its own character; she understood children, and knew how to talk with them, encouraged them in reading and writing. As adults, they thought her books wondrous, and they wanted to do justice to her. The record they left, while quite thin, had been given sensitive consideration from the first. This combination of empty places and depth of understanding seems to correspond exactly with the novels themselves, and the family sensibility from which they grew.

The reasons for the departure from Steventon are a bit dim, but involved many members of the family. Mrs. Austen herself was not entirely well, and it may have been thought that the waters and doctors of Bath would improve her health. Or, perhaps Mr. Austen felt he was getting too old to perform his duties as rector, and that it was time for his son James to have the place for his family. Mortality and dependence must have been in the air. Still an unpublished author, Jane Austen began a novel that she called *The Watsons*, in which four sisters anxiously try to plan how they will survive after the death they anticipate for their clergyman father. In the novel, as in the Austen family, it was a worrisome fact that the income of a clergyman was reserved for the work of the church, and did not remain to support widows or bereaved daughters, no matter how many years of their household life they had put into church work. I imagine Jane Austen talked this future over with Cassandra when they retired for the evening, but on the surface, life went on as usual. The four Austens lived in Bath, traveling a fair amount, and then death began. First, on December 16, 1804, on Jane Austen's birthday, her dear friend Mrs. Lefroy fell trying to get off her bolting horse, hit her head, and was killed. Then, a few weeks later, in January of 1805, the Reverend George Austen, who had had a few attacks, as Austen would report to Frank, of "fever, violent tremulousness, & the greatest degree of Feebleness," which had been successfully treated by "Cupping," was again taken suddenly ill, but, this time, suddenly died.

It was Jane Austen's task to inform Frank, then at sea, and because of the movement of his ship, she had to write to him twice. Her father died in the morning on Monday, the twenty-first of January. One can see, in the two accounts she gave, written on that Monday and then on the Tuesday, both what was absolutely crucial to communicate, so that she would write it almost the same way again, and what shifted in her impressions.

Both letters describe her father's completed life in estranged, conventional language: "Our dear Father has closed his virtuous & happy life," and "We have lost an Excellent Father." But, on the first day of writing, there is a little more ease in those sentences where she can still reach back to the life she knew, the life with him among the living. Yesterday, she says in her first account, he was able to "join us at breakfast as usual, walk about with only the help of a stick," and she seems still partly there with him at breakfast. By the second account, this has become a reflection on the past: "Within twenty four hours of his death he was walking with only the help of a stick, was even reading!"

Both letters refer to the comfort that may be taken from the fact that her father did not know that he was dying. The death feels unreal and formal in the first account, as if seen from a great distance. "Being quite insensible of his own state, he was spared all the pain of separation." In the second, his death has become a part of his life, there is less formality and more feeling, "he was mercifully spared from knowing that he was about to quit the Objects so beloved, so fondly cherished as his wife & Children ever were.—His tenderness as a Father, who can do justice to?—"

At the end of the second letter, she tries to give a last impression of her father, such as might be important to her absent brother, as she imagines him imagining their father. "The Serenity of the Corpse is most delightful!—It preserves the sweet, benevolent smile which always distinguished him." Her cheerful epistolary habit is not natural to the modern reader, but part of the power of early attempts at memorial is that they still carry the feeling of what life with the person was like, the old ways before they have begun to change.

SHOULD I WRITE

Elinor and Marianne are in constant doubt about whether they ought to write, whether they will be understood, whether what they remember has imaginable reality. They read all the time, and they judge the men they hope to marry by what these men read and how. Marianne, we know, "had the knack of finding her way in every house to the library, however it might be avoided by the family in general." But reading and writing—attention and expression—are not, for them, in that ecological balance that a creative life sometimes sustains.

When the two sisters arrive in London, each sits down to write a letter. Elinor tells Marianne that she need not write; she, Elinor, is writing to their mother and there is no need to pay for two letters at once saying they are safely arrived. But Marianne says she is not writing to their mother. From this, Elinor concludes that Marianne and Willoughby must be secretly engaged. Marianne writes to Willoughby several times. The last time it is a day in January, perhaps like the one on which Jane Austen wrote to her brother. Marianne and her grief are extremely exposed:

Before the house-maid had lit their fire the next day, or the sun gained any power over a cold, gloomy morning in January, Marianne, only half dressed, was kneeling against one of the window-seats for the sake of all the little light she could command from it, and writing as fast as a continual flow of tears would permit her.

As Marianne struggles, I feel that odd, memorial combination: an unharbored grief, and also the sense that she is performing the ritual part of the mourner, to be witnessed by whom, exactly; Willoughby, but also people she does not know, the woman he is apparently with, the rest of his life, unknown to her. The writing starts and stops. It is too exposed, and yet it is not entirely wrong; some truth, of record, of inward nature, compels her:

It was some minutes before she could go on with her letter, and the frequent bursts of grief which still obliged her, at intervals, to withhold her pen, were proofs enough of her feeling how more than probable it was that she was writing for the last time to Willoughby.

A FATHER

My father's memorial service was exactly a week after the day he died. My sister and I were both to speak. Each of us struggled alone that week for language. There is a day on which you can still say "This morning, Dad said," and then a day, radically different, in which you can say "Yesterday, Dad said," and there comes this shift: the last continuous action, "dying," is surmounted by a single present, "is dead," that makes all other verbs past, and you cannot believe how estranged an ordinary sentence is from a person you have been accustomed to making ordinary sentences about.

In that week, in the different corners of the house, sitting on the low living room couches, or sorting through the plentiful food brought by kind friends and neighbors, my sister and I strained, separately, for sentences. Now and again we talked of the moments of grief we were having, but we said little of what we thought of saying in public at week's end. I remember she asked me about whether I was going to mention the game my father played with us at bath time, which he called bathematics. My father would set us problems of figuring out how to get a certain quantity of water—if you imagined you had a seven-cup measure and a two, it was easy to get five cups of water, but how would you get six? She asked as if it was quite likely that I would have landed on this instance of my father's playing with us, making learning delightful, which he did, because learning delighted and amazed him, and also being ambitious, which he was. To us, he was kind and supportive, though the support might have been less necessary had the expectations not been so high. There was pressure to get our speeches right.

My father had told my mother something of what he wanted the memorial service to be like, some of his colleagues from the university whom he would like to have speak, that he wanted music by Bach. I am not sure whether he would have guessed that there would be some five hundred people there, but he might have.

The ceremony was held in a large hall. There were my father's colleagues, and his former graduate students, people from my mother's theater company, friends and neighbors, our extended family, the man who ran the hot dog stand where my father got lunch many days. People he had worked with came from Chicago and Utah and Shanghai, and from all across the University of Michigan.

My father had a remarkable ability to understand other people, and to make them feel understood. Strangers came up to us to tell us that my father had seemed to know them better than almost anyone else in their lives. We were writing memorials of a deep internal presence to be spoken both for people we had known since before memory, and for strangers who had felt a great intimacy with our father, but an intimacy unknown to us.

I suppose that one reason to have a memorial service, and advertise it in the papers, is so that people you did not know about may join the mourning. There is a neighbor who keeps a picture of my father in his desk; there are people who worked with him on his research whom I have never met. In many houses of worship, it is a kindness, even a religious act, for a stranger to attend a memorial service. Memorial writing does not exclude strangers, because the meanings of a mourned life will need to be carried by a generality.

A WALK

It was a few days after my father had died, and when I thought of trying to speak at his memorial service at the end of the week, there came a feeling at once noisy and blank. I thought I would leave the house and go for a walk. It was still snowing, as it had been the day he died. I decided to walk out to Gallup Park, where my father loved to walk and where he and I had often walked together. I remember that as I trudged down the snow-thickened streets, I couldn't really believe that he was dead, and at the same time, I had the distinct idea that he was a comet, and I could feel a strange lift in the upper reaches of my mind, of him departing our skies.

When you enter Gallup Park, you walk over a curved wooden bridge, just wide enough for a car to drive over, and from that bridge you can see the Huron River in both directions. Stretching east, you can follow the river path all the way down to the high bridge. But we usually go on so that we can turn toward the west, where the water runs wide and widely sheltered, with trees on both sides, where there are more waterbirds. A little ways on, there is a path to the left where you can walk out on a long protected bit of bog, with planked walkways at low points. There you are really among the trees, they tug at your coat with their winter berries, and the little coves and inlets are full of ducks and other birds. I saw a flock of birds the day I walked out. Because I took pictures, I know that there were thirteen swans, swimming in the icy water and walking about, and four large white ducks with orange bills, and twenty-six smaller dark ducks, many of them sitting huddled in the snow. I took pictures of the tracks, too, from the birds in their coming and going.

Somewhere along the water's edge, I had the idea that I would try to talk about my father's imagination. I had this idea because of his letter. I had not reread it since he had sent it to me, but it rang in my mind that my father had said he wanted the letter published. I had written to the colleague. My father had said, "Thank you, Rachel."

There had been a further confusion. In his first hurried reply, the colleague, Karl Weick, wrote that he remembered that my father had hoped to eventually collaborate on a paper with me. In the hospital room, I did not know whether to say anything about this. At first, I just said that Karl would publish the two papers, and was glad that my father understood and had thanked me. But then I needed to know whether he had really wanted to write together. After a little more time had passed, I mentioned this other thing Karl had said. "I didn't know," I said. Already the morphine had begun to take hold. My father looked a little confused, was unable to give an answer. I could tell from the expression on my mother's face, just the faintest uncertainty, that this was not right, that she would have known if my father had wanted that, had ever said that. We let it go.

After he died, I wrote to Karl, asking what it was that had made him think that, and he forwarded me the email, saying that he was sorry, he had made a mistake. He thought there had been an idea of collaboration, but what my father had written was that he thought "a conversation about Coleridge-Shakespeare-imagination-fancy will soon ensue."

Conversation was my father's medium—in it, he was alert, far-reaching, subtle. His thoughts ran like quicksilver not only through the veins of his own understanding, but through those of the person he was speaking with. He wanted one of his late conversations to be made public. Karl wrote to me that he still thought there was a sentiment of "a father-daughter jointly writing," and I guess I think that there was something right about Karl's misremembering, that there was, indirectly, but force-fully, a parting injunction, to me, to write something together.

A EULOGY

I wrote my eulogy. M and I went for a drive, to be out of the house; S, quiet in her car seat, was in the back. I read out to him what I had written to say. While I was crying, I noticed that it was snowy outside the car, but inside it was humid, and felt like it had just rained.

My sister was to speak first at the service. Then would come ten or eleven people, each of whom had worked with my father. I was to speak last. When my sister and mother and I had talked about it, I had asked for this, to give final expression. I like to go last. My sister thought that she would begin, and we saw that this also would be right.

When the music stopped, and everyone was quiet, my sister stood to walk up onstage to the podium. I was nervous for her, she does not always like speaking before crowds. She was witty and serious, her dark eyes in-tent and clear. She began with memories from childhood. There had been a time, she said, that she decided to go as a box of Cheerios for Halloween. My mother, with training in costume design, stayed up most of the night painting a large box exactly to scale. But once the costume was on, there was a difficulty:

> I couldn't bend my knees inside the box, which made getting up steps impossible. Momentarily panicked at the thought of not being able to collect my candy, I turned to Dad. He quickly devised a system in which at the bottom of the steps of each house, I would fall backwards and he would catch me, support me at a 45-degree angle, and I would shuffle up the steps without bending my legs.

When my sister spoke of her memory of Halloween, I remembered it myself. I remembered the large box, the yellow paint, even the grid my mother drew so that it would be to scale. I remember my sister's shins banging against the edge of the box as if it happened to my own legs.

My sister told me later that she had tried to think how her own observations of our father could offer something to the people there, who had their own memories, and who had come for news of what had happened at the end to the man they knew. My sister said to the assembled people that on his last day my father was very lucid and had been thinking about what to say to us:

> He would not have wanted any of us to regret his absence. He told us, and I'm sure he would tell you, too, to instead look for the qualities in our children, our students and our friends, that they share with him, and to nurture those qualities.

It is a beautiful idea, comforting in its way, and also demanding. From the fragment, the whole may be reimagined. In this way, our characters may continue.

In the words I had written to say, I explained that I was going to talk about my father's imagination. That I wanted very badly to believe that he could still imagine me.

Like my sister, I said, I had thought of my father's playfulness. I said that sometimes, in the evenings, when no one else was at the department, we would go to my father's office at the university. There was a hand truck around for moving supply boxes and my father would give us rides on it, tilting us back and running up and down the halls. I know we laughed, but the memory has gone silent; what I remember is the flat feeling of the metal, and the exhilaration.

My sister and I saw my father differently, but we both thought of how he would tilt a fixed structure and turn it into a vehicle; we both, as children, had leaned to the support of his hands. The difference, for me, between feeling "I am now the only one who remembers this," and feeling

"My sister, too, was there," bears a faint resemblance to the difference between being the last person on earth who speaks a language, and being one of two such people.

I spoke about other aspects of my father's imagination, ones familiar to many of the people gathered, about the games he had invented for his research, his ability to understand people and their different lines of work. I read out the lines from Shakespeare he had quoted in his letter. The last line resonated in the air: "A local habitation and a name."

I spoke of my dad walking through the parks of Ann Arbor in his last years, thinking about John Dewey and what Dewey says of how character is built out of habitual activity. My dad had liked to quote Dewey, that consciousness "is the continuous readjustment of self and the world in experience." Imagination, I said, was the act of a coherent character stretching toward new circumstances. I tried to say what my father would say and slipped into something nearer to the present tense without noticing: "Imagination, I think he would say, is part of how people alone, and people together, learn."

I can see us, my sister and I, ascending to the podium, vulnerable in black clothes, turning to face this audience of friends and strangers. Before that day, I would have said that my sister and I had a private understanding incommunicable before and to those people, and in a way that is right, but in another way, in finding the language that would be expressive to everyone there, we each of us, I think, said something for her sister, something that not only hadn't been said in the previous blurred week in the house but also was somehow not sayable there.

I said how much my father had relished his conversations with my sister when she became "a practical organization theorist." This is true— my sister works with grassroots organizers, she thinks about effective campaigns and about what would make these organizations more themselves. She told me later that she was glad I had said that. If I think of it now, I can see in my mind the graceful gesture with which my father would move his hands to describe the way my sister sees the shapes of political development over time.

For her part she said that "in an uncharacteristically capitalist moment, and with the audacious lack of tact that only a teenager can muster," she had once asked him whether he minded that our mother was not paid well for her work.

I remember very clearly his answer. "If we're lucky," he said, "we get to do work that's interesting to us and that we love, whatever type of work that may be. But art," he said, "is what makes life worth living. All the rest of us do work so that there can be art in the world, and making art is what your Mom does."

I knew this to be a declaration of support for the work my mother does, and also, I think, for the work I do. At the memorial service, my sister and I tried to say to each other, here is how Dad loved what you do, loved you. Saying it more generally, each of us tried to smooth the other's path in the world, to say to the world, here is how you may know my sister, here is how my father's understanding of her could continue among you.

I noticed that as my father's colleagues spoke, and they spoke beautifully, each one opened a space into which it seemed my own experience poured.

A COTTAGE

In the first period of mourning, Austen gave up work on *The Watsons* and never returned to the book. She revised her other manuscripts, but work was slow and it seems she did not start out on new ideas for books. The Austen brothers, all of them fairly well established, gave money, but did not find their mother and sisters a permanent home. Edward Austen and his wife, Elizabeth Austen, lived on large estates with many houses on them, but perhaps Elizabeth Austen obstructed generosity. Neither could room be found for them at the old Steventon rectory, where James and his wife now lived. Jane Austen, who had had her twenty-ninth birthday in December, a month before her father's death, and her sister, Cassandra, who turned thirty-two in that January of their bereavement, now made, with their mother, a transient household. These three spent four and a half years moving from house to house, making the extended visits that were the way poor relations and dependent women cobbled together a life. Four and a half years is a great many days to be Jane Austen and to get up in the morning and to have no way to begin work on a book.

In the fall of 1808, Elizabeth Austen had her eleventh confinement and had a healthy boy, but then, a few days after the birth, she, too, suddenly died. Cassandra was there, as she often was, to help with the nieces and nephews. All the Austens were in shock and mourning. Right away, in the first period of grief, Edward Austen broached the idea of whether his sisters and mother might live in one of two houses available on his estates. The three Austen women accepted with alacrity. Arrangements took some time. In July of 1809, they moved to Chawton Cottage and Jane Austen took up her pen.

The book she chose to work on first was *Sense and Sensibility*. We do not know how radically she changed it. It seems that *Sense and Sensibility* was originally written as a novel in letters. Cassandra later said this was so, and there is evidence within the book, places where the novel shifts into a tone of personal, detailed recounting that seem like a letter from one of the characters. The epistolary novel was a central form in the eighteenth century, many of Austen's first sketches were in letters, and one of the things she was learning to do in rewriting this book was to knit together the perspectives that would have been distinct in letters, and to make of this a novel that moved in the round. The book published two years later is about a household of women, a mother and her daughters, cast out, and then at last able to be "open" and to come to "constant communication," a state like writing, though the characters will not themselves be writers.

When Jane Austen read it out to Cassandra, her sister would have been able to recognize in it different periods of experience and reflection, from the immediate vicinity of death and from further away, as life and language return. I feel sure Jane made Cassandra laugh at the way she had mixed the two of them into the two of them.

It was just enough, their new cottage, to resume her "old habits of composition." The portable writing desk in which she had been carrying her manuscripts about could at last be set down. The books began to be published. Writing was delightful again, and could go on even when she was visiting in other houses. One of Edward Austen's daughters, called Marianne, remembered how her aunt Jane would sit by the fire in the library, sewing and "saying nothing for a good while, and then would suddenly burst out laughing, jump up and run across the room where pens and paper were lying, write something down, and then come back to the fire and go on quietly working as before." Jane Austen never published a book under her own name, but she now heard back from the world that she was being read. She would write to Frank in 1813 that her identity as the writer was "scarcely the Shadow of a secret now." With each successive book, she simply called herself the author of the previous ones. Her novels were her name, and under it, she did after all write for strangers.

RESUMING

My father wrote his letter especially for Karl Weick, with whom he had been talking for several decades. It was for a public occasion, so he also had in mind that it might be read by strangers. He began the letter by remembering a talk Karl had given many years ago. There were certain thoughts, he wrote, that he had been "returning to . . . often through all the years since." One was about the famous distinction Coleridge drew between "fancy," which was more mechanical, like making a Pegasus by sticking wings on a horse, and "imagination," which could open out whole realms.

My father wrote to his friend: "You developed the concept of imagination, as Coleridge did, by invoking that radiant passage from *A Midsummer Night's Dream*:

> And, as imagination bodies forth
> The forms of things unknown, the poet's pen
> Turns them to shapes, and gives to airy nothing
> A local habitation and a name."

Real imagination is not a rigid collage, it "bodies forth" and makes a place. In his letter my father said true imagination, unlike fancy, was "a more fully harmonized combining, a characterization of the whole that organically integrates its parts." The sentence does not seem intended to be poetic or religious, but in it I think I can glimpse my father's idea of regeneration.

Both my father and his colleague were working on ideas of how a school, or an office, or a household has a character of its own. My father wanted to understand how this character continues over time, and can even grow and repair itself and still be recognizable. He had written a paper with a graduate student about a summer camp that had the same culture and rituals every summer, even though it was attended by different people every year.

In his letter, my father thought of my mother. "One of the forces," my father wrote to his colleague, "that kept returning me to your observation was [H]'s work as a theater director. She has a deep interest in how playwrights imagine great characters like Shakespeare's Falstaff or Hamlet and in how actors develop the characters they inhabit on the stage." He thought of this character development, as she does, as evident all through the actors, in their voices and movements. He mentioned Laurence Olivier, "who said he worked first on how a character moved. It might take a week to get the walk, but once he had it, he knew how to say the lines."

It was closer to the Pragmatists' way of thinking about people, my father said, to see a person's character held together in some immediately discernible and thoroughgoing and persistent way. My father worried about the ways that many economists and businesses thought of an individual person as a kind of list of instants in which that person had made purchases or contracted to sell their labor. This so-called rationality misses the older idea Dewey had of a habitual being, one whose habits, my dad wrote elsewhere, "shape and empower" thoughts and feelings. Habit is a kind of generality, the environment of taking an action and of learning. A person lives not in instants but continuously, thoughtfully, from birth to death.

My father thought the individual had been reduced to an economic unit before, in the period leading up to and during the Industrial Revolution, as goods were traded at great distances, people were separated from land and their families, crowded into cities, eventually laboring in factories, or made to labor in fields, restricted and rewarded in little increments of money and time. He saw hope in "the way the Romantics rallied around imagination and metaphor in their reaction to the Age of Reason that preceded them." He believed in a kind of balance in human struggle—that one force would prevail, and then a countervailing one would arise. "I doubt this is an accident," he wrote of the similarities between our own time and the years around 1800. "I hope, in fact, the most recent cycles are a portent."

At the first anniversary of my father's death, I took S to Ann Arbor to stay with my mother. We decided that on the day, we would walk out to Gallup Park. It was very snowy and cold, and we bundled S up in snowsuit, boots, hat, scarf. We went out along the path I had walked the year before, where the birds had been coming and going. The sky was very gray, and there was not even the raw connectedness of recent loss; it seemed a still more desolate day. Carrying S, I noticed the way the air near her face was warmer and moister from her breath under the scarf. At the bridge over the river, we paused to try to say something in memory. I could not really think; my mother had a few things she wanted to say.

After a few minutes, my mother and I returned to talking to each other. She mentioned the time she and my father had walked across that river one winter when it was thick with ice. It makes me a little nervous to imagine it, their sliding and balancing on the ice. It's a wide river and it was daring of them to cross it. I imagine them looking down at their feet, and at the bank across, calling to each other. The few times she's spoken of it, her eyes brighten with the adventure of it.

The winter day on the bridge, with my cold daughter, I wanted to scatter words like bread crumbs, to send something nourishing to the birds fighting their way through winter, to my father, alone in the cold reaches. What would he want to know? Following his wish, we had scattered his ashes in Venice, a city he loved and that seemed very far away. I tried to trace out the movement of those particles, how they might have been carried, in the water, in the air, the water again, and might have arrived here, on the Huron River, running under this winter bridge.

His close friend in Venice, Massimo, had told me that he held long conversations with my father, walking over the canals. That day, as we walked away from the bridge, I said that it seemed like Massimo was able to talk with him. My mother said that she talked to my father all the time, continually. I said, sorrowfully, maybe with frustration, too, that that had not been how it was for me.

My father loved wind, he would hold his head up into it. He had a kind of sympathetic delight whenever he saw a dog with its head out of a car window, the strong wind rushing around its laughing face. Earlier that year, I had been sitting out on the porch with S when the wind came up around a thunderstorm, and she had stood up in my lap and yelled into the wind with all the force of herself, and I had thought they reached toward each other in a way that I could not.

Sometimes I felt I recognized the eerie voicelessness of my disorientation. I had felt something similar twice before: once when my father had told us he had cancer, and I had gotten into analysis; a second time when I had, four weeks before S was born, terminated in analysis.

When my father first told us, he said it was ordinary prostate cancer, and that there was a good chance he would live twenty more years and die of something else. But from the minute he said it, I knew he could die. I had terrible dreams, of dangers and possibilities. The woman I loved did not think it was a coincidence that I ended the relationship we were in, jaggedly, as if terrified, some months after my father told us his news.

I hoped I was not wrong to have left, but I was felled by a loneliness that came both from the raw truth of my actual circumstances and from the accumulation of a lifetime. It was so brutal that I still see an image of bloody flesh every time I think of it. In pain and acutely aware of having caused pain, I walked as if every step might bring about the dissolution of my body. I remember of the spring that, as I climbed the hill from the station platform toward Sarah Lawrence, the cherry trees were incandescently beautiful, and of the summer, that the hot streets of Sunnyside gave a perpetual feeling of grit in my mouth and on my skin.

The sun glared down on the treeless boulevards of Queens, and I seemed to remember slashes of my life, from long ago, even from childhood, with a shocking tactility, as if I could run my hands over the hedges of our childhood neighborhood. These were not recollected moments of being—there was no alignment or resolution, this was an almost terrifying view, of everything broken open and strewn about me. I dreamt of huge animals—birds big enough to carry a person away in their talons, sea serpents miles long.

Once, years before, after a kindhearted dinner with my friend Justin and his husband, Peter, I had told Justin, who is a psychoanalyst, that I needed help. But when he said he could find someone for me to see, I panicked. This time, however, I felt culpable for the injury I had done in fleeing. Justin recommended an analyst. When she called me back and offered a time to meet, I said that time would be "tricky." "Tricky in what sense," she said. I felt the terms of the relationship were established—with this stranger, I would go over every word.

In the five years that followed, I heard her voice in my head at different hours of the day. I explained to her not only during the three sessions we had each week but when I woke up from a dream, when I said something ridiculous at a faculty meeting, on the train on the way home. Telling her my life, I was remaking it. What was so odd was that a great deal of my life hadn't made sense to me until it began to make sense to this listening stranger. It was mostly her part to listen, but once in a while she let me know that things about her own life were also coming to make more sense as we talked together.

When we made the decision to terminate the analysis, it was at first not bearable, not the right time. We postponed for a year. A month before S was born—I was vast, tented in a green dress—M and I drove down to New York for the last session. We walked around the city and M said he felt I was a balloon that might lift up and float away. I wept in bursts. In the months that followed, when I had time to think of analysis, I felt upset and lost. I could not hear her voice at all.

Two and a half years after my father had died, late that summer and in the fall, I set aside Jane Austen for a little while and I read memoirs, and more memoirs. I read Ta-Nehisi Coates's letter to his son, and memorial of his friend Prince Jones, *Between the World and Me*. I thought about how it needed to take the form of a letter, to his son, and how that let the reader, me, a stranger, live into the writer's past as someone intimately connected to it, imagine the future as a father trembling and proud for his child. When I was a student in college, I had first read James Baldwin's *The Fire Next Time*, which begins with his letter for his nephew, and I had talked with my professor about how memoirs often have a kind of letter within them that may teach the reader to be a close correspondent. I became a teacher myself and taught that essay. I would see how my students felt addressed, in the privacy of their own minds, how Baldwin's letter sometimes let them write one of their own.

I sat up one night in the gray striped chair, while M slept on the couch across from me, and read to the end of Edwidge Danticat's *Brother, I'm Dying*, her uncle, having left Haiti, dying in immigration detention in

Florida; water poured from my eyes. There was a moment in *The Long Goodbye* where I seemed to be running with Meghan O'Rourke on that rare day when the green light intensified and she felt the presence of her mother; another, in *The Argonauts*, where I felt within me the tenderness with which Maggie Nelson lay down in the crib next to their baby, gravely ill, and then the relief, that the child got well. Meghan O'Rourke stayed up late at night reading *Hamlet*. As her family transformed, Maggie Nelson read Eve Kosofsky Sedgwick, and Ralph Waldo Emerson. I read of Helen Macdonald, training her hawk, speaking at her father's memorial service, reading T. H. White. I read as much as I could bear of Shierry Weber Nicholsen's book about mourning and the environment, and turned over the question of whether we now grow up mourning nature and are mourners from the first. I can still immediately pick up again with Mark Doty, walking and stumbling to the dunes a few days after Wally Roberts, his lover, had died, lines from Whitman's *Song of Myself* running in Doty's head. In *The Light of the World*, Elizabeth Alexander wrote "if I cannot take a walk with you," toward her husband, Ficre Ghebreyesus, who had died suddenly. Alexander wrote of reading Lucille Clifton, Rainer Maria Rilke, Langston Hughes. I had not lived these lives, but I lived near them. Sometimes, after I put our children to bed, I wondered how Alexander and her sons were managing that night, now that Ficre Ghebreyesus, her husband, their father, was gone.

Most, though not all, of these writers were mourners, most of these rememberers wrote of reading. Language, other people's language, was a rhythm that carried them into the next part of life. There was testimony in their accounts, and there was granular change. But their work was, I thought, not primarily intended either to document or to heal. It was something else, much more like the resumption of a conversation they had already been having. The conversation with the dead, and the past, had become a conversation with the reader. And in a way that made a curious place—where the reader was near to inhabiting both the life of the writer-mourner and the lives of the people who had died.

I remembered Mphahlele ordering his scattered experiences in Pretoria, and I read *Down Second Avenue* again: "Poverty; my mother's resignation; Aunt Dora's toughness; grandmother, whose ways bridged the past with the present, sticking to neither at any one time; police raids; the ten-to-ten curfew bell; encounters with whites; humiliations." I had not forgotten them, Aunt Dora, and the grandmother, whose ways bridged the past with the present, sticking to neither at any one time, as memoirs themselves learn to do. It had been four years since I had taught my students, writing their memoirs. I wanted to tell them that I thought the memoir form might be demanded by our individualistic and immediate and grief-stricken era, as the novel was demanded by Austen's.

The year and the deadly illness have passed. There is a subtle change. The mood at home is one of relief tinged with anxiety. Marianne is too weak to do much, but Elinor notices in "the whole" of her sister's manner "the direction of a mind awakened to reasonable exertion." Marianne does not say much, but "every sentence aimed at cheerfulness." For a few days the weather keeps them indoors, but then "a soft, genial morning appeared," and Marianne, "leaning on Elinor's arm, was authorised to walk as long as she could without fatigue, in the lane before the house."

Jane Austen's characters have private moments where internal understanding deepens, but this is not where her books come to resolution. It is not Marianne recovering and reflecting in bed, or Elinor weeping by herself, neither is it their marriages, which happen offstage, it is the scene of Elinor and Marianne out walking together that relieves the fundamental burden of *Sense and Sensibility*. Just as *Pride and Prejudice* culminates in Elizabeth and Darcy walking together, and as *Emma* completes itself when Emma and Mr. Knightley take another turn around the shrubbery, and *Persuasion* rises to conclusion when Anne Elliot and Captain Wentworth decide upon the "quiet and retired gravel-walk" in Bath, so the seemingly insuperable gap between the sisters is bridged when they walk together.

At a new pace, the pace of recovering, Elinor and Marianne keep together as they never have before. They walk very slowly. Soon the familiar landscape offers them the memories it carries, and they see before them the hill down which Marianne first fell to Willoughby. Marianne has certain things to say to Elinor, but she hesitates. Elinor "tenderly invite[s] her to be open." After this, Marianne says, "I compare [my conduct] with what it ought to have been; I compare it with yours." "Our situations," Elinor replies, "have borne little resemblance." But actually they have been going over similar ground, their possible husbands withholding in similar ways. About the resemblance between their situations, Marianne is accurate: "They have borne more than our conduct."

Reading this, hurrying because it was getting on for two in the morning, I would take a shuddering breath. I thought what I wanted was Elinor's relief, of at last being acknowledged and appreciated. But I think what I really wanted was Marianne's grasp of the relationship between their two situations. After this, Marianne speaks almost as memoirist. She explains to Elinor that, lying in the bed of illness, she had begun from a place before common language. "Long before I was enough recovered to talk, I was perfectly able to reflect." The first work of self-reconstitution is memory. "I considered the past," she tells Elinor, "I saw in my own behaviour . . . nothing but a series of imprudence towards myself, and want of kindness to others." She describes her own manner—for some she had "ungrateful contempt," to others she was "insolent and unjust," toward Elinor herself she has not shown "any compassion." She feels that she has wronged Elinor above all. "I, and only I, knew your heart and its sorrows; yet to what did it influence me?" she cries out. And here her own language, of the heart and its sorrows, mingles with her sister's words of exertion and friendship. "Not less when I knew you to be unhappy, than when I had believed you at ease, did I turn away from every exertion of duty or friendship; scarcely allowing sorrow to exist but with me . . ."

It is complicated, this phrase Marianne uses to blame herself: "scarcely allowing sorrow to exist but with me." At first, I saw that she was saying that she had thought herself to be the only sorrower. When that was the case, her grief often obliged her to withhold her pen. But now that she has both sense and sensibility, it may be within her power to let sorrow exist with others.

When I go back now, I can sometimes see their novel as a double memoir—a record composed by two sisters, each writing for the other of the year of their loss. Each, despite the endless daily intrusions of other people, has been strikingly alone. When Elinor is writing, what she tells Marianne is something like "There are other people who know and remember the same world you do." This Marianne cannot read until she has "leisure and calmness for serious recollection," and she finds her way to it, as it were, the last book in the library of the novel. Then, at last, she can exert herself. This is what Elinor's account has done for her. When Marianne is writing, she could be telling Elinor, "It is not only life in public but inner life that gives us something in common." After their walk, at the very end of the book, when Elinor learns that Edward is free to marry her, she cries, not for Marianne or her mother, but for herself, in joy and sorrow, for the first time that we know of since her father's death. This is what Marianne has done for Elinor.

In the final sentences of *Sense and Sensibility*, the sisters are the only characters named, and their relation the only topic of interest. Between their two houses there was "that constant communication which strong family affection would naturally dictate;—and among the merits and the happiness of Elinor and Marianne, let it not be ranked as the least considerable, that though sisters, and living almost within sight of each other, they could live without disagreement between themselves, or producing coolness between their husbands." Jane Austen takes leave of both sense and sensibility with laughter, combining in their constant communication the merits of Elinor and Marianne. Public exertion and private feeling, their memorial that makes a place for us.

LETTERS BACK

Every year, on the anniversary of my father's death, my sister sends a letter to a group of people who were closest to our dad. The letters are beautiful, eloquent, forceful. She remembers our father so clearly. Can represent what he would have said, how he would have seen the changes in our world. I look forward to those letters in which I will hear him again. Often, it seems to me, more clearly than I can conjure him myself. My sister and I mention my father to each other now and again. It's rare, though, for us to say, "I'm thinking of Dad." We give the finest shape to the things we say more generally, to other readers, in the letters she writes to other people, in the pages I work on here. The work of remembering is different when it is a letter written in freedom, no longer confined to a family, addressed to people more like strangers.

When your father dies, he leaves you a letter of some kind, whether he means to or not. Some fathers make this difficult, ours tried hard to prepare. "For Rachel," the cardboard box of papers and books says. "You are good at filling in gaps," says the note that comes with the letter. He tells a colleague that soon you will speak together of Coleridge and the imagination. His letter goes on awaiting a reply. You write back. But to whom are you writing? It is written for anyone but him to read, yet it must say—*Dad, in the universe, we are still here. We come together, we come apart. We are learning to walk without you.*

And after it has said this, what else will it say? It will say Dad, the years are passing. Sometimes you seem close and sometimes so far away. We are going to have children you will not know. We have had them. They have learned to walk, and to run, they are learning to read. If we could bring them to see you, you would know them in an instant. And we are going on raising them, and what will we say to them, what will we need to understand? The going on we did with you must be a part of the going on we are doing without you.

One of the beautiful things about the myth of Orpheus, I think, is that, climbing with him up the steep rocky path, trying to hang on to the dead, and not to look back, you are walking through a landscape that just is the pained responsibility felt by those who remain alive. There is a time, right after a death, perhaps just a few scattered minutes or hours, when you would do it, venture to the underworld, to get the person back. And then there are other moments when you wouldn't, not quite, you would go in metaphor, maybe, but you are actually alive in the world with all these people and animals and trees and you're not going to stay with Eurydice and, whether you quite mean to or not, you do look back. You look back, to the past, to your memories of the person, which is a kind of acceptance that you are not going to walk next to that person, or just in front of them anymore, you are just going to remember them, and then they are really dead and irretrievable. And you may feel an overwhelming sense, not that by dying they have left you, but that by not accompanying them you have left them. In the years since my father's death, there have been moments when I was angry with death, or with the world, or with him for his goneness, but I think that more of the time I was angry with myself, worried and sad that I had left him, that instead of living in that family from before, I was going to write and remember. Because of course I wanted to stay where I was, with our beautiful, whimsical, howling children, in the family M and I had made together. The days came, I remember some even early on, in the first spring, only weeks after his death, when I felt I was coming back from the netherworld, when I really didn't want to go looking for him anymore, and I could tell that one of these days it would happen, and I would let go.

Four

---◆---

REVISION

The scene that matters most to me in all of Jane Austen is the scene at the White Hart Inn. It is the last great scene in *Persuasion*, and it is almost a scene from a different book. At the inn, in Bath, many of Anne's friends have come together. Among them, she is at last able to declare enough of her feelings that, across the room, Captain Wentworth can hear her. After the many narrow, ostinato scenes that seem confined among a few violins—Anne in conversation with one character or another—this one bursts forth like horns leading the movement of a symphony.

How does a novelist keep several characters alive in the same space together? Austen learned something fundamental about doing this between *Sense and Sensibility* and *Pride and Prejudice*. In all the books from *Pride and Prejudice* forward there are such scenes—they come into my mind whole—I can tell you where each character is sitting or walking, how they are responding to the events of conversation, the entrances and exits. The tone of the whole, that circulating current in which the whole breathes and is alive, is to be entered, distinct and ongoing.

Persuasion has fewer such scenes, which is part of what critics mean when they discern in the book a falling off in Austen's powers and worry that she is already diminished by illness. In *Persuasion*, there is the scene of Louisa injuring herself at Lyme, a physical drama among the characters, and there is the concert scene, where Anne and Captain Wentworth begin to return to each other around and through many interfering presences, and there are smaller scenes of characters out walking, visiting, sitting together in the evening, but there is nothing that has the magnitude and clarity of the scene at the White Hart Inn. It changes the book entirely, makes it a book of a scale and ambition it would otherwise lack; it weights the book toward its conclusion, which opens out vistas. Woolf thought of this scene when she wrote that in *Persuasion* you could see what Austen would have attempted next. What might have happened next in Austen still seems obscure to me. But the scene at the White Hart is the last masterpiece, and I love it as I love the last Schubert symphonies: the air is fresh, the understanding is mature, difficult harmonies are let to transform with honor, among true voices the depths may be revealed.

The room is full of people having different conversations. Not far from the door, two kindhearted married women are talking over the troubles of long engagements. Near the windows, Anne Elliot—quiet, modest, passionate, alone—is speaking to her friend Captain Harville on the topic of who loves longer, man or woman. Captain Harville, whose devoted marriage has withstood many wartime stints at sea, is asserting that men are more constant in their affections than women, while she—her own longstanding feelings for another captain welling up within her—cannot but assert the contrary. She has loved—for so long now, with such fidelity—Captain Wentworth, who is himself in the room, sitting, just beyond hearing distance, so she thinks, and writing a letter on a matter of business. He is, in fact, listening to what she is saying and writing a letter to her, which, just before he departs, he will draw her attention to, "with eyes of glowing entreaty fixed on her for a moment," before he disappears out the door, leaving her to read.

In the spring, a breeze comes through the windows on the upper floors of the White Hart. These windows overlook the entrance to the fashionable Pump Room across the way, and let in the air of both the natural and the social worlds. The Musgroves have taken these rooms for the party of people they have brought to Bath. It is a room of confluences; here, everything can come together.

When she first came in, Anne Elliot found that people were already there and full of activity. Captain Wentworth announced: "We will write the letter we were talking of, Harville, now, if you will give me materials." Pen and paper were "on a separate table; he went to it, and nearly turning his back on them all, was engrossed by writing."

Anne sat down near Mrs. Musgrove and Mrs. Croft; she had little choice but to listen to their conversation. The two good women are enthusiastic that Mrs. Musgrove's two daughters are soon to be married—both agree that it is not right to make young people wait for an uncertain future. If they are in love, let them follow their hearts. Anne could wish that she had received similar advice. Across the room, he, too, was listening. "Captain Wentworth's pen ceased to move." He looked up from his writing and gave "one quick, conscious look at her." She cannot reach him by speaking or writing, has not been able to write to him for eight years. Mrs. Croft and Mrs Musgrove go on talking of "such examples . . . as had fallen within their observation," but to Anne "it was only a buzz of words in her ear, her mind was in confusion."

Captain Harville beckons. When she joins him, his "countenance reassumed the serious, thoughtful expression which seemed its natural character." He is a good friend, a good person to talk with. Captain Harville is pondering questions of faith in love. It was his sister who died of a fever less than a year ago, and left in mourning her fiancé, our friend Captain Benwick, who ought to read more memoirs. It is Captain Benwick who is now to marry one of Mrs. Musgrove's daughters. Captain Harville misses his sister, who was called Fanny, and faults Captain Benwick a little for moving on. Benwick seems to him an exception to a rule he believes in, that it is men who love more fiercely and with more fidelity. "Poor Fanny!" he says. "She would not have forgotten him so soon!"

"No," replied Anne, in a low feeling voice. "That, I can easily believe."

"It was not in her nature. She doated on him."

"It would not be the nature of any woman who truly loved."

Captain Harville smiled, as much as to say, "Do you claim that for your sex?" and she answered the question, smiling also, "Yes. We certainly do not forget you, so soon as you forget us. It is, perhaps, our fate rather than our merit . . . We live at home, quiet, confined, and our feelings prey upon us. You are forced on exertion. You have always a profession, pursuits, business of some sort or other, to take you back into the world immediately, and continual occupation and change soon weaken impressions."

Confinement requires a different exertion. Her own impressions have not weakened.

Captain Harville starts to say "We shall never agree upon this question" but is interrupted when Captain Wentworth drops his pen. Anne is "half inclined to suspect that the pen had only fallen, because he had been occupied by them, striving to catch sounds, which yet she did not think he could have caught." His writing gives way for her declaration.

Captain Harville is a good sort of person to argue with; he recognizes that there may be different points of view:

> "As I was saying, we shall never agree I suppose upon this point. No man and woman would, probably. But let me observe that all histories are against you, all stories, prose and verse. If I had such a memory as Benwick, I could bring you fifty quotations in a moment on my side the argument, and I do not think I ever opened a book in my life which had not something to say upon woman's inconstancy. Songs and proverbs, all talk of woman's fickleness. But perhaps you will say, these were all written by men."
>
> "Perhaps I shall.—Yes, yes, if you please, no reference to examples in books. Men have had every advantage of us in telling their own story. Education has been theirs in so much higher a degree; the pen has been in their hands. I will not allow books to prove any thing."

Now, here it is. The argument for her book that may also be an argument for memoirs, that they offer not proof but, building little by little from private circumstances, space of consideration:

"But how shall we prove anything?"

"We never shall. We never can expect to prove any thing upon such a point. It is a difference of opinion which does not admit of proof. We each begin probably with a little bias towards our own sex, and upon that bias build every circumstance in favour of it which has occurred within our own circle; many of which circumstances (perhaps those very cases which strike us the most) may be precisely such as cannot be brought forward without betraying a confidence, or in some respect saying what should not be said."

She knows so many widows, Anne, knows their faithfulness, though she will not betray their confidences. There is Lady Russell, there is her friend Mrs. Smith, whom she has just been visiting. And, in her own way, she has been a widow of possibility.

Captain Harville describes, with earnest emotion, his own love for his wife and family, the desperation of being separated from them, and the joy in their reunion. He stops trying to prove a point and speaks directly from his experience. And then, in this odd space, across the room from the kindhearted women, at the window with her new good friend, just in or out of earshot of the man she loves, Anne says what she means:

"Oh!" cried Anne eagerly, "I hope I do justice to all that is felt by you, and by those who resemble you . . . I believe you equal to every important exertion, and to every domestic forbearance, so long as—if I may be allowed the expression, so long as you have an object. I mean, while the woman you love lives, and lives for you. All the privilege I claim for my own scx (it is not a very enviable one; you need not covet it) is that of loving longest, when existence or when hope is gone."

She could not immediately have uttered another sentence; her heart was too full, her breath too much oppressed.

She can hardly breathe, she feels again the oppression. But she has spoken to be heard by her friend, and overheard by the man she loves. Captain Wentworth *has* heard her. It decides him. He finishes his letter, which is to her, and leaves it for her to read. But it is because she has spoken to Captain Harville, and to us, that she is to have a different relationship to the world, and to literature.

These reflections of Anne's make a place where I seem to hear women calling back and forth to one another across pages and centuries. Viola in *Twelfth Night*, often noted as a source for Anne's speech, has fallen in love with the duke, whom she serves, cross-dressed and hidden, as if a servingman. The duke says that women do not love as he does, and she says that her father had a daughter, once, loved a man, but told no one, "sat like Patience on a monument, / Smiling at grief. Was not this love indeed? / We men may say more, swear more," but this is show, "we prove / Much in our vows, but little in our love." Two hundred years later, not in a play, in a novel, there is Anne, a woman, speaking of women in general, and of herself. A hundred years after that, she has walked into an essay, not forgetting, though, where she has been. Virginia Woolf is trying to write about "women and fiction" for the talk she is to give at a women's college that will become *A Room of One's Own*. She has got her idea, about "the room and the money." When she explains her own thinking, she sounds, to me, so much like Anne saying "We never shall":

> At any rate, when a subject is highly controversial—and any question about sex is that—one cannot hope to tell the truth. One can only show how one came to hold whatever opinion one does hold. One can only give one's audience the chance of drawing their own conclusions as they observe the limitations, the prejudices, the idiosyncrasies of the speaker. Fiction here is likely to contain more truth than fact. Therefore I propose, making use of all the liberties and licences of a novelist, to tell you the story of the two days that preceded my coming here.

I was in a bookstore, comparing different editions. I don't remember now the reasons for the choice: was it that it had helpful notes, or a cover that was a drawing, not a photograph? Anyway, I bought it, and in this way discovered, in an unassuming appendix, that the scene at the White Hart is not the scene Jane Austen first wrote. We possess the draft of another, quite different scene, the only draft of hers we have. Austen or her family must have been meticulous about destroying her drafts. But, perhaps because it was the last book and not fully prepared for publication, or perhaps because she or someone felt this revision to be of unusual significance, the evidence remains.

Anne makes no speech in the scene Austen originally wrote. The draft takes place not at the White Hart but in the rooms of Admiral and Mrs. Croft, who are also visiting Bath. Mrs. Croft is the sister of Captain Wentworth; it is the Crofts who have rented the Elliot estate from Anne's impecunious father. Now they, too, are in Bath, and they've heard that Anne may be about to marry her cousin, the smooth-spoken Mr. Elliot, and they wonder if she wants the estate back. They tell Captain Wentworth to ask her, and then leave the two of them alone for a few minutes. This puts him in a very awkward position, but true feelings do surface. The winding up is a matter of real estate, and the interview is between the two lovers alone.

It is remarkable how much dimmer the satisfactions of the draft scene are. Anne does not say anything herself; it is precisely her silence that gives him the clue to her feeling. She tries to speak "a word or two, but they were un-intelligible." Then he says, "Pronounce only the words, *he may*," and he will send the message that the estate is to be returned to her and Mr. Elliot. She struggles even for negation, manages to say that she does not want to send this message. They look at each other. "It was a silent, but a very powerful Dialogue;—on his side, supplication, on hers acceptance." She remains mute, and he takes her hand, bursts out, "Anne, my own dear Anne!"

If this were what happened, it would be a profound happiness, the happiness of her life, but it would not allow her character to come to fulfillment. Not as it does, when she speaks out, and he writes her a letter that acknowledges what she has said, that her own struggle has been bitter and that it resembles the struggles of many others, that she, and he, see her as a part of a whole. At the White Hart, she takes her place in the world, even if that world be represented only by the addition of the windows of the inn, of Mrs. Musgrove chattering away in the background, and of the serious questions of Captain Harville.

To revise is to see again, to visit again, to look back on. The work of going back to the past is part of what Anne has learned to do. Her seeing again reaches its culmination in a novel that, although very private, is also about friendship, in a scene full of other people, in a general declaration, "of loving longest, when existence or when hope is gone." Revision, in some important way, must be about both interruption and exertion, about life with other people, and not only the people one was born among or will marry, but friends and strangers. Austen is careful to make this broader canvas clear. When Anne staggers into the chair where Captain Wentworth has sat writing, and she seizes the envelope with the hastily written direction, we know with her that "on the contents of that letter depended all which this world could do for her!"

Revision, its timing and extent, is a subject of tendentious argument among Austen scholars. It is crucial to understanding Austen's development as a writer. Her brother Henry, in his biographical notice, said that when she got to Chawton, some of the novels she published "had been the gradual performances of her previous life." This is often quoted, with good reason; the phrase leaves us with so much matter. The books, then, accumulated layers, as the Austens moved about. Her brother went on to say that "though in composition she was equally rapid and correct," she would "withhold her works from the public, till time and many perusals had satisfied her that the charm of recent composition was dissolved."

Austen does herself describe revising *Pride and Prejudice* when she got to Chawton Cottage after the eight and a half years of wandering, in two very significant letters to Cassandra, and she speaks of the process of revising in one late letter, in March of 1817, addressed to her favorite niece,

Fanny. In that late letter, Austen wrote about *Persuasion* that "I have a something ready for Publication, which may perhaps appear about a twelvemonth hence." And she said of the book that would be called *Northanger Abbey* that, by contrast, "Miss Catherine is put upon the Shelve for the present, and I do not know that she will ever come out." Books were shelved for years, and then set going anew.

Northanger Abbey had, long ago, been accepted for publication, but it was never issued, and the year before this letter, Austen had her brother Henry acquire the rights back, determining not to publish it. After her death, which came later in 1817, her family published both the book she thought was ready, *Persuasion*, and the book she had put on the shelf, *Northanger Abbey*. To me, *Northanger Abbey* is still opaque. The wit is sometimes harsh, the characterizations are less subtle, the proportions are not complex and harmonic. Gilbert Ryle says "it is the one novel of the six which does not have an abstract ethical theme for its backbone," no general qualities being considered in the light of different characters. I think Austen decided not to publish it because she had never found the way to rewrite it to her satisfaction. Virginia Woolf, who had not seen all the manuscripts and letters scholars now use, still made a probing guess based on the draft material Austen left for *The Watsons*: "The stiffness and the bareness of the first chapters prove that she was one of those writers who lay their facts out rather baldly in the first version and then go back and back and back and cover them with flesh and atmosphere." Watching take shape the one scene that we still have from *Persuasion*, you can see how it must have been sometimes in rewriting that Austen was able to make that transparent effluvium in which characters walked free and took up a depth of relation to one another.

In *Pride and Prejudice* certain spacious, visually indelible scenes leap forward from what is mere potential in *Sense and Sensibility*. I suspect that in some way Austen learned to revise differently between the reworking she gave to Elinor and Marianne and the one for Elizabeth. I guess at this from brooding over the way her characters think about changing their lives, which is the experience in the life of a character that is most like an author's experience of revision. The character, or the author, has to see again, so that the next time will have a greater spaciousness, more room for other people. In her last speech, Marianne might have been heading in this direction: "I considered the past," she begins. Elizabeth will be the first to be explicit about revision, and she is so explicit that it is as if Austen is drawing a line under each part of her thinking.

Five

READING AGAIN

FIRST IMPRESSIONS

My room, my childhood room, had a mottled carpet of green shades, mossy, with some beige, and darker greens that shaded toward fern. The rug was probably from the 1960s, and had been there since before we moved into the house. Mine was a corner room, small, with windows east and south. There were trees outside and close by both windows; across the walls, there was the play of shadows, more brittle and more diffuse according to the season.

I was about eleven or twelve when it became my room, so the memories made there were not of early childhood but of youth. Until then, although by day I had professed the desire for my own room, come nighttime I had actually much preferred the comforting breathing of my sister. When I was at last ready, my mother took me to choose a bedspread and curtains, and a desk, fairly large, with a roll top, wonderful in its privacy. I could squeeze behind the desk to open the south-facing window and its screen and from there climb out onto the roof of our back porch. Sometimes I would stay there, under the branches of the trees, and read. This was not actually the wonderful perch that the girl had seemed to have on her fire escape in *A Tree Grows in Brooklyn*—the tar grew hot, the roof was hard even if I brought a towel to sit on—but I did not mind that much that it was not that comfortable.

Out there, in the spring that I was thirteen, I fought my way through *The Hunchback of Notre Dame*, which I did not understand (only at the end of the lengthy chapter called "A Bird's-Eye View of Paris" did I realize

I had been reading a description of Paris seen from above). I read it from the sense that it was a part of what I needed to know, because a girl who had befriended me, she was called Annie and was from Israel, had looked surprised that I had not heard of it. I was a lonely, reading child, and usually had one friend each year, a friend whose parents were visiting at the university from somewhere else, a place to which she would return at the end of that year, and perhaps send me a letter or two that I would never reply to, but would keep, guiltily, in a kind of pincers of knowing I ought to write and not writing, in the drawers of my rolltop desk.

Reading was many things in those years, in that room—it was study and education, it was the marvel of language, the terrible villainy of human creatures, the astonishment of liberty, sometimes just the pure patterns of syntax, and, with a peculiar heat, it was romantic. In my room, on the inside of the closet door, there was a long mirror, in which I fancied I could glimpse reflections of the future. I sat on the carpet near the open closet door, leaning against the wall, hours going by as I read and daydreamed. My journals from that time are often wondering about different boys, recording moments of attraction and bumbling, excitement and shame. But the real romance, I think, was internal. The question that held my attention was: Who will I become? I began to try to etch myself in my mind. I hoped, when I grew older, I would be able to somehow come back and revisit this version of myself and tell her what had happened. It seemed poignant to me that this present self, so desperately curious about the future, might be unrememberable by the time I was actually living in the future.

We went to the theater pretty often, and the stories I read and reread held places in my mind that were in a way like the plays we had seen. In one story I read over and over, *The Swish of the Curtain*, about British teenagers who form an acting company, one of the girls learns by heart the parts of all Shakespeare's romantic heroines—Portia, Viola, Juliet. One night her mother finds her in bed, sitting up but still asleep, reciting. That made sense to me. Reading was learning about the shapes of lives, going over them even in dreams.

Somewhere in these years, I read Jane Austen. I think I probably started with *Pride and Prejudice*, but I don't remember now. I know that after the first, I read them all, as I had read all the *Anne of Green Gables* volumes. To me then, Austen's novels were love stories, coming-of-age stories, the girls not much older than I was. There was no effort, I was just immersed in Austen, lying on my bed with no sense that the afternoon was passing until I had to get up to turn on a light.

But, unlike *Anne of Green Gables* or *The Swish of the Curtain*, both of which I reread and reread and reread, the novels of Austen I read through once, and then read no more. The books did not seem to accompany me as time passed. If you had asked me, I would hardly have been able to tell you the names of the women, or anything that had happened to them. I remember the reading only as a quality of light, barely a contrast with the dim surrounding, like a lamp in the late afternoon. A kind of rose, but without sentiment, the matter-of-fact, pale, interfused rose that the sun leaves in the sky when it sets at the end of a midwestern winter day.

PRIDE AND PREJUDICE

Elizabeth and Jane Bennet are sisters and depend on each other's judgment. Their mother is a woman of small understanding and less generosity: "The business of her life was to get her daughters married; its solace was visiting and news." Their father has understanding and wit but is cynical and lazy. He refuses to take responsibility for Elizabeth and Jane, and their three younger sisters. Mr. and Mrs. Bennet have made no provision for their daughters—if the girls do not marry, and marry well, they will be poor; they have not even sufficient education to be governesses and earn a living. The tone of *Pride and Prejudice*, like that struck by Elizabeth, is all style and verve. "It is a truth universally acknowledged," is its familiar beginning, "that a single man in possession of a good fortune must be in want of a wife." Austen's style, like Oscar Wilde's, gains edge from submerged possibilities. The person who is wittiest about universals may be one often excluded from them.

Into the neighborhood come two interesting men—the first is Mr. Bingley, who is kind and wealthy, and who is immediately drawn to the good-hearted Jane. Mr. Bingley and Jane might soon make a match were it not that everyone interferes: Mrs. Bennet makes ill-advised displays of her intentions, Bingley's mercenary sisters get him away to London, and there he is subject to the dissuasions of his even richer and better-familied friend, Mr. Darcy.

Mr. Darcy's first appearance establishes his haughty and supercilious reputation; he refuses to dance with Elizabeth. Mr. Darcy and Elizabeth find opposition attractive, and the worse they get on, the more powerful the pull they exert on each other. Elizabeth believes herself to prefer Captain Wickham, whose manners are so much easier that it is a while before she realizes he is the real villain of the piece. Though Darcy disdains Elizabeth's social position, he eventually proposes; she refuses him with brilliance, and then they must begin over. Each is forced to acknowledge some validity in the other's actions, and from this unfolds mutual education, which they can see in each other's eyes when they meet again, at his estate, Pemberley.

But they do not find their way together until their new understanding and suitability are put to the test. Wickham, whom Mr. Darcy had previously prevented from running off with Mr. Darcy's young sister, now actually does run off with Elizabeth's young sister, sensual Lydia, who never waits. When girls are run away with in the background of Austen novels, it underscores the peril of all girls' situations. A girl is to grow up and courageously leap—but, as one of the younger sisters, Mary, puts it, "one false step involves her in endless ruin." The ruin will not be his, but hers and her family's, as we learn again at the end of *Mansfield Park*. Austen is caustic: "That punishment, the public punishment of disgrace, should in a just measure attend *his* share of the offence is, we know, not one of the barriers, which society gives to virtue." She decides not to speculate about the hereafter but observes that "in this world, the penalty is less equal than could be wished."

Jane Austen's novels are sometimes accused of not being sexual, and the kind of held-back sexuality they have makes some readers, including Mark Twain, almost "feral" in their anger at Austen. (The word and the thought are Lionel Trilling's; he says Twain's is "a man's panic fear" at being in a fictional world "prescribed and controlled by a female mind.") In four of the novels, unbridled desire runs away; in each one you can tell the wrong man from the right one because the wrong one is capable of taking advantage of a vulnerable girl or woman, and does. Girls, rich and poor, but especially poor, who can neither parry nor repress, and who perhaps cannot bear the restrictions of their parental home, go off, and face either being fallen women, and disgracing their families, or being forced to marry and spend their lives with wicked men. Austen knew what an ill-founded household could grow into; when she was visiting different families, her letters to Cassandra contain sharp reports on signs of anger or violence in the man, whether he took it out on his wife, and how.

Elizabeth and Jane can feel what is wrong with the training they have had; their instincts and intelligence help them, but they are powerless with regard to their sisters. Elizabeth suspects that the way her father looks down on her mother—which she sees as a "continual breach of conjugal obligation," because it means that the daughters view their mother with "contempt"—is related to the way the girls have trouble knowing how to act. Fortunately, she has her uncle and aunt, the Gardiners, who offer better examples of care and esteem, helping with the Lydia debacle, giving Jane and Elizabeth sound advice, acting tenderly and thoughtfully with their nieces and with their own children.

Elizabeth is loyal to her family, and in every Austen novel except *Persuasion*, there cannot be real happiness for a heroine unless her family is also placed on a solid footing by her marriage. The Bennets are not easy to rescue; Mr. Darcy has to take over as head of the family, and take care of the problem of reckless Lydia. There is only one solution. "And they *must* marry!" Elizabeth wonders to her father, and herself, "Yet he is *such* a man!" Lydia is sixteen when she becomes Wickham's wife. The Bennets, waiting at home, learn indirectly how it has happened. Elizabeth has already been learning to better read other people's characters, but now it is perfectly clear to her that not getting carried away takes education, family watchfulness, and patience. The difference between the lucky and the unlucky girl lies partly in the relationship they end up having with time.

ANOTHER LETTER

When, at seventeen, I left my green room to go to college, my father wrote me a letter. I went by myself, on a plane, and I think I read the letter on the plane, or maybe in my dormitory when I got there. I talked about this letter when, at thirty-nine, I spoke at his memorial service. In it, he said, "Seek to feel grateful." I feel sure of this phrase, and I know that the rest of the sentence contained something about sun and rain, "the sun and the rain of life." I knew something of what he meant by gratitude. He had told me, a few times, that when he was growing up he had known a criminal justice lawyer, a defense attorney, I think—my father's family had wanted him to be such a lawyer, not the professor he became. This lawyer had told him that what separated people who would be able to reform themselves from those who would not be able to stop committing crimes was the capacity to feel gratitude. I think I could say now that my father's idea of gratitude was that it was a way of turning outward, to the world, of being in a relationship with what we are of—our long history, the natural realm. To me, reading his letter then, being grateful seemed like being kind, a part of attending to other people. I did not really think about the idea of reform, or wonder about the relationship between gratitude and time.

As the family story goes, I had insisted on going to Cambridge by myself. Some friends of my parents met me at the Boston airport and drove me to my dormitory. I have a memory of struggling with my suitcase upstairs to the second floor of Pennypacker and of a long afternoon of trying to hold my own as my roommates' parents fussed kindly about with microwaves and pillows. This moment would later seem to show what departure was like in our family. Why had I said that I didn't want my parents to come with me? Had I felt that I wanted my independence as soon as possible, or, guiltily, that I should protect them from a break difficult to bear? I wanted them to see me in my new place; it turned out they had wanted badly to come. The misunderstanding, one we all later regretted, went on a long time—it was a year before they visited.

Everyone had done what they could think of. My father wrote a letter; my sister, who was just fifteen, had hidden in my suitcase two photographs, which I found when I was unpacking my bag. They were small three-by-five pictures of the two of us in brass-colored frames. In one of these, she and I were at the piano; the other, which sits near my writing desk now, shows a moment when we were perhaps four and nearly two, both with long hair. I have bent down so that our faces are at the same level, and in the way of pictures from the seventies, the light around our hair is the same yellow-white as the light around the green hedge behind us. In the picture, I look out at the camera with some understanding; she still has the quiet, turned-inwardness of the very small. I worried about her in the reconfigured family I had left behind. She did come to visit by herself, and I think a few of the talks we had were close, but I felt that I was failing her. Picking up the phone to call her, to call home, seemed an effort like trying to run in a bad dream. Once, when I did call, she told me that my father would send her to get the sheets out of the closet of the green bedroom, so that he wouldn't have to go into my room himself.

SENTENCES

Pennypacker was a dormitory slightly outside of the Harvard yard, next to one called Hurlbut, into which, that same week, moved M. He was one of a group of five roommates, and I became, in a diffuse, dining-hall sort of way, friendly with them—their general quality was gangly and witty. M among them was distinguished by thin hair that fell over his eyes, a habit of looking down, and a way of muttering incisive things in a voice hard to hear. I remember once, a bit later, we were on a sidewalk, and had to stand aside for a quite hostile woman trailed by her small and apologetic dog. He said, "That woman's decency is following her at a distance of twenty paces."

We, all of us, enrolled in courses with the kind of urgent errancy I have since observed in my own undergraduate students, choosing classes that we later thought were mistakes but that fairly perfectly predicted what our adult desires and inhibitions would be. In the first semester, I chose a course in ancient political philosophy, and was glad that M and another of his roommates also enrolled. M became a philosopher, his roommate became a political scientist. It turned out to be another course that predicted my future, the section I chose of our required expository writing class. I selected Expos 17, The Essay.

In Expos 17, we studied four writers: James Baldwin, Virginia Woolf, George Orwell, and D. H. Lawrence. Each of the students in our class rapidly found one writer who seemed to speak to her or him alone. For me it was Woolf, and I puzzled, then and all through college, over her sentences and her insistences. Woolf said a woman writer needed a room of her own and five hundred pounds a year. She imagined a writer sister for Shakespeare; she wrote an essay on Dorothy Wordsworth, whom I had never heard of, and several essays on Austen. Woolf said it was remarkable that Austen, living when she did, could have written "without hate, without bitterness, without fear, without protest, without preaching." Woolf said Jane Austen was not naturally as good a writer as Charlotte Brontë, but Jane Austen did not get angry, and Charlotte Brontë did, and this distorted Brontë's prose, whereas Austen's prose came out sparkling and unmarred. All of this held my attention. Sexuality and gender were blurring and expanding, anger and writing were forces, sometimes of clarity, sometimes of disturbance. I felt convinced that Woolf had grasped the essence of these mysteries, and that she would help me.

It was also in that writing class, sitting in the chairs arranged for our small group, that I looked at one of the other women in the class and realized that I was attracted to her. She wore lipstick of a bright dark shade. I have never worn lipstick, the women I was later with mostly didn't either, but I can still see that woman's face and her lipsticked mouth in my mind.

I think I noticed this first thought of attraction in my essay class because I was nearing the tumultuous heart of many things, and because, for me, part of the power of writing was to be able to write of women and to them, an odd power, a masculine-feminine power, harder to reckon with even than sex. It would be another two years, and I would already have been a copresident of the undergraduate queer organization, before I would say to myself that I wanted to be a writer, and an essayist above all.

When I began with Woolf, I did not notice what I would come to realize as I went on reading her, for decades, which was Woolf turning to Austen as guide. She had begun by accepting the then-current image of Austen as decorous. In a way, she associated Austen with her father, Leslie Stephen, who had written the entry on Austen in the *Dictionary of National Biography*. But Woolf's literary understanding moved her away from this more stultified view. Woolf read Jane Austen in the morning and at night, she read her when she despaired of women writing and when she exulted. Austen helped her write—she told her diary that she planned to "gorge on Jane Austen tonight and dish up something tomorrow." Fairly late in Woolf's life, Austen's juvenilia, the bawdy satires she wrote for her brothers and sister, were published, and this confirmed Woolf in her view that those who thought Austen "the niminy piminy spinster" had failed to really delve into Austen. For her, even the smallest bit of an Austen novel was full of vitality: "You cannot break off a scene or even a sentence without bleeding it of some of its life." When she wrote of reading *Mansfield Park* "two words at a time," you can feel that she already held and carried with her the phrases, turning them this way and that. But the fact that Austen had opened a view for Woolf in her maturity, and as a writer, did not register with me in college; I thought of Austen as a writer for the young woman I had been, and I did not go back to her.

The professor of Expos 17 was a man who for many years had been the head of the first-year writing program, an eccentric, muffled man who had found a corner of the university where it was possible to love writing and profess it, although I'm not sure many of us noticed the significance of what he did. Here was the radical thing about the class: for the first three years of college, this was the only course I took in which the professor said about the assigned reading, "That is a beautiful sentence."

I remember which sentence it was. It came in this passage of *A Room of One's Own*, a passage one has to slow down to read:

> At this moment, as so often happens in London, there was a complete lull and suspension of traffic. Nothing came down the street; nobody passed. A single leaf detached itself from the plane tree at the end of the street, and in that pause and suspension fell.

I remember his pointing out to us that the last sentence did the thing it was describing—that it detached itself, paused, and fell. He made a gesture with his right hand that skimmed up to his right, paused, and then descended gently down to center, a graceful gesture. It was natural to feel language in your body, and in your hands. This was a moment I did not notice myself noticing at the time. I think it probably stayed with me with such clarity because it reminded me of home—the kind of gesture my father made while he spoke, the pleasure in language we all took together. I think of sitting on a chair in my parents' bedroom, reading out choice lines of Oscar Wilde and laughing with my mother. A well-turned phrase was a way to be close.

In that course on the essay, I do not believe we were told to write personal essays, but to me it seemed natural to do so, in a way that I am now accustomed to seeing in my own students. When you leave your first home, even very gently, you want to recognize an end.

I wrote about the gravel collection I had had in elementary school. At six or seven, I used to walk to and from school very slowly, looking through people's driveways for tiny stones, and at recess I would avoid the other children and go out behind the brick school building to a heap of gravel that was there. And then I would sit, deliberately turning over those similar stones until we were called back in by the bell.

The stones were a trial, an effort at independence that I found hard to explain to the sympathetic and mordant professor of Expos 17. I felt that I failed, again and again, all semester, but I stayed at it until the class was over. I knew that it mattered to convey the feeling of turning over those small gray stones until there was a dull shine of dust over my fingertips. I just couldn't manage it, because I didn't have names for the necessity and solace of that prideful contemplation. I'm not sure that I know even now, though I've sat on many gravel heaps since.

Jane Austen's sentences gleam and leave no dust, but in some way, my endless turning over of those perfect epigrammatic shapes was a similarly concentrated study, or it became one, once I began to be interrupted.

CHILDREN

When I moved back to Cambridge, to join M at the apartment he was then living in, it was amusing, and a little disconcerting, that we were only a few blocks from Pennypacker and Hurlbut, and that I would pass those dormitories on the way to the library, or the bookstore. Nineteen years had gone by since I had gotten my suitcase up that stairwell. M and I had each been in two serious relationships that had been deep, if still lonely. I had found it very difficult to write, or perhaps to contain the force of writing, while living with a man, and then, although differently, I had been angry trying to write while in a relationship with a woman. M had been to graduate school and then moved back to Harvard to teach. I had lived in New York and taught for nearly ten years at Sarah Lawrence College. It all might have been so different. Especially when I was pregnant, and then when I walked those same streets, in the soft summer light with a tiny baby in a pack against my chest, I used to wish to be able to tell my earlier self, whom I could almost see hurrying along to class, hair wet in freezing weather, inadequate coat blowing about, in a great uncertainty and urgency of intention, that it would come around to this, that she couldn't really make happen the things she thought she could, but that it would come out, and come out surprisingly: though she would still be restless and anxious and uncertain, she would not be lonely. And this seemed poignant in a different way. She had been right; in a way I had forgotten her, or what she had thought of as forgetting turned out to be a way of remembering that she couldn't imagine, one only possible from here, the future of the past, when I saw her, was her, so differently.

I remembered having been on these same streets, living in dormitories on those blocks, having conversations with classmates and roommates about novels. I remembered saying that I had read Austen and mocking the way I had read her. I used to say that I was in such a hurry to see whether she got him that I hardly noticed anything else about them.

For ten or fifteen years, I did not reread any of the novels, and I laughed, when I reopened *Pride and Prejudice*, in my early thirties, to find that I still read it the same way. I didn't seem to be able to slow down. I remember walking down Court Street, near my apartment in Brooklyn, unable to close the book on Elizabeth even when the rain began to fall into the pages.

In *Pride and Prejudice*, each fragment is pressed by geological ages, and in the minuteness a kind of eternality is intelligible, but I only read it this way as M and I reworked our sense of ourselves with S, and then as we all three did with T. *Pride and Prejudice* may have been a gradual performance for Austen, but it never affected me that way—even learning to read it in pieces came sharply and memorably, on a visit to M's parents, and on three indelible nights.

When I went to the hospital to have S, I had with me the second volume of Sigrid Undset's *Kristin Lavransdatter*, which I was reading for the first time. It is a good book, about a strong woman's life and even about motherhood, but I did not glance at it that night, or return to it later.

I could not believe that night, S's first night on earth. The stretching of my body over the last nine months was nothing to the stretching of the veins of my being that went on in that night. Drugged and still more or less cut open, and staying awake, because another being needed milk and a voice in the dark. M, carrying her, sleeping and waking on two chairs in the corner. I had seen other friends, and my sister, with their babies, heard them say how strange it was, that there should be a being where there had been none. I had tried to imagine it, but had thought about it more in what was visible to me—their hands learning to take the shape of their baby. I had not thought they were saying that the change was internal, was a change in the feeling of time.

There were the first, hallucinatory, sunny and smudged days. She seemed to be drinking, but she was also falling asleep, there might not be enough milk, there wasn't enough milk. She was a week old, she was dehydrated. In the pediatrician's office, she became unresponsive. There was an ambulance, we were back at the hospital, waiting again through the night, for a miracle worker in Mickey Mouse scrubs to get a line into her tiny vein. In the morning they told us she was fine, and we propped her up in her car seat and took her home again. That was the second night.

We more or less returned to the ordinary difficulties of keeping a first child going, giving her a lot to drink, probably too much. I was able to say, and usually to believe, that that had been an interruption, not an end, or even the promise of an end. She had resumed her life, which must mean that she had already had her own rhythm in time, even if we didn't know what it was yet.

M and I noticed in the first weeks that we could not get the hang of how to pay attention to S and talk with anyone else at the same time. Either we attended to her, and could not even tell if other people were speaking to us, or we spoke to them and seemed to forget her, and thought we felt her look reproachfully at us. The effort felt like trying to open a blocked passageway in the mind. We didn't have the habit of thinking about her that would just run all the time, that would be her sense of time like a current that ran within ours, and extended beyond ours. Then, when we did, our memories of our own lives had changed.

My old friend William, who died two years ago, used to say that he thought the great mystery of having children was that you could think back to the time before they were born, but you could not actually remember it. I wish I could talk about it with him now; I think he meant that your mind had reformed so thoroughly that that earlier existence had passed away.

Two and a half years went by. Again, we drove through the darkened Cambridge streets to go to the hospital. This time, I felt I knew better what I would need in my bag—the kind of underwear that wouldn't chafe a healing caesarean wound, a few toys that might help S in this strange time, and one book: a copy of *Pride and Prejudice*, so read that its cover was half torn off.

Pride and Prejudice was published on January 28, 1813. On the twenty-ninth, Jane Austen wrote to her sister, Cassandra, of the newly arrived volumes: "I want to tell you that I have got my own darling Child from London."

In Austen's voice are delight and pride and a fondness she could share with her sister, as she watches this creature of her mind, grown already, child and adult both, taking her first independent steps. She told Cassandra that she and their mother had read aloud the first half of the first volume that very night, to an unsuspecting visitor, to whom they merely explained that it was a new book, revealing nothing of its parentage. The visitor "was amused, poor soul! *that* she cd not help you know, with two such people to lead the way; but she really does seem to admire Elizabeth." The name is so lovely in this sentence, as if caressed. Elizabeth was Cassandra's middle name. And how Jane Austen loved her own Elizabeth: "I must confess that *I* think her as delightful a creature as ever appeared in print, & how I shall be able to tolerate those who do not like *her* at least, I do not know."

She had done it. From within her own mind, she had made a character who could learn and grow, and who could never be brought to an end. As delightful a creature as ever appeared in print—with "something more of quickness than her sisters," as we learn from Elizabeth's father before we meet her. The book begins in exposition, but quickly comes to movement in space, at the fateful ball when Mr. Darcy insults Elizabeth and refuses to ask her to dance. The refusal is immediately a wonderful story, one

Elizabeth herself tells while still at the ball: "She told the story however with great spirit among her friends; for she had a lively, playful disposition, which delighted in anything ridiculous." When she talks, she is radiantly attractive, has, as Mr. Darcy's dreadful aunt observes, "arts and allurements," and it is not long before we, like Mr. Darcy, have "never been so bewitched by any woman as . . . by her."

The fiction writers I know, and the ones I have read about, have different ways of talking about the strange moments in which a character they have created does an unexpected thing. I have worked at writing fiction enough to know something of what they talk about. Suddenly, you are writing underneath unfolding events, running to keep up with a person who was of your mind but now seems to be of more than your mind. One of the ways you feel this is that the character begins to move in space and to have her own relationship to time, her own pace, something more of quickness than her sisters. A writer can be frightened to turn away from a character in her first motion—what if she is gone when you return? But, in fact, this is the test of her reality: when she is interrupted, she will resume and still be herself, a being in time.

INTERRUPTION

Jane Austen worked with very little place for herself. There was a constant stream of other people whom it was her duty to attend to. Uninterrupted leisure was a privilege to which Austen, and most women—and most people—did not have access. She was routinely sent to other houses for long stays to take care of nieces and nephews. Even within the household, it was a long while before she became the understood writer. Her older brother James considered himself the family writer and was overbearing about it. The sisters always lived with their mother, and their mother was a good poet, a funny rhymester, and competitive. When the first copies of *Pride and Prejudice* arrived at the house, her mother was the one to read it aloud, too rapidly, to the daughter's frustration. Cassandra was a wonderful confidante, but much of the time it was not at all easy for Jane Austen to get a hearing in her own life.

She had to find ways to work around, through, and with interruption. A clear view of Austen writing arises in the memoir written by her nephew. Austen-Leigh wonders at how his aunt managed to write as much and as finely as she did: "How she was able to effect all this is surprising, for she had no separate study to retire to, and most of the work must have been done in the general sitting-room, subject to all kinds of casual interruptions . . ." He describes the methods she had. First: "She wrote upon small sheets of paper which could easily be put away, or covered with a sheet of blotting paper." Her books could be set aside and taken back up again in an instant.

It may be that Austen's books ring through so clearly in part because in Austen's life, they literally were shuffled under other things. Some of Austen's most resourceful readers—Woolf herself, Stuart Tave, Azar Nafisi, Lionel Trilling, D. A. Miller—notice the inclination to attach oneself to Austen, one or two words at a time. Austen's prose resists interruption and transforms it. Don't break off, stay, revise.

She had another method, as brilliantly adaptive: "There was, between the front door and the offices, a swing door which creaked when it was opened; but she objected to having this little inconvenience remedied, because it gave her notice when anyone was coming." Later biographers have argued that Austen may have had a little more dedicated time and space than this suggests, but still, when I read this sentence of the nephew's, I am entirely convinced of the reality of that swing door that she would not have fixed. She took the very sound of interruption and with it fashioned a room that was not only her own but that could be shared. I think she would have agreed with Woolf that a woman writing needs a figurative room of her own, but, I am coming to believe, they might not have said that one keeps that door closed when it comes time to revise.

I think it would have been a part of Austen's happiness that her father had known her Elizabeth in some form and loved her. When she wrote to

Cassandra on the twenty-ninth of January, in 1813, she would not have needed to remind her sister that the anniversary of their father's death had just passed, on January the twenty-first, or to say that she imagined the pleasure he would have had on seeing her book come into the world. But she had not tried to keep the book as he had known it. She told her sister that she had "lopt & cropt so successfully however that I imagine it must be rather shorter than S. & S. altogether." There are arguments about the extent of revision this implies, but the two letters Austen wrote to Cassandra right after Elizabeth came into the world, which contain some of the most detailed passages we have of Austen's reflections on her own writing, suggest to me that Austen had dug deep.

She indicated to Cassandra that she had been interested in proportion and momentum. "The 2d vol.," she wrote of *Pride and Prejudice*, "is shorter than I cd wish—but the difference is not so much in reality as in look, there being a larger proportion of Narrative in that part." The concern was the balance of the two parts, that of Volume I, in which everything was set in motion at the relatively slow pace of talking about it, and that of Volume II, where the more dramatic actions happened. It was the second part, things happening, that might be "shorter than I cd wish," and pass by too quickly. If readers went by the look and not the reality, they might miss important relations, the way the second half reconsidered the first half, augmented it, reconstituted it. In their later actions, the characters in the book reformed the things they had thought earlier, and readers would need to see this. Proportion is a formal matter and a moral one.

Austen considered the complexity with her sister—the book was to be read at speed, *and* the reader was to learn to slow down. She knew that a strength of *Pride and Prejudice* was its celerity; she had cropt it to be flown through. At the same time, she wondered if she'd rather overdone the quick, bright pace. In the second letter she wrote to Cassandra, six days later, Austen observed, witty as ever: "The work is rather too light, & bright, & sparkling; it wants shade;—it wants to be stretched out here & there with a long Chapter—of sense if it could be had, if not of solemn specious nonsense—about something unconnected with the story." This stretching out, putting in chapters of sense and solemn nonsense, would "bring the reader with increased delight to the playfulness & Epigrammatism of the general stile." Variety of pace would have given the reader a sense of history and time passing, and might have helped readers see that they were to learn to live with Elizabeth over time.

Austen is mocking, for her sister, something they are both proud of, and she is asserting the right of her clear, bright novel to exist without the trappings of more ponderous, more masculine tomes, but she is also naming carefully a shift in history and in her own preoccupations as a novelist, and her letter for her sister is also a set of notes to herself. Because, in the novels she wrote next, she did intend to stretch out. The kinds of things that might stretch the work—she had thought of three, and later she used all of them—were "an Essay on Writing, a critique on Walter Scott, or the history of Buonaparte."

Her reflections had been developing during the period of interruption. Of course, her country and her family had been in a state of continual response to Napoleon Bonaparte. If she had not been writing, writing had nevertheless been her constant consideration, and her novels do contain essays about writing. Finally, she had already been reading Walter Scott's poems with attention, and when his first novel was published the following year, she read it immediately, writing to her niece Anna, "Walter Scott has no business to write novels, especially good ones.—It is not fair.—He has Fame & Profit enough as a Poet, and should not be taking the bread out of other people's mouths.—I do not like him, and do not mean to like Waverley if I can help it—but fear I must."

I think, as Jocelyn Harris and others have pointed out, Austen would have noticed that, in *Waverley*, Scott had complimented, and borrowed, one of her funniest moments in *Pride and Prejudice*, Mrs. Bennet's "Three daughters married! Ten thousand a year! Oh, Lord! What will become of me. I shall go distracted." Scott has Mr. Macwheeble call out "ten thousand a-year, the least penny!—Lord preserve my poor understanding!" It would go on being fruitful for these two novelists to work from each other, as it helped Austen to reread and rework Fanny Burney and Maria Edgeworth, two novelists she admired still more than Scott. Arguing with the more conservative Scott in her mind would have been a way to frame her thinking about the individual moving in the world, pulled simultaneously by Enlightenment principles and Romantic feelings. Sometimes she might have thought that the older classical principles of liberty had promised more for the place of women, Romantics could be quite conservative about who got to live in their old stone houses; at others, that the Romantic feeling for imagination, and for nature, in the poems of Wordsworth, perhaps, was close kin to her own feeling. Taking apart Scott's novels might have helped her to see how ideas of history and of the present day could be not a backdrop but a part of her characters.

I imagine that *Pride and Prejudice* found something of its "light, & bright, & sparkling" tone in the first period that Austen worked on it, nearly twenty years earlier, in the 1790s, a period not without dark incident. Already in 1793, the French had declared war against the British, and her brother Henry had joined the Oxfordshire Militia. Her cousin Eliza's husband was guillotined in 1794, and Henry and Eliza were married at the end of 1797. Still, I imagine that by 1813, after twenty years of war, and all the new works of literature that had appeared in those decades, the earlier tone now seemed to its author at variance with her times. I suspect that Austen experimented with how much she could change the historical world in which her characters felt themselves to be living. In *Sense and Sensibility*, Marianne Dashwood does read Scott's poems, and is clearly a character who would find congenial his moonlit Scottish abbeys and ladies rowing to the rescue across lakes. Although *Sense and Sensibility* was revised and published first, it is a book with much clearer affinities to the Romantic than its successor, *Pride and Prejudice*. The Bennets live amid the movements of troops, but the holiday atmosphere of these military maneuvers does not seem to have room for the seriousness of the real military engagement with Napoleon, who, at the time Austen was rewriting *Pride and Prejudice*, was the ruler of seventy million European subjects and in the process of invading and retreating from Russia at the cost of more than a million lives. These things really did not fit, even as an aspect of the future, on the stage she had designed for Elizabeth.

I can't imagine Austen shoehorning in a few pages on "the history of Buonaparte," and, obviously, I do not wish for changes to *Pride and Prejudice*, but I sympathize with her concern. I know that I stay up late worrying over how the world will make room for our children, and whether we are preparing them to take a place in the world as it is and is going to be. The tone we try to set among us—of safety, merriment— may be too much at odds with the world. And, when I consider the distance at which Austen was revising, then certainly the things I thought fifteen years ago seem outmoded when I am trying to see the children in the future from here. In all her subsequent books—in *Mansfield Park*, in *Emma*, in *Persuasion*—her heroines would inhabit definite, recent years, and the fine grain of lived history would be more evident. Change would be slow to emerge, and sometimes indistinguishable from stasis or forgetting. But, for this book and this character, it must be managed differently.

Austen reflected on her decision with her sister, but the decision was made. The book had its locus. Elizabeth could neither be nor imagine Napoleon, as, later, Emma and her community could. Instead, in *Pride and Prejudice*, Austen brought her attention to bear on that inward reform by which two people can get into the habit of each other. Not reform as it may go on, slowly, among many people, but between two, with the effervescent quick timelessness of a turn at a dance.

READING AGAIN

When I took *Pride and Prejudice* back up, some ten years further on, we had one child. I was pregnant and nearing forty-one. I still read it straight through. Its swiftness was of the clouds racing by. Elizabeth was uninterruptible. My own hours, though, broke into minutes, and those into seconds. There were days that seemed nothing but interruption, nothing but one minute task breaking apart within another.

You can only be interrupted by someone else, who has been active in other things elsewhere, while you have been doing the thing you have been doing. When someone else demands your attention, it is a sign of the multiplicity of life moving forward. From interruption comes the necessity of balancing, again, the different streams of activity in your mind. For me, learning to sustain this is still the central task of domestic life. The writer who could stay with me was one who had learned to live in her own busy household with her own darling child, not her first child or her last, and who was perfectly lucid about what such reform necessitates. If I stopped reading, even after a few words, the epigrammatic completeness of each Austen sentence left me still in the story and with something to think about.

While I was pregnant with our second child, I worried differently about the coming change to our lives. I knew better how really difficult it would be to hold the attention I needed for writing during the early months, and I guessed that the sense of interruption would be still greater, and more complex. I felt, though, more sure that years would come when space would open again. I worried less for M and for me, more for S. She was so little, carrying her tiger up and down the stairs of our house securely tucked under her arm. I knew, and had learned again in detail during psychoanalysis, what a hard time I had had after the arrival of my younger sister. I had felt that something special that I had had with my mother was never the same after that.

I found myself reading smaller and smaller favorite pieces. I read the happy scene where, at last, Elizabeth and Darcy walk together, and he tells her again of his feelings, and she lets him know that hers have changed. Then I found myself favoring off-kilter bits: the impossible proposal Mr. Collins persists in making even after Elizabeth's very definite refusals, that wonderful mercenary speech of Mrs. Bennet's, even the awkward late scene Elizabeth has with Wickham, whom she has come to detest, and who is now married to Lydia. All this orbiting around the book gradually spiraled in toward what came to seem to me its center. I remember the place where I was and the copy I was reading when I began to see the book this way, funneling into a scene that led, backward and forward, to all the other scenes.

I had found a copy of *Pride and Prejudice* at M's parents' house. He and I had brought S, and we were all staying there on a visit. This house, even now, can seem to me to be oddly missing a room, and to be oriented somehow sideways. I had first been at the house twenty years earlier, when we had been in college, and I had talked M into driving home to the Midwest together one Christmastime. I had more or less invited myself to stay one night at his parents' house en route to my own, and slept that night in a room close to his old childhood room, where he was sleeping. I was up most of the night in a state of longing that was probably also a state of alarm. The room I remember myself in—with a narrow bed meant for a child and a red plaid coverlet—was situated across the stairwell from the door behind which M slept, and it is still, in my mind, the only room in that house, the room around which that whole house turns. But, although elements of my memory are to be found in different rooms of the actual house (there really are two rooms that belonged to the boys as children, one does have a plaid quilt, though it is blue), there is no room that actually aligns with the one I remember. The way I lay looking out the door and across the landing is not possible in any actual room in the actual house, but the house of that night is stronger to me than any subsequent impression. Every time we visit, I have a moment of wondering where that other house is.

It was in the actual house, the house I have since come to know, a large and ordinary house that faces forward, in which dishes are washed and children leave their toys about, a house of chores and kindness that does not catapult its guests into a state of uplift and unrest that will endure for sixteen years, it was in the actual house, on that visit with M and little S, that I found a copy of *Pride and Prejudice*, a worn old Signet paperback. This felt providential: I was only reading Austen, but I had not brought *Pride and Prejudice* with me. The pages had a few penciled definitions of obscure words in the margins, which I believed had been made by M, and which made me feel I was reading alongside his younger self. I learned later that they were actually his brother's notes, though the copy is one M read early on. In that house where M had been a teenager, where he and I, still teenagers, had slept in adjacent rooms, within that chipped cover that had been at the beginning of the brothers reading *Pride and Prejudice*, I read it again, and I was suddenly taken with Mr. Darcy's letter.

In a way, it is the point of inflection in the book. Elizabeth refuses Darcy, with ferocity, and he writes her a letter—in which he investigates what he remembers, and reflects on his own conduct—and she reads it, and at first will not believe she has so mistaken him, and then reads again, and remembers, too. The only thing I wanted was to have that dim but real sense: that I had written for her and then been, half her, half near her, holding Mr. Darcy's letter in her hand, walking about the park at Rosings, not even heeding where she was walking and first exclaiming, "This cannot be!" and then reading again and learning that indeed it can.

First Impressions was a good first title for *Pride and Prejudice*. "Impressions," to my ear, suggests that our understanding of events and other people impresses itself in our substance and being. In the first part of her novel, Jane Austen has been at pains to establish the intensity and fixity of Elizabeth's impressions. When he proposes to her, Elizabeth tells Mr. Darcy that she has an "immoveable dislike" of him. "Immoveable" is important—in Jane Austen, to stand still is to resign. Life is movement, life is continual response to ever-changing conditions.

It is coming to be spring, "the five weeks which she had now passed in Kent, had made a great difference in the country, and every day was adding to the verdure of the early trees." The morning after the proposal, Elizabeth Bennet, agitated, goes out to walk. Her favorite walk is "along the open grove," edging a side of the park, "where there was a nice sheltered path." At first, she thinks she will go to the grove, but recollecting that she has several times encountered Mr. Darcy there, that he has seemed to come there almost thinking to find her, she chooses another walk; then, either from wanting to see him or from reverting to habit, she turns for the park, and there, in the grove, he finds her again. He gives her a letter, saying only, "Will you do me the honour of reading that letter?" She is surprised on opening it to find that it is very long.

Mr. Darcy's letter is like a memoir. He has written to be unmistakable to the woman who, the night before, rejected him on the grounds that he has not behaved sufficiently like a gentleman. He intends his letter to be a study in character. As he declares at the letter's opening, he would not be writing it, he would have spared both himself and her "the effort which the formation, and the perusal of this letter must occasion," if it were not for one crucial thing: "my character required that it be written and read."

His character is his own recognizable combination of virtues and flaws, as distinct as a fingerprint, as regular as his habits, as historical as a diary, as precious as his place in the world; in fact, the thing without which he does not have his place in the world. He and she could well be strangers thenceforth; nevertheless, he wants her view of him to bear some relation to his view of himself. More than that, by writing, he is in a way acknowledging that he will not completely have a view of himself until he has written it out for her.

He looks inward. He writes of himself and of his family, of his boyhood, when he had first known the dissolute Wickham, and of a later moment when his own father died, and then of protecting his young sister from Wickham's designs. Mr. Darcy writes of things that, he tells his reader, he "would wish to forget," but which the desire to make himself understood requires him to remember. Angry and proud though he is, he is refusing Elizabeth's refusal. It sounds grudging, but it is a change to the past, the present, and the future, for both of them, when he says, about interpreting her sister Jane's demeanor, that he is willing to learn from Elizabeth: "If *you* have not been mistaken here, *I* must have been in an error."

When Elizabeth first begins to read the letter, she does so "with a strong prejudice against every thing he might say." She is in a state of per-turbation, and reads "with an eagerness which hardly [leaves] her power of comprehension." When she comes to the account of how Wickham had importuned Darcy for money and then tried to entice Darcy's young sister to run away with him, "astonishment, apprehension, even horror, oppress her." She exclaims, "This must be false! This cannot be!" and puts the letter away. Her thoughts can "rest on nothing." She walks on. But it will not do. She unfolds the letter again, and "collecting herself as well as she [can] . . . command[s] herself so far as to examine the meaning of every sentence." Sentence by sentence: this is Austen's idea of the work of reading again. "Widely different," Austen tells us, "was the effect of a second perusal."

The rereading of the letter is the moment of reversal, the throat of the hourglass through which the whole novel passes, and from which it issues out with everything in opposite form. Wickham had been the hero and Darcy the villain; the opposite is to be true. Mr. Darcy's conduct, which she had thought could not be "less than infamous," is instead "capable of a turn which must make him entirely blameless throughout the whole." Darcy's study of his own character becomes Elizabeth's study of hers. "How despicably have I acted!" Elizabeth cries out to herself. "Pleased with the preference of one and offended by the neglect of the other . . . I have courted prepossession and ignorance, and driven reason away . . . Till this moment I never knew myself."

M studies self-knowledge, not usually in instants but as a continuous condition. He thinks of it as running all through a person, our capacity to know ourselves being what makes a person a person and like no other kind of creature. An odd thing about an epiphany, a moment of knowing yourself to be yourself, is that it feels at once like a change and like a return.

Elizabeth goes on rereading her letter. "Mr. Darcy's letter, she was in a fair way of soon knowing by heart. She studied every sentence." Knowing by heart, we say, when we want to talk with children, or with tenderness, about remembered language. Like Elizabeth, I reread Mr. Darcy's letter until it became one of my favorite occupations. Austen must have written it thinking how it would be known by heart, by her character and perhaps by other readers. The first rereading is the occasion of realization, and then memorization may give the change of heart its reach.

When I took *Pride and Prejudice* to the hospital, prepared for my third night of holding a baby until dawn, the glue on the spine had given way not between Volume I and Volume II, but nearer to where I had divided the book and Elizabeth had, "Till this moment I never knew myself." In my mind, I see her lifted upward from the book's division, as the children were lifted from me.

IDEAS OF CHARACTER

On the first day of psychoanalysis, I talked about M. The session was a somber one. I pictured a vast, low concrete dome over my life, but saw a thin glare of light toward the far edge. I was worried about my father. And the six months that had gone by since his surgery had been difficult for me. There had been spring, when I had ended the relationship I was in, with the woman I loved, and there had been raw seasons of loneliness. The first month of analysis was October. I went, three days a week, and lay on the couch, and spoke and fought and longed and remembered. Almost every day, I tried to write to M. In early November, I sent an email.

In the years since college, what I had written to M were anxious letters that implored his attention. M, lucid and unflinching, thought that we were too alike, bookish and anxious in too much the same way, and that he wanted something different. He would write, or call, or, when we visited, say, in different forms, no.

If I let my mind go, I can still remember the points of contact as if seared by them. A hot day in summer, in a dim interior, at an exhibition of black-and-white photographs on Ninety-Fourth Street, we stood with only a few inches separating our arms and shoulders. A walk, two or three years out of college, where we saw a dozen blue herons; I had taken the train to Princeton, where he lived with his girlfriend. They had recently acquired a giant water mattress. This bit of information like a bludgeon. Years, the occasional message, the physical effect of his voice on my answering machine. Another visit, he slept on my couch in Brooklyn; nothing, but the man I was then with broke up with me afterward. A year and a half later, the same man and I broke up again. I flew to Berkeley, where M was living, I was to go to a concert, I had nervously explained, to be performed by the musicians I then worked with. After the concert, I told him I had nowhere to stay. He said I could stay in his apartment; there was only a mattress on the floor. I thought, surely, but he had just written a letter to the next woman he was in love with. We lay, backs turned, and I waited out the night in slow seconds. Perhaps something, though. In Pittsburgh, was this before or after Berkeley, I spilled beer all over the front seat of his car; later, one minute, music playing, we danced together in his kitchen, I forgot the dancing, much later he reminded me. He came to Brooklyn, I think to see about me, now by himself, we walked to the Promenade to look at Manhattan across the water, I told him I was happy with the woman I was with, which I was. He got a job, moved to Cambridge, I wrote an email, abroad again, now less happy, three years, he didn't write back.

That later fall, living in Sunnyside, the drafts I wrote of letters to him were also anxious, elaborate, breathless, but I did not send them. After the month of trying, I had managed to write in a quieter, more truthful way, with just a few words in each sentence. I said that it had been a hard year. That I was doing my best to work on the book that I had been working on when he and I had last been in touch, three years before. I said I was alone, and that I had started analysis. I thought I might hear back. I waited a month, and another, but I did not.

In my work, I was dissatisfied with my own sentences. I was trying to write to the bottoms of words, using pieces of sentences balanced against one another like brushwood, or angled like limbs of trees. In the mornings, I got up and labored over long phrases broken apart by dashes, trying to get them to move in and through space. I read about the origins of words, and tried to use words so that their roots would grow downward for a reader. I hardly spoke of my writing at all, not even with the quiet listener whose black-shod foot rotated gently in my peripheral vision while I chased my dreams.

Every session finished with the same sentence. She would say: "It's time to end." I struggled with this and found it hard. It was painful to think that we might not see each other again, that one of these days it really would end. But it was worse to think that things would never change, that I would just go on coming into the office in the same way, talking of the same things, three days a week forever. She watched how I handled the breaks, between sessions, in the summers, my ability to resume. We were practicing, for death, and for the end of the story we were writing together. Analysis was expensive, and I used some money that had been left to me for education. I was lucky to have the money, but it was my savings and I was teaching a lot. I resented the expense, but I didn't want to interrupt. About money, and time, I held back anger and distress.

With her, as with every other person, I was afraid of staying and of going. My fears could be seen in the way I felt about marriage. I did have real objections to the institution and its history of subjection, to its prominent place in society, and the lavish industry around it, but my real refusal was for the prolonged intimacy, the terrible endlessness. And yet, how badly I wanted to be with another person. I would sit on the subway, looking at the ringed fingers of everyone else in the car, wondering how this state was possible for so many, and not for me. I had conspicuously failed to go to any of my friends' weddings. Finally, in a state of fierce feeling, I stood with my friend Tara when she married her husband, and by the time my friend Justin married his husband, I had begun to see another possibility. Something was there, on the days of my friends' marriages. In the photographs, there was a quality of sunlight that spoke of a kind of regard, known between two, knowing, and known in the world. You will be able to try again; someone else will be seeing with you.

I spoke of my dreams of huge birds, of others where I furtively kept what I called "second accounts." Early on, I read Melanie Klein's book on envy and gratitude in part because my analyst cared about Klein, but I think I would have given it the name of gratitude even without that. What else could you call it, the relief of telling someone the things within your-self that had isolated you and that you had found terrible, and of finding that you and they were still there?

Three mornings a week I went to analysis on the Upper West Side. The trees in Central Park were bare in the slumbering way of November and then in the stark way of January. It had been a year since my father had told us he had cancer. At the end of each session, I ran for the C train. At Forty-Second Street, I joined the crush of commuters to get across to Grand Central, where I plunged into the lower corridors and hurriedly purchased, if I could get one, the same kind of cranberry-orange muffin, before dashing out along the dark and fluorescent platform to board the Bronxville-bound train. My students were learning to write their charac-ters for strangers. It would be another nine years before I tried to write about this, but I guess so was I.

The Austen family read Dr. Samuel Johnson together on many an evening. In 1798, Jane Austen carefully set aside funds to purchase Boswell's *Jour-nal of a Tour to the Hebrides* and his *Life of Samuel Johnson*. She often refers with laughing admiration to the great essayist and lexicographer, with his incisive and flexible categories for emotions, morals, literature, words. The groundwork Johnson laid saved her so much time. In a piece that she must often have turned to in her father's library, Johnson had written, in 1750 for *The Rambler*, on "the new realistic novel." He looks into the combina-tions of qualities in a literary character that may make them seem not lurid and full of "incredibilities" but derived from "general converse, and accu-rate observation of the living world." He takes it as right that art ought to imitate nature, and that realistic characters are agreeable to read of, and may provide important examples to young readers "easily susceptible of impressions," for whom they serve as "introductions into life." Realistic novelists must exercise care, for their "power of example is so great as to take possession of the memory by a kind of violence." Some, he says, like Swift, are too given to thinking of the qualities of character in opposition, or to thinking that certain virtues are inevitably accompanied by correspondent faults. One must be more precise, more variegated, more attentive to interaction, and to something like the volume of qualities, the way they expand within a life. He turns to particular examples. "Pride," he says, "which produces quickness of resentment, will obstruct gratitude." The workings are clear, and must have stayed in Austen's mind after she came upon this passage: "It is very unlikely that he who cannot think he receives a favour will acknowledge or repay it."

For Johnson, "it is of the utmost importance to mankind" that writers not be reductive about the relationships among qualities of character, otherwise we will all simply forgive our vices as being necessarily attached to our virtues, all will be jumbled together and "the colours of right and wrong" confounded. Qualities of character in Austen are not to be seen in opposition, or on a continuum. It is not that gratitude is the opposite of pride, or that removing degrees of pride will increase corresponding degrees of gratitude. Stuart Tave points out that when Anne Elliot's qualities of fortitude and gentleness are seen by Captain Wentworth to have found "the loveliest medium," that medium "is not attained by having a little of one thing and a little of the other . . . but by a simultaneous completeness of fortitude and gentleness." In the earlier draft, Austen had called the medium "just," but the better word, which allowed for more of the art and scope of these effortful combinations, was "lovely." The qualities no longer interrupt or obscure each other, they exist together.

A SUITOR

Jane Austen commenced work on what would become *Pride and Prejudice* in 1796, about eight months after what she described as a "very gentlemanlike, good-looking, pleasant young man" named Tom Lefroy appeared at a ball in their neighborhood. Austen wrote of Lefroy in the first letter we have of hers, penned with delight to her sister the next day. "Imagine to yourself everything most profligate and shocking in the way of dancing and sitting down together." He was in Hampshire because he was visiting his uncle and aunt, the Lefroys, who were near neighbors and close friends of the Austens. Both Austen and Lefroy were then twenty. She thought him very attractive, though she had reservations about some of his clothes. After the first excitement, Jane Austen looked forward "with great impatience" to the next ball at which she was to see Mr. Lefroy again, and joked to her sister, "I rather expect to receive an offer from my friend in the course of the evening. I shall refuse him, however, unless he promises to give away his white Coat."

Austen probably knew that her genteel but by no means wealthy family would not be considered a good prospect for this young man. But it seems there was passion on both sides, and that their neighbors the Lefroys were too worldly and observant not to attend to it. Mrs. Lefroy was Jane Austen's first grown-up woman friend, her closest mentor, a serious reader, a writer of poems. Jane Austen thought of her as her "Beloved Friend." There were other connections by marriage between the two families. But Mrs. Lefroy, knowing this engagement to be an impossibility, apparently sent Tom away; her sons said this was "because he had behaved so ill to Jane."

All contact ceased. But, nearly three years later, long after she had a draft of *First Impressions*, Austen still hoped for news of him. One November afternoon, Mrs. Lefroy called. Jane Austen wrote to Cassandra, "I was too proud to make any enquiries," but her father, sensitively, asked where Tom Lefroy now was, and from this she learned that he had "gone back to London in his way to Ireland, where he is called to the Bar and means to practise." Jane Austen's letters are often suggestively enjambed; she goes on immediately to say that Mrs. Lefroy then showed a letter from a friend whom Mrs. Lefroy hoped would interest Jane Austen. This other possible suitor said that he would like to be better acquainted with the Austen family "with a hope of creating to myself a nearer interest." Jane Austen commented to her sister, "There is less love and more sense in it than sometimes appeared before . . . It will all go on exceedingly well, and decline away in a very reasonable manner." She thought it "most probable that our indifference will soon be mutual." One wonders a little which man she might be thinking of.

Some seventy years later, in 1869, when James Edward Austen-Leigh wrote the memoir of his aunt's life, it was still the family understanding that there had been powerful, mutual feeling, although, like all else, different branches of the family thought differently about the matter, and his sister Caroline Austen hoped he wouldn't be too much influenced by the Lefroy part of their family playing up the story. Austen-Leigh decided to report how the Austens had kept track of Thomas Lefroy and his distinguished career, and the care with which he remarks that Lefroy did not forget his first impressions suggests to me that Jane Austen didn't either:

> At Ashe also Jane became acquainted with a member of the Lefroy family, who was still living when I began these memoirs, a few months ago; the Right Hon. Thomas Lefroy, late Chief Justice of Ireland. One must look back more than seventy years to reach the time when these two bright young persons were, for a short time, intimately acquainted with each other, and then separated on their several courses, never to meet again; both destined to attain some distinction in their different ways, one to survive the other for more than half a century, yet in his extreme old age to remember and speak, as he sometimes did, of his former companion, as one to be much admired, and not easily forgotten by those who had ever known her.

This is most of the romance we know of in Austen's own life. There was one later proposal, from the brother of close friends of hers, a man she did not think herself well suited to, which she nevertheless accepted, and then, twenty-four hours later, declined. And there were a few other possibilities, including someone whom Cassandra mentioned to a daughter of her brother Frank (Catherine Hubback, who became a novelist). This someone, suitable and handsome, had been "met at some watering place, shortly before they settled at Chawton," and Austen "perhaps regretted" that nothing came of it, but perhaps not so very much.

The other romance in their life, one that interested Jane almost as nearly, was that of her sister, Cassandra. At the time that Jane Austen met Tom Lefroy, Cassandra was engaged to a Tom of her own, Tom Fowle, and very much in love. Tom Fowle was less of a stranger; he had been a student at the school the Austen family ran in their house, and had become a clergyman. After the engagement was announced and celebrated, Tom Fowle decided he couldn't refuse the request of his patron, the well-named Lord Craven, to take the chaplaincy of a regiment sailing to the West Indies to fight the French. Lord Craven himself had just purchased the colonelcy; his mother, Lady Craven, said he had "all the military furor of the times upon him." In 1795 and the winter of 1796, the French were supporting and instigating rebellions by enslaved people in the West Indies as a way of attacking British rule. (The mobilization also affected Jane and Cassandra's brother Frank. Frank was aboard HMS *Glory*, one ship in the convoy escorting nineteen thousand men, including Lord Craven's troops, to the West Indies.) In the West Indies, Tom Fowle contracted yellow fever, from which he died in February 1797. Later, Lord Craven apparently said he never would have taken Tom Fowle had he realized he had a fiancée. For the Austen sisters, the fates, and the war, were more relentless in life than in fiction. Neither sister had the chance Jane Austen's heroines and heroes get—to go back over the ground of errors and assumptions and to come to romance and marriage—but this does not mean that the sisters did not know themselves in the world.

Their mother once, perhaps dismissively, said to a granddaughter that her daughters were "wedded to each other." This may also have been perceptive. The Austen sisters were one of the generations. Their characters did become clear to themselves and to other people. Catherine Hubback remembered that her aunt Jane "always said her books were her children, and supplied her sufficient interest for happiness; and some of her letters, triumphing over the married women of her acquaintance, & rejoicing in her own freedom from care were most amusing." Jane and Cassandra Austen had room and occasion to feel grateful, an adult household, with the space in it to raise darling children of their own.

He wrote back. M did. Three months later. The name in my inbox produced in me an intensity of feeling that made my eyes temporarily blind. When I could see, I read, in such a hurry to find out whether he was with somebody that it was almost as if I held the computer upside down. He was not, he was not with somebody. He might come to visit in a few weeks.

When I told Justin that M might be coming, Justin, who had followed the course of our repeated turning aside for the whole fifteen years of the story, said, "It's very Jane Austen." Which pleased and embarrassed me— although, because I had not then really read Jane Austen carefully, part of what embarrassed me was the triteness of longing for traditional happy endings, which, I now know, Austen herself is not that interested in. The ends of her books are not in weddings, about which Austen generally strikes a note of uncertainty, if not outright mockery; instead, the real endings point toward adjustments that make way.

M did come to visit, and over the course of an evening that had its awkwardness, but during which we had a long walk in the dark under the black trees that arch from Central Park over Fifth Avenue, it began between us. Two years later, we married in the park. In the ceremony itself, our parents, all four of them alive and there, spoke. M's parents talked movingly of his growing up, of what they knew of his character; his brother spoke, with love, of time rushing by. My father said that he was grateful to be part of that day. My mother spoke of what my grandmother and grandfather would have felt had they been there. My sister and my friend Tara organized the day, let it be effortless for us. When it was my sister's turn, she talked of books from our childhood, and the books she hoped would come in the future. It was a very green day in May, with beautiful light, and a breeze.

Later in *Pride and Prejudice*, when Jane is surprised by Elizabeth's confession of whom she loves and intends to marry, Elizabeth says merrily of her former dislike of Mr. Darcy, "In such cases as these, a good memory is unpardonable. This is the last time I shall ever remember it myself." Elizabeth acknowledges the gradualness of change, but once the change is complete, it obviates all that went before. Jane wants to know how it began. "It has been coming on so gradually, that I hardly know when it began. But I believe I must date it from my first seeing his beautiful grounds at Pemberley." Of course Elizabeth knows how this may have the mercenary tone of her mother, or the bleakness of their actual dependence, or the triumph of good fortune, but she might also just mean that seeing that land—"she had never seen a place for which nature had done more, or where natural beauty had been so little counteracted"—she saw the ground of what their life might be.

She had gone with her aunt and uncle Gardiner to visit Pemberley, as one visited private estates among the sights of the country. Darcy himself had not been there, and a housekeeper reported the good, private, unseen side of his character. With the Gardiners talking to the housekeeper in the background, Elizabeth had stood before Darcy's portrait in the picture gallery, and there had come a moment of mutual understanding:

> Every idea that had been brought forward by the housekeeper was favourable to his character, and as she stood before the canvas, on which he was represented, and fixed his eyes upon herself, she thought of his regard with a deeper sentiment of gratitude than it had ever raised before; she remembered its warmth, and softened its impropriety of expression.

Austen does not say Elizabeth fixed her eyes on Darcy, but that she fixed *his* eyes on her. It is his regard that raises "a deeper sentiment of gratitude." To revise, well, whether the revision is of your own writing or the life you are living, is to be able to see with someone else's eyes, or from care for someone else. In revision, as in gratitude, we see ourselves with, and through, the world. Later that day, Mr. Darcy himself returns, and, with the Gardiners, Elizabeth sees how strikingly he has changed.

The next morning, Mr. Darcy brings his sister to call, and that night Elizabeth lies awake—Austen teases her—"two whole hours." Elizabeth goes over the revisions that each of them have made. Her own hatred has vanished and become respect, esteem. After the day's events, she even feels something of "a friendlier nature." He, who has been so disdainful, is now eager to make their families known to each other. Only "ardent love" could have wrought "such a change in a man of so much pride." She tries to determine what it is that she herself is feeling. "It was gratitude.—Gratitude, not merely for having once loved her, but for loving her still well enough, to forgive all the petulance and acrimony of her manner in rejecting him, and all the unjust accusations accompanying her rejection." When Elizabeth then has to rush home to support her family after Lydia runs away, and she feels still more strongly for Mr. Darcy, Austen investigates her feeling as if the reader might have doubts: "If gratitude and esteem are good foundations of affection, Elizabeth's change of sentiment will be neither improbable nor faulty." With gratitude as foundation, affection will blend through and soften interruption, become capable of revision, continue in time.

Because of an earlier uterine surgery, my doctor felt it would not be safe for me to labor, and with each pregnancy I had a C-section. S waited, as scheduled, and I did not go into labor. T came a few days before the planned date of the surgery. I woke in the night and, after some time and disbelief, realized I was in labor. The contractions grew more intense and frequent as we called our friend Anna, collected the bag I had packed, tiptoed out of the house, drove in the dark, walked up and down in a waiting room, and as I struggled on the gurney while they could not get the anesthetic to take. Then, again, the strange disembodied sensation of being cut open beyond a hastily rigged curtain, M able to see my innards, I able to see his face, a drawing forth, and then, red and held up from behind the curtain, a baby, a baby I loved as if my need to hold her, and then him, might blow my body to pieces.

In the blurry night and days that followed, struggling to stay awake and stay with the second child, I worried about S. I knew she was going to have to make room within herself and in the world around her, that she would have to make that vault into a new sense of time that M and I had found hard. I wanted not to leave her alone in that change. And yet, in all my forethought, the thing I hadn't done was tell her that we might have to go to the hospital in the night, and that she might wake up and find Anna there in the morning. I reassured myself that it was only a few hours before M had been able to go back for her, but she had to do those hours herself, as, in the weeks that followed, she had to spend many hours on her own, when I, though I longed to be with her, could not. I cannot know yet whether I have passed on to her my own childhood's sadness over separations, my own sense of injury, the pride with which I held myself apart. Perhaps, anyway I sometimes hope, these experiences will have prepared her to find, in reading again, an answer to interruption.

ENDINGS

Jane Austen's novels often end a bit unexpectedly, and there are generally clues near and at the ending, last notes to the reader about what she herself has thought the book to be about, and how to let it go on in your mind.

The two main characters almost always take a walk together, and arrive at a form of mutual understanding that fits their characters and their novel. After many days of frustration, Elizabeth and Darcy manage to escape her mother and her siblings, and to be alone together. The first thing she must tell him of is her gratitude for his help with Lydia. She speaks immediately, "while her courage was high." "Mr. Darcy," she says, "I can no longer help thanking you for your unexampled kindness to my poor sister . . . I have been most anxious to acknowledge to you how gratefully I feel it. Were it known to the rest of my family, I should not have merely my own gratitude to express." He, too, takes courage, asks her again, and is accepted "with gratitude and pleasure." When it is settled between them, they look back at the past together; each faults himself or herself, but she says they must not quarrel over who deserves greater share of the blame. "You must learn some of my philosophy," she tells him. She can mean this differently now that he will be remembering in his own way beside her: "Think only of the past as its remembrance gives you pleasure."

Before this day, they had walked together but never in rhythm; they had been awkward and frustrated, each paying more attention to himself or herself than to the other. But as they have this conversation, they walk "several miles in a leisurely manner, and too busy to know anything about it," find at last, "on examining their watches, that it was time to be at home." They have made time continuous together.

Perhaps it is easier for Austen to consider the workings of gratitude without slowing down for a critique on Walter Scott and a history of Bonaparte because gratitude is not like progress in time, but like a rhythm in time.

In the very last two sentences of *Pride and Prejudice*, Darcy and Elizabeth are living happily ever after, and Austen finds an elegant way to let us know how well they will tend to each other, and the children they will have, by reminding us of the good Gardiners: "With the Gardiners, they were always on the most intimate terms. Darcy, as well as Elizabeth, really loved them; and they were both ever sensible of the warmest gratitude toward the persons who, by bringing her into Derbyshire, had been the means of uniting them."

Anne Elliot labors long over what comes to Elizabeth in a moment, but time in *Persuasion* is related to time in *Pride and Prejudice*. Time in *Persua-*

sion is often ambiguous, not a sequence at all, more like a running river, currents, over and under. What seem like periods in life are really some strange mingling of the present with the past and the future—unexpected patterns arise in looking back, the anticipation of the future shapes present movements, and it is all changing, again and again.

Anne, meeting Captain Wentworth's friends, looks backward to look forward into what seems a hopeless impossibility, but turns out to be her actual future. Time comes to be shared in *Persuasion*. Nearly everyone in the book proves themselves capable of real friendship, and of revision. "These would have been all my friends," is one way to describe the shape of *Persuasion*, which has such an odd shape.

Perhaps four years ago now, I left the children in M's care and took a train to meet my friend Jessica in Old Lyme, Connecticut, at the house she and her family have there. We took a winter walk in the woods, late in the afternoon. Jessica and I have always walked together. She is Jessica and a novelist now, but she was Jess when I first knew her. We grew up three houses apart, on the same street. Our knowing each other goes back before we can remember. We weren't each other's closest friends, but we walked to middle school together every day. And some summer evenings we would fall to talking, and we would walk each other back and forth from one house to the other until long after dark.

In Connecticut, talking and turning about as we used to do, it once again was dark before we knew it, and we found our way down the last rutted hill by feel. We talked about what we were trying to write—the sketches on painting and musicians that I had been unable to form and make sense of, the novel she was writing and was near to finishing and did later finish, these memorial pieces that I was beginning to work on. I missed my father, and she had known him most of her life.

Some days or weeks later, I had a dream in which I was staying at that house, but Jessica was not there. I had gone there to write. When my time was over, I was going to return the keys to her. My friend and I were taking turns revisiting, in writing, the houses of our childhood, marking our losses, refiguring our memories. At the dream's end, I meant to take a train, which I missed, to where she was. I set out instead in a car, driving along a long, incredibly straight level, of train tracks, and of a midwestern plain. In the sky was a dark rose color mingled and blotted with darkness. This was the color reading Jane Austen had been, when I had first read *Pride and Prejudice*, in my green room, but the color had changed, now it was transmuted in the sky—like a book, like a friend—that knew me again now, my father dead, two children of our own.

There was a while, in Cambridge, when, reading together, T would close a book and say "The End," whether we had gotten to the last page or not. I think he had the sense that we were looking into the book together, as if it was a window, and that to say "The End" was a form of acknowledging what we had seen, and repairing what would otherwise be a break, like saying "Thank you." I still, every night, close the book for T and bid him good night, and it is a kind of prayer, or a belief I am working on—that looking together now will, in some sense, never be forgotten.

In Cambridge, before we left that house we loved, with the purple door, and all the windows on the second floor, I began noticing something that the children still do. They both will occasionally pause, transfixed, when they see leaves moving in the wind. It comes over them suddenly, in the middle of what they are doing. Sometimes I am cutting up food for them at the table, and the room is silent, and I look up, and they are both looking out the windows, fallen into reverie. I think to myself, "They see the world," and I wonder what it will be to them.

Elizabeth is capable of every adjustment in a flash. She has only to take a long walk and give a quick glance at her watch. Still, once in a while, really thinking of the world and its people, I catch an echo that I believe I share with her, an awareness that I am part of movement in time, that we are coming to ends in the river of unending time.

Six

MOURNFUL WORLD

MOVING HOUSE

It was the summer of 2016—more than three years after my father had died, and five years after I had stopped teaching. We moved to Chicago. For the journey, M drove the family car with some precious items in it. I flew with the children. We waited at the airport, and S hoped for a good omen, that ours would be the plane with a rainbow painted on its tail. It was, on the scale of things, a comfortable move, an exciting one, and we were also anxious and sweaty and sad. We took a taxi to Hyde Park, to the temporary apartment where we would be staying, and the taxi driver kindly welcomed us to our new home. Old friends brought food. We found a playground, the stores where we would buy goods in familiar packages. We began to learn the neighborhood, and the South Side. Places I knew from reading were before my eyes—a few blocks north, on Woodlawn, was the very spot where James Baldwin had dined at the house of Elijah Muhammad in *The Fire Next Time*; some while after we moved to the neighborhood, a new statue of Gwendolyn Brooks was unveiled near the streets that figure in *Maud Martha* and in the Bronzeville poems for children that S likes to read.

When I tried to talk to the children about history, they knew I was talking to them about death. There were enduring reasons for the Black Lives Matter signs in the windows of houses and cars. The university we worked at had played a complicated and often destructive role in the neighborhood's history. I thought of what Claudia Rankine had written the previous summer, quoting a friend: "The condition of black life is one of mourning." In the first months, my point of view was that of a visitor, trying to get my bearings; this was gradually subsumed by different, more extended experience: pride in the neighborhood, gratitude, to be part of its life, and for the ways we all tried to watch over one another's children. The change turned out to be a little like reading Austen—years, two words at a time.

We were all trying to learn. My last memory of that summer is of carrying T back from the playground one evening in September when the first leaves were changing. As we passed under them, he was struck by the reddish purples that veined and edged the green leaves, "like flowers," he said, "like grapes."

In the study I claimed in our temporary apartment, I was, I thought, completing my book about the years I had spent reading Austen. I hurried. I went on writing as if, at least in the book, we were still living in Cambridge. First grief and first domestic life, *Sense and Sensibility* and *Pride and Prejudice*, really did seem to settle around that earlier place. I hoped we would soon be done and join ourselves here. I did not think there would be a second half to the book I was writing, and to my Austen years. If asked, I told people that I was done reading Austen. We were not yet settled in Chicago—that would come later, the neighborhood, students, a house, a garden, more years—and I did not realize that I still had not reckoned with the books Austen wrote from a place of settledness, the exponentially more complex *Mansfield Park* and *Emma*.

That summer, I was excited and nervous to begin teaching again, and had difficulty preparing the class. The world had changed so much in five years, and so had I. The refugee crisis was again worse, the map of the world was scored with new lines. When I looked back through essays I had often taught, many seemed encased, unaware of the world, while books that now called out as sufficiently complicated and painful to be relevant were ones I felt uncertain about how to teach. I had taught writing about voyages and islands before, and I decided to do so again, but to think more about forced migration and flight. I would teach V. S. Naipaul's *The Middle Passage* as I had, but I would add some of Edwidge Danticat's essays on Haiti, and chapters from Olaudah Equiano's *The Interesting Narrative of the Life of Olaudah Equiano, or Gustavus Vassa, the African, Written by Himself.* These are all books where violent history is full of voices—you can hear so many different people speaking in them. I wanted to talk about this with the students I would have. As had been the case with reading memoirs, I thought these books were the opposite of reading Austen. Olaudah Equiano's autobiography, written from his own experiences as an enslaved person and his observations of the Atlantic trade in people who had been enslaved, was published in England in 1789, and was widely read and hugely influential, but I did not yet see a history where Equiano and Austen might play interwoven parts.

In the event, the class was bisected by the 2016 election. There was the Tuesday. We met the next day, Wednesday, in the morning. I could see on the students' faces a kind of double estrangement, each one having both the shock of what had just happened and the recollection of other shocks they had been through in their lives. They had been assigned to read Elizabeth Bishop's poem "Crusoe in England" and we read it out loud, slowly, each student taking a few lines, reassured not so much by its bleakness as by the patient attention of the whole—she had worked so carefully at it, it was something we could do.

The first summer we lived in our house, the children, five and two, their faces still soft and unformed, helped me to take care of the garden, bringing out their blunt scissors and pruning. That was a summer of scooters, certain swimsuits through sprinklers, the trailing tinny music of ice cream trucks not quite where we were. Also a summer where I was editing an anthology of migration stories that a colleague and I had collected from people at the university and in our neighborhood—stories beginning in Vietnam, Bolivia, Puerto Rico, Mississippi, India.

The next summer, each of our children was injured at a playground, we took each to an emergency room in a different state. A picture book in which a mouse breaks her leg and goes to the hospital still gives me a panicked, dizzy feeling. That was also the summer of the midterm elections. Some evenings and middles-of-the-night anxiety immobilized us in purposeless vigilance. War in Syria, in Libya, in Yemen, the Rohingya were trying to survive in Bangladesh. In June, we went downtown and walked with the children at a protest against the family separations at the border and in our city. S held up her sign, a drawing she had made, of a mother and two children, and carefully lettered in high, wobbling capitals, FAMILIES BELONG TOGETHER. The sign is in our basement now, and when I pass by it, I remember the hot day of her holding it, and how T wept because he could not yet write, and it seemed like making signs might be a way to save themselves and other children.

In the study at the top of our house, I fought with *Mansfield Park* and with *Emma*, shape-shifting spirits of enormous power. A phrase ran through my mind, "Hold tight or let loose." From a Swedish fairy tale I read when I was little, in which a princess is turned into a giant swan, and the young man who is to rescue her must hold on to her while she transforms into one terrifying creature after another. While he struggles, his hands gripping feathers, claws, fur, the scales of a dragon, she calls out, "Hold tight or let loose! Hold tight or let loose!" In the way of fairy tales, his trial and her enchantment have a strange duration, lasting forever and resolving overnight.

The other day, a spring morning in 2019, I went to a colleague's class to talk with her students about *Emma*. My colleague was saying that it was hard to get a grip on the book she had been at work on for ten years, begun in such a different place, with different ideas and aspirations, and now only barely kept coherent, so much later. I found myself saying to the class that books are like that, they very often have more layers than they can quite contain; it is part of what makes a book a place a reader can return to, at different times in their own life, that a book is made that way.

It interested me, talking with the students after years of fighting with it myself, to see how eagerly and painstakingly they read *Emma*. They did not feel that to read Austen was to avoid the contentious world. To them it was natural to argue over Austen and the institution of slavery, Austen and the position of women, Austen and the Napoleonic Wars. I thought about Lionel Trilling, in his essay "Why We Read Jane Austen," puzzling over a course he had taught on Austen in 1973, in the midst of presidential scandal. Trilling had assumed he was just offering another literary seminar at Columbia, and was astonished when more than 150 students pleaded to enroll, as if to read Austen were not an exercise but a "vocation." Before that his most popular course had been one on William Blake, given in 1968, when "the large majority of the students at my university were either committed to or acquiescent in its disruption."

Trilling notes that the passions for Austen and Blake may be related, both resulting from different kinds of "disgust with modern life." The dystopian cries out for the utopian; his students

> who so much wanted to study Jane Austen believed that by doing so they could in some way transcend our sad contemporary existence, that, from the world of our present weariness and desiccation, they might reach back to a world which, as it appears to the mind's eye, is so much more abundantly provided with trees than with people, a world in whose green shade life for a moment might be a green thought.

A green thought may not be mere avoidance. Paring away weariness, sadness, desiccation, one may come to an ideal that still has meaning, or to a restriction that must be acknowledged. The world of each Jane Austen novel—permeated, saturated with an environment, qualities, concerns that she had culled from years of her experience and observation—has a principled consistency. The more intently you read each one, the more firmly they insist that you learn to see the relationships among ideals and foreclosed possibilities.

A MOURNER

Anne Elliot is the person in her family who is most attached to the grounds of their estate at Kellynch Hall, and she often slips out for a stroll there. When the decision is taken to leave the family home, Anne, like her author, dreads "the white glare of Bath," and we learn that she is "grieving to forego all the influence so sweet and so sad of the autumnal months in the country." Kellynch is the place shaped by her mother, and her grief for her mother's death is a part of the grounds she walks over. When the Elliot family are forced to leave their inherited estate, and they rent it to Admiral and Mrs. Croft, Anne returns to her childhood home a final time. *Persuasion* makes careful distinction between true conservation and sentimental or reactionary clinging. Anne does the Crofts the justice of seeing that they are better caretakers than her own family. The one place, though, that she cannot yet relinquish is her mother's: "Except when she thought of her mother, and remembered where she had been used to sit and preside, she had no sigh of that description to heave."

Her attachment to a fixed place and role for her mother has held Anne back all along. When she was eighteen, and engaged to Captain Wentworth, Lady Russell, who was her mother's dear friend, was the one who persuaded Anne to renounce him. Anne was too young, her mother had been dead only four years, she could not let her go. Even if Lady Russell was not giving the advice Anne's mother would have given, it was a chance she could not take. She had inherited this friend from her mother. She let go of Captain Wentworth.

Now Anne goes to Bath, where her father and sister have fallen in with the man who is eventually to inherit Kellynch, their relation Mr. Elliot, untrustworthy and rich, very gentlemanlike in manner. He is interested in Anne. Lady Russell tries to persuade her to think of Mr. Elliot, which would mean a return home. Lady Russell says that if she could "look forward and see you occupying your dear mother's place . . . if I might be allowed to fancy you such as she was, in situation, and name, and home, presiding and blessing in the same spot." And Anne feels the pull of this so strongly that she struggles "to subdue the feelings this picture excited. For a few moments, her imagination and her heart were bewitched" by the idea of "becoming what her mother had been . . . being restored to Kellynch, calling it her home again, her home for ever." If she never settles in a new place, if she takes a selfish husband as her mother did, maybe she would get back to that place she and her mother shared.

Everyone in *Persuasion* is in mourning. Mr. Elliot's first wife has died, and he wears "crape round his hat." The first time his cousin Anne Elliot encounters him, she realizes it is likely to be the relation she has heard about, "both master and man being in mourning." Mrs. Musgrove mourns for her ne'er-do-well son, who actually had been a sailor under Captain Wentworth, and later died abroad. Captain Benwick gets over his mourning for his fiancée a bit too rapidly according to Captain Harville, whose mourning for his sister is more steadfast. Mrs. Smith, Anne Elliot's good friend, is a widow; so is Mrs. Clay, the companion of Anne's sister. Lady Russell herself lost her husband long ago and never remarried. In *Persuasion*, the characters' mourning is as finely calibrated as how they attempt to persuade.

When Jane Austen was writing *Persuasion*, everyone in her world was in mourning. She began the book in August of 1815, two months after the Battle of Waterloo, and wrote it during the next year as people began to take stock of the wars and what had come with them. There were many millions of countable deaths, but as to how many people had starved, or gone to early graves after they were widowed by the war, as to how many children had not survived to grow up, these losses were not countable but pervaded the air. In daily life, when you went into a shop and the woman behind the counter had one less child, or you checked the library list for new books and thought of those who would have written other books, and differently, or when you walked through the cemetery after church, it would be in your mind.

In their mourning, perhaps they also felt, I think they must have, that the ways of life in which they had grown up, with every expectation that these ways would see them through, had, quite suddenly, in the space of two decades, become almost completely unrelated to the world that had come to be. What should they do with all of these habits and ways of navigating, all this remembered life that seemed now like it hardly touched the world moving on.

In English, words for mourning and for memory probably all branched from the same Proto-Indo-European root. The root is *(s)mer-*, which meant "to remember," and which wound its way through Latin and Old French to give to English "memory," "memoir," and "memorialize." But *(s)mer-* had actually already found its way into Old English, which had two related versions of this word: one was *gemimor*, which meant "known," and the other was *murnan*, which meant "to remember sorrowfully" and "to mourn." I thought about these murmuring sounds, running through our language, in my high study, leaves out the windows north and south. *Persuasion*, with its unanswered questions about remembering and being known, was still with me. Anne knows what has happened for the Austen heroines who go before her—Fanny's sharp sense of the constraints and endurance of history, Emma's steps toward a future ideal. I went back down to what lay beneath the foundations of *Mansfield Park*.

The other night, in the kitchen, I was talking with M about how writing memoirs may have become more necessary of late, when each of us carries our own mourning and still hopes to know others and be known. He said that as a graduate student, he had taken a seminar on Marx, and he had been struck by the fact that one of the things we are robbed of as we are divided into tiny functioning cogs in vast machines is general understanding. We cannot grasp the whole picture of which we are a part, but it is still human nature to work for, and sometimes to accomplish, general understanding.

A person who posts a few words about recent life to be read by friends and strangers may of course be insisting on the past to the exclusion of the present, or may be burying the past and making it unrecognizable. But that person may also be trying to take a broken bit of a recent day and, remembering, place it so that it doesn't lose touch with the hurrying present.

A POINT OF INFLECTION

When Elizabeth Bennet, her own darling child, arrived in her volumes from London, and Jane Austen knew the light, bright, sparkling young woman would be rereading her letter forever, she herself was already immersed in *Mansfield Park*. What was it to be about, exactly? In the same letter of January 1813, in which she described for her sister *Pride and Prejudice*, "lopt & cropt," she wrote a few suggestive lines. The letter goes on, and she mentions the transition, but does she mean to a new part of her letter, or to a new book, or both? "Now I will try to write of something else;—it shall be a complete change of subject—Ordination. I am glad to find your enquiries have ended so well." Cassandra, apparently, acted as Austen's co-researcher, and ordination was to be an event in the life of the next characters. Edmund Bertram, loved by both Fanny Price and Mary Crawford, is a second son. He will not be wealthy; by both inclination and necessity he is to be ordained as a clergyman in *Mansfield Park*. Cassandra was doing her research at Steventon, staying with their brother James, who had taken over their father's rectorship. To write of ordination was to write of their father's profession, convictions, and situation, of their brother's, and of Tom Fowle's. Because women did not have formal educations or the

145

chance to choose professions, a woman was born into, and married, the professions she was going to, proximately, have. When Edmund is ordained, either Fanny, who is very thoughtful about religion and would have been a gifted clergyperson herself, or Mary, who isn't and wouldn't, will be ordained, too. Their children will grow up in the parsonage, as the Austens had.

I wonder if Austen would have thought of "ordination" in its root senses of ordinary, and of ordinal numbers—the finding of coordinates, making regular days on the turning globe. The very next sentence of that same dense letter—she was ever particular about the landscapes of her novels, and ever more so for the novels coming—asks Cassandra "if you could discover whether Northamptonshire is a Country of Hedgerows." The request has given rise to books of speculation. Austen-Leigh says his aunt must have answered in the negative. A hedgerow, the name for those capacious wooded walks the sisters had loved at Steventon, does obscure Anne Elliot while she eavesdrops; he says there is no such device in *Mansfield Park*. There is, though, the barest mention of a hedgerow in *Mansfield Park*, and the hedgerow itself has been effaced. Fanny Price walks in the shrubbery with Mary Crawford and wonders over the hedgerow it used to be, and "our powers of recollecting and of forgetting." *Mansfield Park* is about the thinnest possible views—a transparency, a silhouette, a garden walk, a windowpane, a rehearsal—through which one may hold one's past and let it go, keep, or make, a place.

Seven

FORGETTING

TRYING TO RECALL

I think that *Mansfield Park* is the book I took home when my father died. I was only reading Austen, and I do remember grabbing a paperback from next to the bed. I had then been reading Austen for about a year, but I still had very little sense of what the novels were about. *Mansfield Park* would have been the right one to take. It held, in refracted form, a story of my father's early life, and of my feelings about our childhood home. But, although for all the rest of Austen's novels, I know exactly when I was most absorbed by them, for *Mansfield Park*, my most definite impression is that I can't remember.

I first tried to write about *Mansfield Park* two years after my father died, in the summer of 2015, the summer after the ferocious winter that we four had spent having our daily life inside together. It fascinated me that nearly a quarter of *Mansfield Park* shows the characters rehearsing a play. I had spent a lot of time, as a child, at rehearsals of plays my mother was directing. In particular, my sister and I had been fairies in her production of *A Midsummer Night's Dream*. Every time I sat down to write about *Mansfield Park*, I had more memories of being in *A Midsummer Night's Dream*. I had been about ten, and the play had seemed so splendid. I wrote and wrote about the costumes, and the set designer, and how Oberon had come to rehearsal on a motorcycle and how our rude mechanicals, as part of their play within the play, had had among them not only a man who played a wall but a real dog, and, oh beautiful scene, the dog had barked, comically, and we children fairies had hung about backstage to watch the dog.

That summer, I picked up Claire Tomalin's biography of Austen and discovered that in their barn, a little ways from their house, the Austen children had had a theater, and that they had rehearsed a dozen or more plays, from the time Austen herself was seven years old. I saw the theater influencing her books. She seemed to think of her characters as being almost like a company of players, moving through the rooms of a house. I settled on the theater as the center of *Mansfield Park*. I wrote of the sensual rehearsals by which the young people are consumed: "We are rehearsing," Mary Crawford says, laughing, "all over the house." I was interested in how Fanny Price often slips into rehearsal to watch, and how she works to teach plodding Mr. Rushworth his lines, "trying to make an artificial memory for him." I wrote of the influence of the theater on Austen's celebrated dialogue; she often gives what seem like stage directions in parentheticals, "(smiling)" "(looking significantly at his father)." I wrote of how, in *Mansfield Park*, when Sir Thomas is away, the others have the freedom to rehearse. And I wrote of the world with my mother and sister in our rehearsals of *A Midsummer Night's Dream*. I wrote of Fanny's longing to conserve the green lands around the park, and of Titania's sorrowful speeches about "the mazed world," with its seasons out of order and its rivers flooding and overbearing the continents. When I learned that Jane Austen, in both *Mansfield Park* and *Emma*, had been reworking the scenes from *A Midsummer Night's Dream* of the lovers roaming in the woods, it seemed like a distant confirmation that I was on a right track.

In *Mansfield Park*, one of the things the characters are trying out by rehearsing is the death of their father. But Sir Thomas comes back in *Mansfield Park*. I worked out ways to believe that we had, by rehearsing so much, with my father absent but nearby, memorizing the whole play, as my sister and I both did, somehow conserved our childhood in that play.

MANSFIELD PARK

Fanny Price is the only one of Jane Austen's heroines who is represented as a child. In all the other novels, the childhood of the heroine is given in a few biographical notes, but we actually see Fanny from the time that she is ten years old. She is the second-eldest child in the large Price family; they live in Portsmouth and scrape together a living near the sea. But Fanny's aunt has married very well, to a baronet, Sir Thomas Bertram, and when Fanny is ten, she is told she will go to these relations at Mansfield Park.

Fanny is timid, a creature of habit. From the first moment of her arrival, it is clear that the Bertram household is not to be a place of happiness for her—her uncle is severe, her aunt Bertram lazy and vague, her cousins have the glitter of pride and self-concern. She experiences the move as a complete destruction, "the separation from everybody she had been used to," Jane Austen says, from every cherished habit and relationship. "[T]he despondence that sunk her little heart was severe," and she "ended every day's sorrows by sobbing herself to sleep."

To be Fanny is to be the child who has just come to the neighborhood, who does not have the right clothes, or know the wide world, whose own parents do not speak the language of the new place. Her cousins are condescendingly surprised that she "cannot put the map of Europe together." Fanny's sole support is her cousin Edmund, who is generally kind to her, and with whom she is raised as if they were brother and sister. She loves him, tremulously, and, as time goes on, passionately. First cousins were allowed to marry, but in the novel this nearly incestuous love is disquieting, it has been outlawed from the third page, by her other aunt, officious Aunt Norris, who declared any romantic love between her nephews and this soon-to-arrive niece "morally impossible." No one thinks of it but Fanny.

Fanny writes letters with her beloved actual brother William, who is just a year older than she is. They are survivors of childhood poverty together. A couple of years after her removal, he is sent to sea, and he makes a short visit to her on his way to board the ship. She waits years to see him. And, when he is at last onshore again and invited to visit at Mansfield, their reunion is so joyous that it makes the rest of the characters envy the sincerity and depth of their love.

Everything in *Mansfield Park* exists in two forms, or along two paths. There is a birth family in Portsmouth, an adoptive family in Mansfield

Park. There is a brother William, much loved and worried over in the perils he encounters at sea; there is a cousin-brother Edmund, nearby and in need of guidance. The novel itself actually divides, early on, to pursue two paths, one at sea, one nearby.

Some twenty-five pages into the book, about the time that Fanny turns seventeen, Sir Thomas leaves Mansfield Park and goes to his plantation in Antigua. We are told the measure is necessary "in a pecuniary light." The estate would have been troubled, scholars surmise, because of declining sugar prices, and competition with the French, and perhaps because of the resistance of the people who have been enslaved and made to work the land. Sir Thomas takes his son and heir Tom Bertram along, and they are gone many months. Tom Bertram returns, but the father and his estate are still in difficulties, and he does not come back. Many of the meanings of *Mansfield Park* turn out to be hidden in this seemingly forgettable absence.

Meanwhile, in the immediate vicinity of Mansfield Park, another brother and sister arrive, the clever and alluring Henry and Mary Crawford. The Crawfords are parentless, loyal to each other, supported by extended family, in particular a rich and debased admiral uncle, who gets a very good living from the sea. Fanny's cousins fall for them. Edmund is more and more taken with the vivacity and pointed wit of Mary Crawford. The Bertram sisters, Maria and Julia, promptly succumb to the flirtatious charms of Henry Crawford. The young people decide to put on a play called *Lover's Vows* (a German play, Romantic and sexual, which had been translated and reworked for the English stage by the talented playwright Elizabeth Inchbald, and was presented in Bath some seventeen times during the years Jane Austen and her family lived there). Fanny refuses to be in the play, but also memorizes all its lines. Like some other displaced children, she has developed powers of observation and a memory of great exactitude— it is what she can do, her force and her habit, to notice and remember.

Mansfield Park is a bit like *Cinderella*, and the two stepsisters are Fanny's cousins Maria and Julia, who ridicule her and expect her to be of service to them. Maria and Julia are fitted out to marry wealth, and fairly early on, Maria makes what is considered a good catch, the very rich Mr. Rushworth, "a heavy young man, with not more than common sense." But he owns Sotherton, and the grounds are so very extensive. It is decided that Sotherton must be "improved," by bringing in Humphry Repton, an actual landscape architect, omnipresent in Austen's time. She was a bit skeptical of Repton's vaunted powers.

Talking over the improvements, it transpires that Mr. Rushworth will probably begin by cutting down the great avenue of trees that has been the estate's glory for generations. "Cut down an avenue!" Fanny says under her breath to Edmund. "Does it not make you think of Cowper?" And she quotes the poet's line: "'Ye fallen avenues, once more I mourn your fate unmerited.'" Edmund understands how important habit is for Fanny to uphold her places. At another moment, he says she is "of all human creatures the one, over whom habit had most power, and novelty least." Now he only says ruefully, "I am afraid the avenue stands a bad chance, Fanny."

A day trip is arranged so that the characters may lay plans for the estate's improvement, and Fanny's one hope for the day is to see the avenue before it is cut down. Then she will hold a picture of it in her mind. The other young people wander about the grounds, seeking and losing one another like the lovers in the wood beyond Athens in Shakespeare's play. To Fanny, experience often comes in negation. She is fatigued and sits waiting; no one comes to her and she misses the avenue by a few minutes and steps.

GAPS

If I took *Mansfield Park* home when I thought my father might be dying, it was not because I had connected Fanny's childhood to my father's. But, trying to write of our childhood and the play inside *Mansfield Park*, I kept losing the thread. Intruding into my happy recollections of *A Midsummer Night's Dream* came other, more uncertain memories. In particular, one very vivid one of venturing out into the lobby on opening night, in costume, and realizing that I had made a real error and gone where I should not be. Working at this memory, I thought I might have been looking for my father, because he had not been a part of our making the play.

I looked through the diary my father had kept for us of some years of our childhood and found that, disappointingly, the play had been elided in a gap of several months. I tried to remember if he had said anything about the play, then tried to think of sharing something similar with him, even his reading out loud to us, which he did every night when we were little, but couldn't get any real memory to come back. It seemed my father was disappearing from the very places I had thought would hold him most securely.

My father was sent away from home when he was five. He referred to this fact, now and again, and quite openly. I have sometimes held it back. It took me more than a year to tell the story in analysis, even though it was so central to my father's character, and to mine. I wasn't sure whether to write about this aspect of his life, and I asked my mother. She said that, while he might have hesitations about the whole idea of being written about, of that part of childhood he always spoke openly.

When my father was five, his parents were divorcing. His mother was schizophrenic and seriously ill. He was sent to live with his father's sister and her husband. Both his birth father and mother subsequently married other people. His birth father was a successful bookie in Las Vegas; his birth mother married an architect and they moved to live near my father. My father grew up in the home of his uncle and of his aunt, whom he always called mother, and he visited in the other households. Nearly all of these six parents had had difficult, impoverished childhoods; four of them, I believe, had not finished high school, and had run away to the city in adolescence. There were jealousies, bitter arguments, a fight for custody.

We knew many stories of my mother's childhood, which had had pranks and adventures, and also the long voyages and repeated migrations that made her family, despite their great sociability, close-knit and isolated. We heard few particulars of my father's childhood. Once, when I was a college student, visiting his adoptive mother, I realized that I had no idea which room in her small bungalow he had slept in from the time he was five. There were five rooms in the house, only one could have been his, but it didn't seem possible that it had been. He left exceedingly light traces.

As an adult, he made certain renunciations. When he and my mother married, he gave up dancing, and gave no explanation. There is a lilting picture of them dancing together at their wedding. He used to tell us, over birthday candles, and after eyelashes, that he always wished the same wish; I do not know what that was either. In college, he had studied history, but he went to graduate school for political science, and he worked early in computer science. His work looked to the future, and it was only in his last years that he was really reading back—to John Dewey, and to Wordsworth. He would never act in plays, though all the rest of us often dressed up and performed.

My father had known rupture from a very young age. He and my mother, with good luck and with the money to buy a house, with force of character and a dedicated belief in making a family history, shielded us from any similar break. Yet we sometimes played it again in metaphor, departures that felt like abandonments, continuities that felt like sacraments. There was a day, on a holiday visit home, when he knew he was ill, that he and I went together to buy the wine for dinner, and when we returned, we sat in the car in our driveway to talk a minute longer. He said that my mother had a great gift for ritual, for filling a day or a holiday with specific tasks and pleasures, certain foods, certain anticipations. He was at the edge of crying. Steady character was his guide in uncertainty. When you are five, or ten, and you are without your mother, any discernible habits are something to attach yourself to. A sentence from *Persuasion* that I have wanted to read to my father comes when Anne Elliot is in Bath, and, unexpectedly, a number of her friends turn up. She learns how it has happened: each wanting to be with others, they have all ended up coming. She is amused, finding in it "a most characteristic proceeding." He would have liked that.

Our home was intact, reliable, and a place of tenderness for all our growing up. This, both the reality of it and the force with which my parents needed it to be so, gave us what seemed to me for a long time intractable difficulties of leaving it. I loved it so much, the atmosphere of our family life, and it seemed vulnerable. In the drawers of my rolltop desk, while I was growing up, next to the gravel collection, I kept souvenirs—a piece of the worn linoleum from the kitchen floor, the steering wheel cover from our faded first family car.

ROOMS OF MEMORY

In our house in Ann Arbor, my mother's study was in the basement. It was dim down there, with a low ceiling. In my memory, there were rows of bookshelves, a little taller than I was, that I could wander among almost as I did at the library, and these were full of mysteriously promising volumes. In this room, my mother finished her dissertation on ritual and theater, furiously typing away after my sister was born. In this room were books I intended to grow up to read, among them the plays I did later share with my mother, who would coach me for the parts I took in *Hansel and Gretel* and *Annie*, who would give me Oscar Wilde and tell me to read Artaud's *The Theater and Its Double*. The rooms of a house are shaped around the regular activities of their inhabitants; the basement for me held the excitement of writing stories, and of the theater. In high school, I sat down there at her desk to write essays and to attempt two novels. By that point, the dark study, now nearly empty, was almost continuous in my mind with the rehearsal spaces, empty, with their black rubber floors, where we watched plays my mother was rehearsing; sometimes we were in them and rehearsed ourselves.

They had given away the library. Early on, after I learned to read, perhaps around the time I was sent to kindergarten and sat on the gravel heap, my father decided that they had too many books that they would never read again, and that they should give them away. He was zealous about this and persuaded my mother. Later, she was sorry that she acquiesced. They cleared a great many of her books, though not the plays, but all the French novels, all the delightful English possibilities, and probably quite a lot of his German literature, too, and his poetry and history. The books he worked from were at his office, and he kept those. Although we were taken regularly to the library and the bookstore, I felt that the landscape of books in which my mother wrote, and in which I might have grown up, had disappeared from beneath my feet.

I became a hoarder of books, unlending and thieving. I still keep borrowed books that I know are important to the friends who lent them; I cannot even bring myself to return the library books I've finished. I stockpile and barricade with books as if being a woman writer depended on it. And whatever native tendency to duplicity I had found a channel in literary work. When I was very little, I liked to hide precious objects. I took furtive delight in stealing sugar, my strategy in games was to play last: I saw the power in withholding. Perhaps this aspect of my character would have become associated with books and writing even had they not given the library away. In any case, I never said to other people, or to myself, that I wanted to write.

At Mansfield Park, Fanny has a room of her own, the old schoolroom, which is cold because a fire is a luxury above her station. In this cold little sitting room at the top of the house are keepsakes William has sent to her, and a few cast-offs from her cousins. Edmund comes to her there now and again, and they talk about the books she is reading, ambitious works of history and geography. Most of the other characters are hardly aware of the room's existence. It is not until late in the book that her uncle realizes no fire is ever laid for her there, and decides she may have one. The cold has been the atmosphere of the room, given entirely to the rigors of remembering: "She could scarcely see an object in that room which had not an interesting remembrance connected with it." There are her geraniums, the books she has been a collector of "from the first hour of her commanding a shilling," and there are images. Over the fireplace, a set of family silhouettes, the photographs of that day. A drawing of a ship, made by her brother William when he was in the Mediterranean, "with H.M.S. Antwerp at the bottom, in letters as tall as the mainmast." The tall letters are those of a child, as William was when first sent to sea. In the three lower panes of one window are transparencies: "Tintern Abbey held its station between a cave in Italy, and a moonlight lake in Cumberland." Jane Austen very probably knew William Wordsworth's great poem of nature and remembering, "Lines Composed a Few Miles Above Tintern Abbey, On Revisiting the Banks of the Wye During a Tour. July 13, 1798." Whether or not Fanny herself read Wordsworth, a spirit like his—brotherly, near to Tintern Abbey, finding sustenance in the beauties of nature—hovers over the room she inhabits.

ARE THEY FORGETTING

When I began rereading *Mansfield Park*, pregnant the first time, in a crowded apartment in Cambridge, I spent an afternoon on the couch watching Patricia Rozema's film version. In the movie, the son and heir Tom Bertram has sketchbooks of what he has witnessed of slavery in Antigua, and his subsequent illness involves a hallucinatory reliving of what he has seen. Violence is explicit and memory is difficult to bear. This makes a psychological portrait of effects of empire that run through the whole of the empire. In *Culture and Imperialism*, Edward Said observes about *Mansfield Park*, when he points out the significance of Sir Thomas going to Antigua, that Mansfield Park itself is set up as a kind of center of the traffic of empire. I hadn't read Said, but having seen the film, I had encountered one idea of *Mansfield Park* with its undercurrents as overcurrents.

In the film, also, Fanny is made into a writer. This is not like her personality in the book, but it is a way of thinking about certain historical roles, ones that were actually closing off in Fanny's present, but that had belonged to her past. The film has been criticized for anachronism, for displacing our present into the past, but its time movement is stranger: it also displaces Jane Austen's past onto Fanny's present. Fanny confined herself to letters, and never would have written for strangers. But it had, just recently, been true that a woman, or someone vulnerable for other reasons, could make a place for herself in language that was less at the mercy of presiding powers. In the eighteenth century, certain Enlightenment ideas had been opening the way for people with less power to be educated, and to write, to correspond with the powerful, to partake in public conversation, and to invent imagined worlds. The Napoleonic Wars and the clash of empires that Fanny lives in the midst of were closing these possibilities down, drawing attention to battles in which women had no role, making domestic politics more reactionary and religion more compensatory and apocalyptic.

Jane Austen watched these developments with dread. She defended the novel—and the talented women writers like Fanny Burney and Maria Edgeworth, at whose heels she followed—in a well-known argument, likely added to the manuscript of *Northanger Abbey* in the Chawton years. Austen spends an unusual two pages ridiculing the largely masculine establishment for the way it derides the feminine profession of novel writing, pages that would not be out of place in *A Room of One's Own*:

> Let us leave it to the Reviewers to abuse such effusions of fancy at their leisure, and over every new novel to talk in threadbare strains of the trash with which the press now groans. Let us not desert one another; we are an injured body. Although our productions have afforded more extensive and unaffected pleasure than those of any other literary corporation in the world, no species of composition has been so much decried . . . there seems almost a general wish of decrying the capacity and undervaluing the labour of the novelist . . . 'It is only Cecilia, or Camilla, or Belinda;' or, in short, only some work in which the greatest powers of the mind are displayed, in which the most thorough knowledge of human nature, the happiest delineation of its varieties, the liveliest effusions of wit and humour are conveyed to the world in the best chosen language.

"We are an injured body," she says. The injury is past, but the tense is present; the injury, often overlooked, is still in our bodies, and had been in some measure anticipated by those works that displayed the greatest powers of mind. Writing may see forgetting coming.

In *Mansfield Park*, Fanny does not write. It is through the rehearsals—the stage being another place where women found certain freedoms—that she is beginning to shift her understanding of the past, her desires for the future. But even though she memorizes the play with exactitude, rehearsals for her may have more to do with effacing, and this troubles me. I am used to taking the part of remembering, believing that sharp recollection and exact evidence are infinitely preferable to indistinct presences or a worn story. In *Mansfield Park*, all the characters are, through the play, forgetting things about their history and family. There was a period when scholars thought this was a sign of Austen's disapproval, and would criticize her for her prudish attitude toward the theater. It is not usually wise to deride Jane Austen for having a trivial understanding. Now it is a commonplace that she was instead attending to the power of the theater and to restrictions on it.

Elizabeth Inchbald, who translated *Lovers' Vows*, was also an admired novelist and actor, and certainly a member of that injured literary corporation whose liberty Austen sought to defend. The "licence which every rehearsal must tend to create" may not be the only kind of liberation to hope for, but Fanny's life would have unfolded with fewer, or different, constrictions had it been possible for the play to go on. Sir Thomas might have died in the West Indies—everyone knew someone who had—and, through the play, the characters have been rehearsing the liberties and licences his death would create. But he comes back, right in the middle of a rehearsal, which breaks up in consternation. He puts an end to every trace of the play in *Mansfield Park*. He is dignified, to cover up the disturbing possibility that his death would have mattered little to them. There is a conflict of different kinds of forgetting. Sir Thomas means to try to "forget how much he had been forgotten himself," and to do this he hopes "to wipe away every outward memento of what had been." Even, and it is a bit shocking when you think of the trouble Fanny and Jane Austen had to get books, "even to the destruction of every unbound copy of 'Lovers' Vows' in the house, for he was burning all that met his eye."

Mansfield Park is Austen's harshest book, the one that most seems to me like a play by Beckett, or Nathalie Sarraute. Beckett once wrote to a friend, "Now I am reading the divine Jane. I think she has much to teach me." Uncomfortably neither comedy nor tragedy, in tone *Mansfield Park* is like another play it refers to, *All's Well That Ends Well*, classed with the comedies, and yet it is something more painful that the wonderful Helena marries her own Bertram only by trickery, that he is so much above her in station and so much beneath her in humanity. *Mansfield Park* is about succession, and power; the question is a historical one, not of romance but of belonging. It's just a little harder to see it as a history because it is about the rise in station of a young woman who is not a queen. In life and in novels, there are seasons that are plainly joyful, months that grieve, but so many years are this other thing, power and place, sharply felt, full of internal dimension, taking up the life that has been and changing it.

When I look through the eight and a half years of transience in what turned out to be the middle of Jane Austen's life, and try to find a season that has the preoccupations of *Mansfield Park*, I come the closest in reading about the summer of 1805. All the elements are there—the ships, the menace, the dead father, the play, the green summer, the books, the children sent away from home, the forgetting.

1805

In the summer of 1805, Jane Austen was at Godmersham. Her brother Edward's house at Godmersham Park was in Kent, between Ashford and Canterbury, by current roads about seventeen miles from Dover, so that the channel, France, and its hostile armies would have seemed quite near. It was the third year of the Napoleonic Wars, and Britain knew that Napoleon planned to invade England. The Royal Navy was vigilantly holding many French ships in blockade, preventing Napoleon from having the ships he needed for invasion. The British also hoped to engage the French and allied Spanish ships that remained free to move around the world. A decisive defeat of these would more quickly scuttle the possibility of invasion. The British had the superior navy and officers (France had executed many of its most experienced officers during the revolution), but France was ambitiously building ships and the British might not hold their advantage much longer. Naval battles could be fought anywhere in the world, and one of the great naval games of cat and mouse was played that summer of 1805, as the French, hoping to get position and time to break the blockades, went from the Mediterranean to the Caribbean and back across to Gibraltar, with Lord Nelson and his squadron in pursuit.

Jane Austen could have followed the movements of the ships in the paper and also in her brother Frank's letters, as he was aboard HMS *Canopus* in Nelson's fleet. The squadron arrived in Barbados on June 4. They went on to Trinidad and arrived in Antigua on June 12. By June 15, the *Canopus* and the rest of Nelson's ships were sailing fast toward Europe; they would make landfall at Gibraltar a month later, on July 17.

Military campaigns on sea and on land took their shapes during summers, when energy and food were more abundant, and the sheltering and transport of ships and soldiers easier. In the summer of 1805, clouds of war gathered across continents and oceans. Napoleon laid the groundwork for two enormous victories; he would destroy the bulk of the Austrian army, and the Holy Roman Empire, in the Ulm campaign in September and October, and would win the Battle of Austerlitz against the Russians and Austrians that December. If Lord Nelson had not succeeded in provoking the Battle of Trafalgar that October, which did, indeed, make French invasion of England logistically almost impossible, the course of the Napoleonic Wars, and the life of the Austen family, would have been very different.

In the Austen family, this was the summer after the death of their father. George Austen had died, in Bath, in January of 1805, and now Jane and Cassandra had their first experiences of passing their time at other people's houses without the sense of their own establishment to return to. It would seem that their circumstances in Bath had been quite impoverished; perhaps—like Fanny Price when she has to leave Mansfield Park and wait out a long season in Portsmouth—they were reduced to evenings without candles, bluish milk with motes of dirt in it, and the mere hope for a clean roll of bread. Fanny Price misses the coming of spring in the country acutely: "She had not known before what pleasures she *had* to lose in passing March and April in a town. She had not known before, how much the beginnings and progress of vegetation had delighted her.—What animation both of body and mind, she had derived from watching the advance of that season which cannot, in spite of its capriciousness, be unlovely."

Summer in Kent, out on the North Downs, must have seemed very lovely. Edward was the Austen brother in the best position to offer Jane and Cassandra something of a place. Charles was also at sea, and neither naval brother was yet married, though Frank began to speak urgently of the possibility, perhaps in hopes of having a household his sisters and mother could join, which they in fact did, shortly after Frank's marriage, which took place the next summer, in 1806. In his brief 1805 movement through the Caribbean, pressed as the fleets were to keep the French in their sights, Frank would not have seen Charles, who was in Bermuda aboard HMS *Indian* in June.

For Jane Austen, tracking her brothers in the naval news, and on the map she had in mind from many years' experience, it was not unusual to have two brothers in the Caribbean at once, or to think of the map of those islands as a place of strong associations and family connections. Her brother James's first wife had been the daughter of the former governor of Grenada. Many of their neighbors, and some members of their extended family, were involved in colonial administration or held property in the Caribbean that was worked by people who had been enslaved. From 1804 to 1811, Charles Austen was assigned to the North American station, patrolling the Eastern Seaboard of North America. His job was to keep the United States from trading with Napoleon, and, after 1807, to intercept the trade in enslaved persons between the British West Indies and the American South. Charles's posting brought him often to Bermuda, where, in 1807, he would marry Fanny Palmer. Her father had been Bermuda's attorney general. "We do not call Bermuda or Bahama, you know, the West Indies," says Mrs. Croft, who has often lived aboard ships, in *Persuasion*.

That summer of 1805, Charles and HMS *Indian* left Bermuda in July, setting sail for Halifax.

Jane Austen and her mother and Cassandra arrived at Godmersham on June 19, 1805. We know this from the diary of the eldest child in the household, Fanny Knight, a great favorite of her aunts Jane and Cassandra: "Grandmama, Aunts Cassandra & Jane, Anna, & Fanny Cage arrived here at 6 in the evening." At that time, Edward and Elizabeth had nine children, ranging in age from Fanny, at twelve, down through five boys and three girls, the youngest of whom was little Louisa, just one year old. It was to be a summer of children's games. In Jane Austen's letters are mention of cribbage, and of "Battledore & Shuttlecock" (she and her nephew William managed six consecutive hits). She was thought by her nieces and nephews to have a rare talent at spillikins. Above all, it was a summer of playacting and acting. The day after their arrival, writes Fanny, "My doll was christened '*Fanny Eliza*.' We gave a grand entertainment in honor of the Christening." Six days later, they spent all day as imaginary characters and in the evening put on a play, "Virtue Rewarded." Their governess, Anne Sharp, a particular friend of Jane Austen's, seems to have enjoyed putting on plays as much as the Austen family did. She took the masculine roles. Fanny's diary:

> June 26th, Wednesday
>
> We had a whole holiday. Aunts & G'mama played at school with us. Aunt C. was Mrs. Teachum the Governess Aunt Jane, Miss Popham the Teacher Aunt Harriet, Sally the Housemaid, Miss Sharpe, the Dancing Master the Apothecary and the Serjeant, Grandmama Betty Jones the Pie woman, & Mama the Bathing Woman. They dressed in Character & we had a most delightful day—After dessert we acted a play called "Virtue rewarded".

"Virtue Rewarded," their play, which some think had been written by Anne Sharp, is a common enough subtitle. The phrase would have turned

Jane Austen's thoughts to Samuel Richardson's *Pamela; or, Virtue Rewarded*, in which a landed gentleman repeatedly tries to have sex with his fifteen-year-old maidservant. Young Pamela resists, writes, notably, a sad diary for her impoverished parents to find, and her eventual reward is that her employer marries her. Her nephew tells us that Austen's "knowledge of Richardson's works was such as no one is likely again to acquire." The year before, in 1804, a new edition of Richardson's correspondence, with an excellent and readerly introduction by Mrs. Barbauld, had been issued. Somewhere in or around 1805, Austen herself completed a five-act play, a burlesque of Richardson's novel *Sir Charles Grandison*, that she had begun twenty years before. In the first years of the new century, when Austen was unpublished and uncertain, Richardson's novels, and novels like them, in which young women are explicitly kidnapped and raped, were the backdrop against which she was working out her ideas. Part of what would give her characters their depth is that her readers were well aware of what menaced an unprotected young person in a predatory household.

Paula Byrne's *Jane Austen and the Theatre* and Jocelyn Harris's *Jane Austen's Art of Memory* study the influence of Richardson and others on Austen's novels—how Austen not only borrowed and transformed plots, characters, phrases, and epistles but got better at borrowing as she went on. Marianne Dashwood falls in love with Willoughby, who actually did make off with a vulnerable young woman, and left her destitute with a baby. Unlike Marianne, that young woman does die. *Sense and Sensibility* cannot quite figure out what to do with this and is by turns tragic and satiric, but by *Pride and Prejudice* this possibility had become a subtle, permeating, consistent edge.

At Godmersham, on June 26, there were two plays—the evening's *Virtue Rewarded* had been preceded by a whole day in which they dressed up and played characters. These, too, held ideas of what domestic virtue and service may be for women. "Mama," the mistress of the large house, played the bathing woman, whose hard job it was to physically lower the gentry into the ocean. Aunt Jane and Aunt Cassandra were the governess and teacher they might have been, had Edward not been adopted into this wealthy household, and that they might yet become if family support ran out. Miss Sharp, who actually was in service as the governess, played the emerging lower middle class of professions—the dancing master, the apothecary, the sergeant. "They dressed in Character & we had a most delightful day," says the happy recording child who does not see the adults' anxiety about their stations and future.

The rewards and punishments of fate, how quickly life could change for a child of twelve like her niece Fanny, this was there ready to be recollected when Jane Austen watched her family perform a play. Frank and Charles had both gone to naval school and then to sea when they were about twelve. Edward had first left the Austen household and come to Godmersham when he was thirteen or fourteen. He was formally adopted—the family expression was "taken more entire possession of"—by Thomas and Catherine Knight, probably in 1783, and he was the only child in their large house for the rest of his growing up. Knight money made many things, including writing books, possible; Catherine Knight also gave Jane Austen small sums, and may have helped support the publication of *Sense and Sensibility*. Now Edward had inherited all this bountiful space, and the house he had come into was full of children and had become a kind of sanctuary for Jane Austen and her dispersed siblings. Experience had taught her to know the transience of fortune, as hindsight instructs us.

MANSFIELD

In the summer of 1805, there was a great deal of visiting about, different families of the country were received at Godmersham, there were regular trips to Goodnestone, Ashford, and Canterbury, which were all so close that one might dine and return or stay overnight. On August 24, Jane Austen wrote to Cassandra, who was then staying at Goodnestone, that she had the previous evening been to dine at Eastwell, the estate belonging to the Hattons. Paula Byrne looked into this episode with new depth in *The Real Jane Austen*. Austen reported in her letter that she had been well pleased to be seated next to Mr. Finch-Hatton, rather than his wife, Lady Elizabeth, who Austen thought had "astonishingly little to say for herself." Perhaps it was particularly frustrating that this wife had not much to say for herself because, by Austen's lights, she ought to have been quite interesting. The wife was niece to, and had been raised by, Lord Mansfield, who had been lord chief justice, and had decided two of the most important cases about slavery, in 1772 and 1783. Each decision had significantly advanced the cause of abolition, and had become a part of how Austen thought about domestic and national life.

The trade in enslaved persons went on during Austen's entire life. Until she was about twenty-five, Britain was the largest slave-trading empire in the world, eventually responsible for the embarkation of 3.2 million people. Of these, about 2.7 million disembarked. Reading through the careful work of many scholars brought together at the website *Slave Voyages* (www.slavevoyages.org), you can see the movements of the men, women, and children being taken to the sugar and cotton plantations of the Caribbean and the southern United States while Austen was coming of age and learning to write. Austen did not have the numbers, but she knew the conditions of the middle passage from her brothers.

We know that she read with deep engagement the works of Thomas Clarkson, a central figure in abolition, a friend of both William Cowper and Samuel Taylor Coleridge. In January of 1813, as she brought *Mansfield Park* to conclusion, she wrote to Cassandra about another writer, whom she was reading on military policy and the British empire, and she remarked, "I am as much in love with the Author as I ever was with Clarkson." No one who had read Clarkson's history of the slave trade with passionate attention would be unaware of the two decisions Lord Mansfield had made.

In the first case, Mansfield had ruled, in 1772, that James Somersett, who had been brought as an enslaved person to England, and had escaped, could not be removed from England by his master. Mansfield's ruling stated that the sovereign law of England did not recognize the condition of slavery: "No authority can be found for it in the laws of this country." In 1785, William Cowper published his poem in six books, *The Task*, which included a passage on the situation of enslaved people that became a common-language understanding of Mansfield's ruling:

> They themselves, once ferried o'er the wave
> That part us, are emancipate and loosed.
> Slaves cannot breathe in England; if their lungs
> Receive our air, that moment they are free,
> They touch our country and their shackles fall.

Like many other readers of her day, Jane Austen would have known these lines well. Austen's brother Henry, in his biographical notice, wrote that "her favorite moral writers," both resolutely abolitionist, "were Johnson in prose, and Cowper in verse." Lines from different Cowper poems appear in nearly all Austen's books. Reading Cowper—on the surging life of the city, the troubling but not-to-be-overlooked newspaper, the quiet steadfast reading and conversation of a winter evening in the country, and then, the expanse of a prospect, a walk near favorite elms and through hedgerows—I feel near the home life of Austen and her family, and of William and Dorothy Wordsworth. Like these writers, Fanny Price has quite a bit of Cowper memorized.

In Cowper's lines are both familiar gray days and a growing understanding of the intricate ways those days were connected—through the air, across the waves—with other places in the world. Cowper's ideas of purer English air do sound to my ear wishful, nationalist, but there is something to be learned from seeing how his image of breathing the air brings international events home. I think Austen took to heart from the successful sugar boycott of the early 1790s that when you put sugar in your tea, it was *at once* a domestic and an international act, and that this was an important understanding. *Persuasion* closes by describing the navy as "that profession which is, if possible, more distinguished in its domestic virtues than in its national importance." In her sentence, the national may not exclude or enclose the domestic virtues; there is a question of practicing both to their fullest, and a question of which actually entrains the other.

Lord Mansfield was also a judge in the appeal, in 1783, of the *Zong* case. The background circumstances of the case were that the slave ship *Zong* had taken on far too many enslaved Africans and then been poorly captained, and had been about to run out of water. The crew knew that if the enslaved people died of thirst due to the captain's incompetence, the ship's owners would redeem none of their investment, whereas if they died by drowning, an insurance claim could be filed. There ensued three days of mass killing, resulting in the deaths of at least 130 men and women. This might have passed unnoticed, but the underwriters of the insurance did not want to pay, and the case went to court. A jury decided the insurance company was obliged to pay, but Mansfield and the King's Bench agreed to hear the appeal. The King's Bench ruled that the deaths had been the result of incompetence, which prevented the owners from collecting their insurance. Perhaps more important, because of the appeal, because, at the conclusion, Mansfield called for a retrial (which did not take place), and because, through the efforts of Olaudah Equiano and Granville Sharp, the case had the time and exposure to capture the public imagination, the *Zong* became a part of a more general understanding of both human nature and the natural world—the calculations by which human intelligence will debase itself, the ocean full of death. Both are suggested by J. M. W. Turner's painting *Slave Ship*, of 1840, based in part on the *Zong* case, and exhibited with a poem about enslaved persons thrown overboard that Turner himself had written in 1812, when Jane Austen was turning themes over in mind for *Mansfield Park*.

It is now widely accepted that Austen took the unusual step of naming her third novel for Mansfield, his rulings, and his household. It is the novel of hers in which a historical name figures most significantly. But it is not easy to see what Austen meant by giving this name often associated with liberty to a fictional estate that had been built by profits from the slave trade. In the novel, Mansfield Park is called a "plantation," suggesting a similarity or an interconnectedness but not, I think, an equivalence. Jane Austen carefully did not write that the life led by enslaved persons was in any way equivalent to the life led by her characters. (In *Emma*, Jane Fairfax, the one character who does raise the possibility of an equivalence between enslaved people and being a governess-for-hire, reveals something of her own self-preoccupation in her speech.) Rather, the shared Mansfield name makes a kind of locus of overlaps where you have to think about history and power, where you must reckon with kinds of restriction, and kinds of forgetting.

Reading *Mansfield Park*, I feel its relentlessness. Sir Thomas and Edmund speak at such ponderous length. Aunt Norris, who also subsists in part on Bertram charity, continually subjects Fanny to afternoons of cutting commentary and fatiguing demands. (In *Jane Austen's Names*, Margaret Doody reminds us that Aunt Norris was likely named for the "cruel proslavery delegate" John Norris, who betrayed the abolitionist movement at a key trial, and was written about by Thomas Clarkson.) The green world of trees and gardens is Fanny's only respite, and even this is frequently denied her by other people's selfishness—they take her horse, keep her from walking in the shrubbery, abandon her or tell her to wait instead of walking with her in the avenues, order the trees cut down, and later on banish her from Mansfield Park entirely. Fanny wants the green lands, wants charge of them, but her voice hardly rises above a whisper.

A judgment the novel does seem to make, and that may seem terrible, though it may not, and that is certainly religious, and that may be instructive for us trying to live in our age of refugees and extinction, is that everyone who lives at Mansfield Park is confined, and that flight from there is impossible. The place may be named for an ideal of liberty; it may not be bereft of hope; it is constrained and structured by human character and its organization; and you can never get out of Mansfield Park.

The actual Mansfield estate was, like Godmersham, an adoptive household. Lord Chief Justice Mansfield was the first Earl of Mansfield and his wife was Countess of Mansfield. They had no children of their own but raised two young relations together: their niece Lady Elizabeth Murray, who would become Lady Hatton, she who had so "little to say for herself," and a great-niece who it seems was of interest to Jane Austen; this other young woman was called Dido Elizabeth Belle.

Jane Austen would have known the story of Dido Belle's history and might have heard something of it from Mr. Hatton when she was seated next to him. Elizabeth Hatton would just then have been coming out of the first year of mourning for Dido Belle, who had died the previous July, in 1804. Dido Belle was the child of Maria Belle and a nephew of Lord Mansfield's, Sir John Lindsay. Lindsay was a naval officer and eventually an admiral. He had met Maria Belle when he had taken a Spanish ship, on which she was held as an enslaved person by one of the ship's officers, and must have taken her with him and then had a child with her. Maria Belle's later history has not yet been uncovered, but the child, Dido Belle, was taken by her father back to England to be raised by her great-uncle Lord Mansfield.

Dido Belle's position in the Mansfield household, and in British history, was complex. We have record of at least one guest at the home of Lord and Lady Mansfield complaining that there was "a Black" present in the company on an equal footing, linking arms to walk with her cousin, which lets us know about levels of prejudice, how she was treated, and how she acted. In the celebrated painting of the two nieces, both are dressed gorgeously, Lady Elizabeth starched, forward-facing, and empty; Dido Belle, caught in motion, is clearly the person who, if she were onstage, would be the only actor you'd watch, radiant and animated. Dido Belle also worked as Lord Mansfield's private secretary, a position of some importance, which suggests she had been given a fairly good education. Lord Mansfield died in 1793. He left Dido Belle a legacy and an annuity. Probably trying to protect her from future constraint, he also included in his will that she was officially at liberty. Either other people, or she herself, could have felt she did not have possession of herself before this death and document.

There were then in England a significant number of free black men and women working and living, and there were relatively untroubled marriages across racial lines. It is not at all outside the realm of possibility that

Jane Austen was at least as unprejudiced as a curious, humanist novelist of two hundred years later might be, and that she, too, would have thought with concern of what might have happened to Dido Belle's mother, of what that separation had been like, and of how it had felt to be raised in England in the Mansfield household, and not be able to leave.

Jane Austen kept track of the stories of neighboring families with great interest—they formed an ongoing drama of curious characters that she caught with her pen for her sister. Cassandra destroyed these letters in part so their neighbors and relations would not read the epistolary novel that had been practiced on them. The characters in Austen's novels were fully imagined, condensing observations of many years. They are often introduced to us as if we, too, might have grown familiar with such people sitting at dinner tables. How Austen's imagination was at work that summer of 1805 is suggested by a character who arises in her last unfinished novel, now called *Sanditon*, about a newly created, pushing little seaside spa town, whose proprietors are anxious to welcome three young women among the summer guests. Questions of property and exploitation are acrid:

> Of these three, and indeed of all, Miss Lambe was beyond comparison the most important and precious, as she paid in proportion to her fortune. She was about seventeen, half mulatto, chilly and tender, had a maid of her own, was to have the best room in the lodgings, and was always of the first consequence in every plan of Mrs. Griffiths.

As in *Mansfield Park*, cost and costliness pursue a young woman, press her into property. Miss Lambe is given in language that suggests all this is familiar to us, "about seventeen, half mulatto, chilly and tender, had a maid of her own." (There is some speculation about how Jane Austen intended the label "half mulatto," as it was not a designation any other writer used.) Seeming to come from two worlds, Miss Lambe is seen as important, "precious," she has a servant herself, but she is still treated as other people's income. The more we make an idea of property, the more it makes us. Miss Lambe, chilly and tender, must have been separated from a parent by people who had interests in the Caribbean, and she finds it almost impossible to get warm.

It is just after Sir Thomas has returned. Edmund says to Fanny that her uncle admires her, and the admiration has an unpleasant undertone that Edmund says is not unpleasant:

> "Your uncle thinks you very pretty, dear Fanny—and that is the long and the short of the matter. Anybody but myself would have made something more of it, and any body but you would resent that you had not been thought very pretty before; but the truth is, that your uncle never did admire you till now—and now he does. Your complexion is so improved!— and you have gained so much countenance!—and your figure—Nay, Fanny, do not turn away about it—it is but an uncle. If you cannot bear an uncle's admiration, what is to become of you? You must really begin to harden yourself to the idea of being worth looking at."

This has all the insidious endlessness that makes *Mansfield Park* so hard to bear. It is immediately after he has told her to harden herself and to be "worth looking at" that Edmund says to Fanny,

> "I only wish you would talk to him more.—You are one of those who are too silent in the evening circle."
>
> "But I do talk to him more than I used. I am sure I do. Did not you hear me ask him about the slave-trade last night?"
>
> "I did—and was in hopes the question would be followed up by others. It would have pleased your uncle to be inquired of farther."
>
> "And I longed to do it—but there was such a dead silence! And while my cousins were sitting by without speaking a word, or seeming at all interested in the subject, I did not like—I thought it would appear as if I wanted to set myself off at their expense, by shewing a curiosity and pleasure in his information which he must wish his own daughters to feel."

Everything is expense, inertness. To express curiosity, humanity, is to "set myself off at their expense." Fanny is too silent; after she speaks the silence is dead. In 1993, Edward Said wrote that this dead silence meant that Fanny Price, and perhaps Austen, assumes "there simply is no common language" with which to talk about Mansfield Park and slavery in Antigua in the same breath. He did not have access to publications—some inspired by his underscoring of "the slave trade"—of the last twenty years, as to how Mansfield Park had come by its name, and he does not seem to have known the history of Jane Austen's brothers and their involvement with abolition. I wish I could ask Said, with his brilliant spatial sense of *Mansfield Park*, to write again, more, about its geography of deliberate forgetting, the way its characters learn not to ask, but to let one another sail right off the map.

Edmund repeatedly bemoans how Mary Crawford speaks "as she ha[s] been used to hear others speak," and of how this means she has "a corrupted, vitiated mind." He does not remark on it, but through his speech and Fanny's we can see it, the way everyone at Mansfield Park has learned to speak of themselves and everyone else as aspects of the property. They have all been made mute ornaments. Though "beyond comparison important and precious," though "of first consequence," though sitting on soft sofas, possessions still.

"TIME, AND MANY PERUSALS"

If all this became a part of *Mansfield Park*, it happened gradually, in stages. It is not 1805 that matches the tone of the novel, it is 1805 seen through the varying lenses of the next eight years. Or, the arrangement of lenses is still more complex—it is 1813 seeing back to 1808, looking toward 1805, which holds a version of 1797 that is now interestingly at odds with the way 1797 looks in 1813.

Austen probably worked on scenes for *Mansfield Park* on and off for twenty years. She used almanacs to help her keep track of the progress of the days in her novels, and it seems the Austen household didn't save almanacs, so she used ones near to hand in any given year. One can work out layers in her drafts by the occasional specific date that creeps in. In *Mansfield Park*, in one part of the book, Easter comes "particularly late"—it would seem on Sunday, April 16, as it did in 1797, when the Austen sisters were still at home with their parents in Steventon. In 1797, Frank was about twenty-two and had been away from home, in training and at sea for ten years; Charles had been gone for six. When Charles was on land a couple of years later, in 1799, Austen would write fondly to Cassandra of "our own particular little brother" in the great happiness of being with him again. In *Mansfield Park*, Fanny waits seven years for the return of her brother William. The year 1797 was also when Cassandra's fiancé, Tom Fowle, went to the West Indies as a chaplain with Lord Craven and died of yellow fever in San Domingo. He was buried at sea.

In another part of *Mansfield Park* there is a ball on Thursday, December 22. December 22 fell on a Thursday in 1808, a year when both of Austen's brothers were at sea, and Jane Austen was living with Frank's family in Southampton, which they chose because it was near the hub of naval activity in Portsmouth. The Abolition of the Slave Trade Act had passed in 1807, and Frank's ship was part of the patrol, headquartered in Portsmouth, that began, in 1808, working along the coast of Africa to pursue and apprehend slave ships. Later, his recollections of some of this work were gathered by his grandson for *Jane Austen's Sailor Brothers*: "Chaced a ship which proved to be a Portuguese bound for Rio Janeiro. She had on board 714 slaves of both sexes, and all ages. She appeared to be about 300 tons!! And in those days the St. Albans was compelled to let the craft proceed on her course."

Frank was an evangelical Christian, and strongly abolitionist. Brian Southam, in his book on Jane Austen and the navy, points out that the two exclamation marks in "300 tons!!" likely come from the horror of thinking about such a small ship with such a huge human cargo, many hundreds more people than would be allowed by the regulations that Frank knew well. Because the ship was "a Portuguese," nothing could be done. In 1808, writing some remarks about St. Helena, Frank wrote that England, jealously guarding "her own liberty . . . should pay equal attention to the inalienable rights of all the nations, of what colour so ever they may be." We don't have many of Frank's letters to Jane, nor what we believe was the monthly epistle she wrote to him—though we have one letter she sent containing a congratulatory poem about the birth of a son and the safety of his wife. But we know what his letters were like. Austen wrote to Cassandra, in March of 1814, of Frank's "thinking, clear, considerate Letters." Frank's opinions and observations were a part of her understanding of ships, bodies, confinement, and had become a part of the novel she was then about to publish.

In 1808, Jane Austen had returned to Godmersham in the summertime and wrote to Cassandra that it was not as nice as it had been in 1805: "Three years ago we were more animated with you and Harriot and Miss Sharpe." Animation seems important here—as is true for Fanny when spring comes with "animation, both of body and mind," the sense is of the soul, the anima, that which makes a being move. A few more months passed. Cassandra took her turn at Godmersham. Edward's wife, Elizabeth, died, just after the birth of their eleventh child. Niece Fanny, whom Austen told Cassandra she thought of as "almost another sister," began, at fifteen, to run their large household. Of the littler nieces in new mourning, Aunt Jane wrote to Aunt Cassandra, "One's heart aches for a dejected Mind of eight years old." Two of the small sisters were sent motherless away to school. So many of the Austens had been in this position, sorrowfully guarding memories alone. As in Fanny's novel, with its curious layering of memories, through which time pools and runs backward.

The Austen sisters and their mother left Southampton and nearby Portsmouth for Chawton Cottage in 1809. At some point in Austen's reworkings of her material the central character became Fanny, like her beloved niece, Fanny Knight, and like the young woman from Bermuda whom her brother Charles had married and brought home in 1811, Frances Palmer. In the book, Fanny Price's family is from Portsmouth, and Fanny returns there in the later part of the novel.

In 1811, Charles and his wife, Fanny, and their small daughters began to live on HMS *Namur* in harbor duty in Portsmouth. The *Namur* was a storied ship, it had been in the wars for American independence, and it had seen action at Trafalgar. (It was also a ship that Olaudah Equiano had served on in 1759, which makes me wonder whether Austen would have read his autobiography. It has become a part of my *Mansfield Park* to imagine how interested she would have been in every detail of battle scenes and of the customs in Turkey, and of Equiano's experiences in Antigua, and the *Namur* under sail, how she would have admired the prose, so full of voices, every figure alive and active and peculiar.) Finishing *Mansfield Park*, in July of 1813, Austen asked permission to include the name of one of Frank's ships, *The Elephant*, and "two or three other of your old Ships?" She put in both the *Canopus*, on board which Frank missed the Trafalgar action, and the *Endymion*, on which Charles earned his first prize money, money he used to send his sisters topaz crosses, like one Fanny gets from her brother William in the novel. William Price's ship is said to lie close to the *Canopus* and the *Endymion* in Portsmouth harbor.

The first advertisements for *Mansfield Park* appeared in June of 1814. In September of that year, Charles's young wife, Fanny, who had just given birth to their fourth child, died of a fever on board HMS *Namur*. The three surviving little girls were sent to live with their mother's family and Charles went grieving to sea.

Mansfield Park is a story of a large ensemble, and in it, efforts at remembering flow from and around removals. Characters are continually being shuttled: to sea, to Antigua, to Mansfield Park, to London, to Portsmouth. In *Mansfield Park*, a smooth life is not surprisingly interrupted, life is the continual survival of rupture. Like *Persuasion*, it is a book about long-absent presences, how as we grow up we may remember, and how we will forget.

They had actually all been separated even earlier. Jane Austen's biographer Claire Tomalin brings out the way Austen, and her brothers and sister, had been reared with what was then a common double separation built into earliest childhood. Nursed for the first three months by their mother, they were then sent out to a nearby farm and taken care of until they were around eighteen months, "the age of reason," as Tomalin says, at which point they were allowed to come back home. Even at the time, some recognized the terrors this caused little children. Tomalin quotes the reformer and naturalist William Cobbett: "Who has not seen these banished children, when brought and put into the arms of their mother, screaming to get from them and stretching out their little hands to get back to the arms of the nurse?"

One never knows how much of Austen to assume in the speech of her characters, but it is striking when the warmhearted Isabella Knightley exclaims to her sister, Emma, of a young man who has grown up entirely in an adoptive household,

> "But how sad it is that he should not live at home with his father! There is something so shocking in a child's being taken away from his parents and natural home! I never can comprehend how Mr. Weston could part with him. To give up one's child! I really never could think well of any body who proposed such a thing to any body else."

Austen had written to Cassandra, in October of 1813, that she approved when Charles's wife, Fanny, kept their little Cassy on board HMS *Namur* with them, even though the child did get seasick: "Indeed the only difficulty with mama is a very reasonable one, the Child's being very unwilling to leave them. When it was mentioned to her, she did not like the idea of it at all."

The Austen girls themselves had been sent away, again, at just a little older than Cassy was. Jane Austen had been only seven to Cassandra's ten when they went to join a cousin who was being tutored by a lady who then took the three girls from Oxford to Southampton, where the children were hardly allowed to communicate with their parents. There, Jane and Cassandra were severely ill with typhus; Jane was in danger of dying when finally her cousin managed to get a letter out. The parents came to take the three girls home, and the cousin's mother eventually died of the fever.

Later, the Austen girls and their motherless cousin were sent to another boarding school. Mrs. Austen, sounding flip, and irritable, seems to acknowledge the harsh permanence of some of these departures, giving the responsibility for them to her daughter—"It was her own doing; she *would* go with Cassandra; 'if Cassandra's head had been going to be cut off, Jane would have her's cut off too'" was the explanation she gave to her granddaughter Anna Lefroy decades later.

Jane and Cassandra formed very young the habit of relying completely on each other. The relationship meant many things, but in *Mansfield Park* it meant a bond of memory in a forgetful world. "Children of the same family," Austen wrote in *Mansfield Park*, "the same blood, with the same first associations and habits, have some means of enjoyment in their power, which no subsequent connexions can supply." This is the chance to go over again "all the evil and good of their earliest years." With siblings, one may retrace "every former united pain and pleasure . . . with the fondest recollection. An advantage this, a strengthener of love, in which even the conjugal tie is beneath the fraternal." Childhood is short in Austen, but sisterhood is long.

We have few letters written by Cassandra, and she burned what some conjecture were hundreds of her sister's. Cassandra took most of the household duties at Chawton Cottage so that Jane Austen could write, though Jane Austen did not want the whole burden to fall to her sister, and did succeed in being the one to prepare breakfast each morning. Jane Austen always said her sister was the wise one, and their niece Anna Lefroy, thinking of them together, felt that Jane Austen's mood varied considerably, "when grave she was *very* grave," but was "not sure but that Aunt Cassandra's disposition was the most equally cheerful." Cassandra, at the periphery, is a contrasting, shaping presence. Anna remembered how, one summer's visit to Chawton, she would get novels from the circulating library and then relate their ridiculous stories to her aunt Jane, who "sat busily stitching away at a work of charity . . . Greatly we both enjoyed it, one piece of absurdity leading to another, till Aunt Cassandra fatigued with her own share of laughter wd exclaim 'How *can* you both be so foolish? & beg us to leave off—" Delightable, but a moderating influence, who took responsibility for the progress of time.

Theirs was a family brilliant in continuity, but they made metaphoric ruptures. Their brother James had sold their father's library, much to Jane Austen's regret. Burning intimate letters was a fairly common practice, but did Cassandra burn them because she was private, or possessive, or because she knew they would be very interesting, or intolerable, to the world she and her sister lived in? Perhaps the letters had sex in them, and anger; Jane Austen could be mean, and was. The letters would have embarrassed the families they knew and lived with. I do think that Cassandra wanted the novels to live with a fervor that almost equaled Jane Austen's, and she might have feared that, only just beginning to be accepted and to garner renown, they would be forever set aside if people became too early acquainted with the Jane Austen she knew.

Perhaps she and Jane had often talked it over, the feeling they had of not wanting to know the writers of books from too nearby. Jane Austen, when she was invited to be at an evening with the celebrated Madame de Staël, whose works she admired and imitated and recommended, was immediate and decided in turning the invitation down. She wanted the clear, untrammeled voice of the author, and Cassandra must have known what she meant. It does seem to have been a part of their idea to, in some measure, disappear. Leaving behind mostly the mountaintops, and some lists of supplies and pack trains, but no maps of routes, or descriptions of ice storms, no account of how they got up, or down.

When she was, in her own way, widowed by her sister's death, Cassandra carefully parceled out the remaining letters, and even her memories of her sister, among their many nieces and nephews, choosing who would know what. It was a delicate, family labor, and they all played their parts. Cassandra understood the whole quite well, and Jane Austen, who certainly *seems* to have had a good understanding of character, and of time, may have been rightly grateful to her and confident in the literary executor she had chosen.

Close by—that is the hallmark of Austen's work—we are so close by her characters, listening to them thinking, living in a few rooms and going for walks, as close as we are to the families we grew up in, or to the households we made, whatever they were like, when we were grown. When this is given the slight abstraction of fiction or a play, we still sometimes call it domesticity, but don't we really just mean the core of life, whatever it is about our lives that we hope to be in charity with when we die. This requires remembering and forgetting. Sometimes let us go over "every former united pain and pleasure"; sometimes, as Elizabeth Bennett says to her sister, a good memory is "unpardonable." A shared record is truth, is the possibility of freedom, but a too-exacting record may mean living only in service to the past. Close by but not suffocated, room enough to think and change. Circumspection is one of the deepest and most moral qualities in intimate life.

They did not know, Cassandra and Jane Austen, whether it would happen for the books they had worked to make, but it was how they themselves lived with books, working day and night to come near to living in them, for them. They wanted to leave the possibility. There would have to be just enough to suggest that there had been people there. A stage set, a few hats, a few stories, the possibility of a love affair, some books read, one scene in draft, a list of opinions. If we, readers and writers, were going to live in their household, read these books and write of them as if the books formed the core of life, then they would have to get out of the way.

READING AND BELONGING

It was odd, in a way, that my father should have had the idea of giving away the library—for he loved our reading, and he loved going to the theater with my mother, her research and her ideas about plays. And, more generally still, my father abhorred a gap. If we went into the next room, he followed. If I said I had been thinking about anything—self-portraits or exile or adverbs—it always turned out he had been, too, and generally had been for a long time, and he would remind me of when he had begun the inquiry. This was sometimes competitive, but more than that it came, I think, from a great need not to have been separate, even in thought. He read to us himself every night all through childhood. In the books he chose—*The Wind in the Willows*, *Stuart Little*, *Peter Pan*, *Charlotte's Web*, *The Little Prince*—there was, often, a tinge of regret about the lost world of childhood.

In that first, shared room, we had bunk beds and the carpet was a mottled red and pink. I think my father sat on a chair and we lay in our beds or sat on the carpet, but I really don't remember it. My mother has told me that she didn't want to get in the way of the reading, but that it was so nice that she would walk quietly up the stairs and sit near the top, where she could hear the sounds through our bedroom door. I can almost feel the edge of it in my mind, but it is more like her remembering than mine.

In an entry in my father's diary, he remembers how I learned, early, to read, and how he felt then, among many feelings, the regret of realizing that "in a small way having children learn to read is a warning of their growing up and leaving home."

When I read this, I was struck by the depth of his anticipation of separation. S, too, learned to read at three, but I did not think of her leaving home. She seemed safe to me, I felt she and I would always know how to find each other. My father used to remind me, now and again, that until I could read, I cried every night before sleep. I just needed to, my parents felt. There was sorrow in going across from the day to the night. After I learned to read—I used to hear his relief when he would tell me this—I stopped.

My father knew and loved that reading was a liberation for me, and yet he was sad, and that sadness that perhaps was a part of my crying before sleep became a part of reading and writing. I did not want my reading to have his sorrow in it, but it does. And in another way, I did want it to, because I wanted to be with him. The difficult borders between people in a household run through every aspect of life.

In the evenings, when the desire for narrative is strongest, in the Austen household people often read aloud to one another—from letters, from plays, from novels. One could enter into the experience of any one of these forms, hearing a character go on telling about her life. It came through the voice of someone one knew, who read not exactly as an actor but as a supple reader, giving shape to the different figures. One sat, with one's stitching, in the half-light, and one rejoined the characters one had played at being the night before, as they went on with their story.

Fanny Price has been reading out loud to her aunt from Shakespeare. "She often reads to me out of those books," the indolent Lady Bertram explains to Henry Crawford, "and she was in the middle of a very fine speech of that man's . . ." Sir Thomas has returned and put an end to the play, but not to ideas about the theater in *Mansfield Park*. Henry, now in pursuit of Fanny, sees a chance to make a fine impression. He says he will continue from the place where she has left off, takes up the book, "and by carefully giving way to the inclination of the leaves, he did find it." Fanny will only look at her work and determinedly says nothing. "But taste was too strong in her. She could not abstract her mind five minutes; she was forced to listen; his reading was capital, and her pleasure in good reading extreme." Henry Crawford is an actor born,

> The King, the Queen, Buckingham, Wolsey, Cromwell, all were given in turn . . . and whether it were dignity or pride, or tenderness, or remorse, or whatever were to be expressed, he could do it with equal beauty.—It was truly dramatic.—His acting had first taught Fanny what pleasure a play might give, and his reading brought all his acting before her again; nay, perhaps with greater enjoyment, for it came unexpectedly, and with no such drawback as she had been used to suffer in seeing him on the stage with Miss Bertram.

Fanny does not seem to mind, as I do, that he silences her in order to read himself. She loves to listen—her cousin Edmund reads "very well; but in Mr. Crawford's reading there was a variety of excellence beyond what she had ever met with."

When Henry has done reading, Edmund compliments him, and

Henry says one can hardly help but know Shakespeare well: "His thoughts and beauties are so spread abroad that one touches them every where, one is intimate with him by instinct." Edmund, though seeming to agree with Henry, then says something that is less lyrical, more exact. He says: "One is familiar with Shakespeare in a degree . . . from one's earliest years. His celebrated passages are quoted by every body . . . We all talk Shakespeare, use his similes, and describe with his descriptions." Henry Crawford explains in nouns, ones with which he is a bit too free and intimate; Shakespeare's phrases are objects, "beauties" that one touches everywhere, picking them up and putting them down at will. But Edmund says, with more restraint, more attention to conduct, "We all talk Shakespeare . . . [we] describe with his descriptions," we "use his similes." Language is not a possession, it is ways of acting.

After the brief interlude of reading and reflection, Henry forces Fanny out of her role as observer and insists that she return to the room where she is constrained to live, replete with acquisitions, of which she herself may soon be one. Lady Bertram lies on her couch with her pug dog and her demands; in Fanny's hands are the cloth and thread, the work she has constantly to do. Henry traps her in a conversation that makes her miserable; she cannot escape him. To me, there is an almost physical menace in the way he pursues her, telling her for seventeen sentences how he deserves her until "(seeing her draw back displeased)" he tells her to forgive him before asking two self-satisfied rhetorical questions that he himself answers. Austen does not say that he touched her, although he has been touching her cousin Maria at every opportunity, but her drawing back shows the oppressiveness of his demand. She is saved by the servants. She is not a servant; the language links them together: "The solemn procession, headed by Baddeley, of tea-board, urn, and cake-bearers, made its appearance, and delivered her from a grievous imprisonment of body and mind. Mr. Crawford was obliged to move. She was at liberty, she was busy, she was protected."

These words that are applied to Fanny, perhaps a bit ironically— "grievous imprisonment of body and mind," "at liberty," "busy," "protected"—are words that draw on the experiences of enslaved persons and of servants brought from the far empire. Her vulnerability, the poor niece brought from Portsmouth, is not the same as would be a servant's, and certainly not as would be an enslaved person's, but the language deliberately forces a conjunction and a consideration. Henry has learned ways of treating people with less power than he has, "one touches them every where," ways that are spread about and degrade the world by forgetting what else it might be. We learn from the language we are continually hearing and using, and we are described with its descriptions. Henry and Fanny have learned their parts playing over in imagination the stories of plantations and empires in which they have been raised.

For a long time, I read of the play. And then, for an even longer time, I read the last third of *Mansfield Park*, in which Fanny is returned to Portsmouth. The trip that would have meant so much when she was little has now been contrived by her uncle, who intends the poverty of her birth home, which she may have forgotten, to incline her to accept the proposal of Henry Crawford. Fanny is very lonely there, in Portsmouth. The day they arrive, William's ship, the *Endymion*, goes to sea again, and she is desolate. The household is slovenly; she is hungry for even a piece of bread that is not dirty and stale. She waits there in the house of parents and younger siblings who have all but forgotten her, and who are careless and loud and disorderly.

When I am reading Edward Said on Fanny's impressions of her return, I find myself dolefully agreeing with him that Fanny misses being at the center of the empire, with its "larger and better administered spaces." He is humane about this—knowing that part of the redistribution of empire is to make of the centers pleasant places in which it is possible to "see clearly," and to "think clearly," while relegating "lonely insularity" and "diminished awareness" to the impoverished edges. The clear places "are not available to Fanny by direct inheritance, legal title, by propinquity, contiguity, or adjacence." Said sees it this way: "To earn the right to

Mansfield Park you must first leave home as a kind of indentured servant or, to put the case in extreme terms, as a kind of transported commodity—this, clearly, is the fate of Fanny and her brother William."

Fanny's metamorphosis, though it can take place only in precisely her constrained circumstances, also says something in general about leaving home when very young. Austen had seen her brother Edward transformed in a related way. He was not an indentured servant, or a transported commodity, but he had been just one of the children in their noisy, though still genteel, parsonage, and then, having charmed the Knights, who needed an heir, he had been "taken more entire possession of," and made into a Knight, and become the proprietor of Godmersham Park, a part of a system of property, a gentleman often quite generous with his poorer sisters, who lived near Portsmouth.

In the last third of *Mansfield Park*, Fanny's ideas of home are traced with great delicacy. On first arrival in the Portsmouth disorder, she recoils but thinks the fault is in her. Gradually, in her introspection, the history of her allegiances clarifies: "When she had been coming to Portsmouth, she had loved to call it her home, had been fond of saying that she was going home; the word had been very dear to her; and so it still was, but it must be applied to Mansfield. *That* was now the home. Portsmouth was Portsmouth; Mansfield was home."

What she has gripped in memory is not in Portsmouth. She has held things in their earlier proportions, as exiles and mourners often do, has remembered affection with her mother that her mother no longer displays. This is not exactly a flawed memory, it is a historical one. In the deepest part of ourselves, where we hold an idea of home, remembrance and forgetting are inevitably woven together.

Fanny goes through the grief of separation again. She subscribes to a library and reads with her sister Susan, hoping "in this occupation . . . to bury some of the recollections of Mansfield which were too apt to seize her mind." When her cousin Tom falls dangerously ill, she longs to be home among those who, in their own ways, also seem to have forgotten her, and her longings "were such as to bring a line or two of Cowper's Tirocinium for ever before her. 'With what intense desire she wants her home.'" The "Tirocinium" is a poem against sending one's children away to be educated in a system. Fanny, who was sent away to be educated, now remembers the poem in the opposite direction from its original meaning; she misses the second home, of her education, and finds it requires great effort to bury her recollections. It is now that she is sad to "lose all the pleasures of spring," and that "animation, both of body and mind," which would have come from seeing the season's "increasing beauties from the earliest flowers in the warmest divisions of her aunt's garden, to the opening of leaves of her uncle's plantations, and the glory of his woods." She is wan. Sir Thomas has remanded her to a fate that seems likely to lead to serious illness. His is the power of confinement and liberty: "To be losing such pleasures was no trifle; to be losing them, because she was in the midst of closeness and noise, to have confinement, bad air, bad smells, substituted for liberty, freshness, fragrance, and verdure, was infinitely worse."

From this remote vantage in Portsmouth, Fanny follows one more play, looking out through a brilliant sequence of letters, to watch the doings of her cousins and the Crawfords. Mary Crawford is predictably hopeful that Tom will die, and Edmund will inherit, and she will be able to marry rich after all; Henry Crawford is flirting with Maria, who is now married. Fanny knows their characters so well that when it does all collapse, and both Bertram sisters run off with their lovers, she is shocked but not disbelieving—"her judgment told her it was so."

For his part, when he has had time to consider, Sir Thomas cannot believe how he has raised his daughters. They have been told to pursue "elegance and accomplishments," and never "self-denial and humility." They know how to acquire and to be acquired, but not how to act. "He feared that principle, active principle had been wanting; that they had never been properly taught to govern their inclinations and tempers by that sense of duty which alone can suffice. They had been instructed theoretically in their religion, but never required to bring it into daily practice."

His solutions, though, are as unforgiving as burning all the copies of *Lovers' Vows* that he meets. Maria and Mrs. Norris are dispatched into exile, a place "remote and private," and, the narrator tells us, "shut up together . . . it may be reasonably supposed that their tempers became their mutual punishment." Julia and Mr. Yates are quickly incorporated into the smooth proceedings. Edmund will be married off to Fanny, about whom Sir Thomas now has "the high sense of having realised a great acquisition in the promise of Fanny for a daughter."

There may be genuine happiness, there may be "life for a moment . . . a green thought," and still there is so much silence in what Fanny acquires. The concluding scene Fanny does have with Edmund comes when he wants to know if she has loved Henry Crawford. Backing her into a corner, Edmund sounds like Captain Wentworth in the draft scene Austen rejected:

> "You do not wish me to be silent?—if you do, give me but a look, a word, and I have done."
> No look or word was given.
> "Thank God!" said he.

When the resident clergyman of Mansfield dies, Edmund succeeds to the living. I find the last sentence of *Mansfield Park* Austen's most enclosing ending:

> On that event they removed to Mansfield, and the parsonage there, which under each of its two former owners, Fanny had never been able to approach but with some painful sensation of restraint or alarm, soon grew as dear to her heart, and as thoroughly perfect in her eyes, as every thing else, within the view and patronage of Mansfield Park, had long been.

Living under and within a structure of power means that, becoming an owner yourself, you will forget the history of former sensations of restraint and alarm. And you may forget ambitions you had: writing, speaking aloud. At the same time, gentler and freer aspects of life and devotion may also involve rubbing away parts of the past and its authority. Samuel Johnson wrote of an art of forgetfulness. Austen's own memory, her brother wrote, was "extremely tenacious."

FORGETTING

The theater—the lines memorized by actors and auditors, the sudden strong memories that come to us when we sit at a play, and perhaps also the cathartic way that a play may allow you to let go of something too tenaciously and disproportionately remembered—was a favorite pastime of Sigmund Freud and of his Viennese patients, who dreamed of the theater and felt changed by it. Sometimes one of these burnished, exilic memories stands out just when you are learning a new way of being and forgetting an old one. A rehearsal, like a dream, like a several months' stay at a home that used to be yours, may bring out the particulars that are to be eroded.

Fanny has seen that Edmund and Mary Crawford are drawing closer together through playing lovers in the play. Edmund and Mary both feel uncertain about the scene in which their characters are to declare their passion for each other. Each decides to seek out Fanny and ask to rehearse opposite her in order to prepare for playing opposite each other.

It is because of this that rehearsal comes to Fanny's cold and quiet room. Mary arrives first and says to Fanny, "I have brought my book, and if you would but rehearse it with me." A few minutes later, Edmund enters with the same idea and is delighted to find Mary there. They decide to rehearse together, with Fanny as prompter and spectator. Once the play is there, her room can't really be held apart as an archive of keepsakes; it becomes a part of the house through which the moving currents of life run. The scene is an emotional one, with the pain that the joining of fixed memories to living practice does have—Austen mentions surprise, consciousness, pleasure, joy, animation, pity, weariness, and suffering.

Fanny is still Fanny, whose brother William has sent her the drawing of a ship hanging on the wall, but something is happening that is a part of her growing and surviving. "In watching them," Austen says of Fanny, "she forgot herself."

In *A Midsummer Night's Dream* the rehearsals are *in* the woods. The place of dreams and the theater of practice are the same place. At the end of *Mansfield Park*, we are told in a few jocular sentences that Fanny and Edmund spent a lot of time under the trees, but we are denied any actual scene of them measuring their steps together and reaching happy resolve. Cassandra, purportedly, wanted her sister to change the novel's ending and let Fanny marry Henry Crawford, but, holding aside the unpleasantness of his character, the book is a history, not a romance. Fanny walks with neither possible lover, but with someone else, and in the middle of the book, Mary Crawford, who has never really seen the value of the country, and lingers in it because of her interest in Edmund. Fanny tries to explain how astonishing the change has been for a rough hedgerow that in just three years has become a lovely walk: "Perhaps, in another three years, we may be forgetting— almost forgetting what it was before. How wonderful, how very wonderful the operations of time, and the changes of the human mind!"

Most important is not what the hedgerow allows her to remember but the ways it may allow us to forget. The thoughts are complicated, and she pauses as she tries to give them words:

> She soon afterwards added: "If any one faculty of our nature may be called *more* wonderful than the rest, I do think it is memory. There seems something more speakingly incomprehensible in the powers, the failures, the inequalities of memory, than in any other of our intelligences. The memory is sometimes so retentive, so serviceable, so obedient—at others, so bewildered and so weak—and at others again, so tyrannic, so beyond controul! We are to be sure a miracle every way—but our powers of recollecting and of forgetting, do seem peculiarly past finding out.

Forgetting, too, is a power, and Fanny works at the intricacy of remembering and forgetting that a green walk may allow, and that devotion to a
place may both offer and require. Miss Crawford, after this reflection,
"untouched and inattentive, had nothing to say."

"Rehearsal," meaning the activity of actors learning to play their parts, became a word in English in the 1570s, a little before Shakespeare began
using it in *Hamlet* and *A Midsummer Night's Dream*. A little before that
time it meant more simply to repeat, to say over again what had already
been written or said. And before that, it meant to go over the ground. It
was to establish a relationship between a body in motion and the earth.
This meaning of the word "rehearsal" came from "rake over," to turn over
the ground—from the Old French *re*, meaning to repeat, and *hercier*,
which was to harrow, or drag or trail upon the ground. Thus it was always
a way to struggle with what lay, remembered and forgotten, beneath.

Hercier is also the word from which we have "hearse," which carries the
last movement of the dead above the earth. Before it was a vehicle for the
dead, a hearse was a flat display of candles that went around a coffin; this
display was thought to look like a harrow or a herce, a rake for breaking up
that ground into which the dead would be returned. When we rehearse a
play, we go over the ground into which what we love has gone.

In my father's diary, I found something else that had been in the background of our having done the play that I hadn't remembered. When I
was nine, the age Fanny Price was in her last year in Portsmouth, my
mother was told she would stop teaching theater at the university. I knew
then that her job had been more precarious because she was a woman,
with children. My father described it in his diary, in November of 1982:
"The girls have taken this very calmly . . . For me it felt like a mild form of
a death in the family." He noted how tired he was and that my mother
seemed to have a worse version of the same effects.

Perhaps my sister and I did not speak of it much, but I knew that my mother was a gifted director. In the basement were posters from her productions of Sheridan's *The Rivals*, and Beckett's *Endgame*. For my mother, the theater was a radical space of ritual and self-creation. The possibility of certain kinds of work closed, but she made a theater company with three other women and directed there.

In other entries from that fall of mild bereavement, my father remarked upon how much I was reading, especially plays: *The School for Scandal*, and "something by Shaw," comedies my mother gave me. It was the following spring that she was asked by a large community theater to direct *A Midsummer Night's Dream* and cast us in parts in the play.

I had not been wrong, not exactly, to think our family life was held by the play, it was just a different family life, more pained and mortal, in which the world had more power over us. I memorized all the lines, I would *not* forget. But there seemed no getting away from it—it undulated with forgetting. We made it without my father, and he had been afraid that in reading we might forget him, and had given the library away.

It happened to me once in analysis, after a long while in which I had been trying to make out some of the benevolent aspects of childhood, that after a dream I saw a kind of dimensional shape, something like a shape that putty or clay would make stretched and hanging down, and I knew it was the shape of our family. It was small, and I felt sadness. Not a memory, more like the presence of a forgetting. It rushed upon me and I thought, "That is exactly the way it was."

Eight

◈

A FRIEND

If I picture a map of the five Austen novels in my mind, the first four are like the orbiting bodies of a planetary system, widening outward in concentric circles, from the tight binary star of the two sisters in *Sense and Sensibility*, to the family life of *Pride and Prejudice*, to the wider ellipse of *Mansfield Park*, all the way out to the perfectible community resonant in *Emma*. *Persuasion* is something like an asteroid that moves, irregularly, repeatedly, among the different spheres.

Persuasion is about mourning, again; it is like seeing mourning after you have visited all these other planets, seeing mourning as it manifests around a body in motion, one that is not in a predictable orbit but hurtles toward a future, uncertain but not entirely separated from what has gone before. It is connected to the experiences of each of the other books—to memorializing, seeing again, forgetting, learning, and imagining, but it is different because Anne says how it has happened for her. She says it in public, at the White Horse Inn, but before that she has spoken in private to another, an intimate, friend.

Jane Austen knew that friendships between grown women was one of the subjects of *Persuasion*, and she knew that this was an unusual subject for literature, and that some of her readers might overlook it. For a long time, I was on Captain Wentworth's side when, two pages from the novel's end, he and Anne talk over whether he will forgive Lady Russell for her inter-ference. Anne says she has been "thinking over the past," and that "much as I suffered from it, that I was perfectly right in being guided by the friend whom you will love better than you do now. To me, she was in the place of a parent." She says that she herself would never have given that advice, but that following it was a kind of duty, and that "a strong sense of duty is no bad part of a woman's portion." I never liked this, and am relieved that Captain Wentworth says: "Not yet. But there are hopes of her being forgiven in time. I trust to being in charity with her soon."

Lately, though, I have more sympathy for Lady Russell, "the friend . . . in the place of a parent," who has tried to honor Anne's mother. She may have helped to extinguish Anne's hopes, *and* without her how else would Anne have survived the years that followed?

Now, as Anne finds other friends, who hear her better, she and they still inherit something of the friendship that existed between her mother and Lady Russell. On the evening when all the characters go to the concert, Anne and Lady Russell can both think of Anne's mother, who used to be able to hear Anne playing with a "just appreciation." At the concert, Anne becomes aware that Captain Wentworth "had a heart returning to her," and listening to the Italian songs, giving quick and accurate translations of the Italian to her neighbors, and watching everywhere for Captain Wentworth, that is the beginning of the rebirth of happiness for her. It is a different friend, Mrs. Smith, who can see it, the next day, when Anne comes to visit, how Anne is illuminated by the return of music, the ready flow of syllables.

Another memorial service, in 2018. Jessica and my mother and I all were there together. It was for a woman who was our neighbor growing up, a pianist called Susan Kister. Sue lived in the house next to ours and four down from Jessica's. She was the presence of music on our block. It was Sue who had found the pianist to play at my father's memorial service. It had also been Sue who drove me to the hospital when my father summoned me there on his last day. Sue's was the first house I walked to by myself, when I was three and four. My mother would watch from our front steps and Sue from hers, and I was always in sight of one or the other, except for the brief, thrilling moment when I passed the hedge that divided our two front lawns.

We have our own children, and I begin to guess what it might have been to my mother, to see her child walk out of her sight, and to think, "She will be sheltered by my friend." It is not morbid that when I see Jessica's tenderness with our children, and hear shades of my voice in the way she speaks to them, I think that if I should die, they will be comforted by my friend.

My mother spoke of friendship at Sue's memorial service. Being friends grew from being neighbors, slowly:

> Sue was a private person and I think many of you know fiercely independent . . . She liked the hedge between our houses.
>
> But our kitchen windows faced each other and as our friendship grew so did the way we came to greet one another through our windows. Except for my family, Sue's face was the first I saw each morning and the last at the end of the day. We always smiled and waved. Even now, three months after her passing and two years since she moved to Glacier Hills, I still sometimes find myself expecting to see her at her kitchen window.

At the end of what she said, my mother spoke of how Sue looked out for her in the years after my father died, and always had dinner ready for her each time my mother came back to the empty house, even after Sue became ill, and forgetting began to set in. I felt the idea of character that my father and mother had worked out together in what she said of friendship. It was "so fundamentally a part of who Sue was," that

> still she would be waiting at her front door, looking out for me when I turned up from wherever I had been with a smile of welcome and friendship, inviting me in for a dinner that she could no longer remember to prepare.

My mother sat down in the seat on my left. From the seat on my right, Jessica, in her dark dress, stood up and walked to the stage. She began:

Almost thirty years after my last lesson, Thursday evenings still have a special feeling to me. They remind me of music, and Sue, and all the hours I spent with her.

Sue liked her students to open her front door and come right in, even if the previous lesson was still under way. We were to wait on the sofa at the far end of her living room from the piano. Opening a door without knocking first was impossible for me, but if I knocked, then I interrupted the lesson and Sue had to come open the door. I spent a lot of minutes in a state of suspended animation on her front steps. When Sue realized what was happening, she never said anything, but she started leaving the door just cracked open a bit for me—and somehow that made all the difference.

The door, the concrete squares of sidewalk in approaching it, imprinted with the mysterious initials of a cement company, the walk to Sue's house.

I think I generally looked down on my way to Sue's house—I had the sidewalk memorized—but I looked up on the way home. I watched the trees against the evening sky and thought about music. Often I was filled with a sense of calm purpose I can't quite account for, but it served me well.

Jessica caught at what eternality was for Sue: "For her it was about the music, I think, which came before and continues after."

There was a time, very late in Sue's life, when Jessica and I were both visiting our mothers, staying a few houses apart, going to sleep with our windows that looked toward each other. My mother, who went often to visit Sue in the place of assisted living where she had gone, drove Jessica and me, and we sat with Sue in her room, together. When Jessica spoke of this, she remembered that my mother put on some music; it was Mozart, "and Sue turned toward the sound, peaceful, as if a door had been cracked open for her."

It is hard to send the dead on their way. They entrust us with so much. At my father's memorial service, music was played by the pianist Sue had thought of. Jess sat holding S, who was asleep, on her lap, while I spoke. For years, Sue waited at her door for my mother. Then, Jessica and my mother spoke for her.

When I came home to Chicago, I sat at our kitchen table in the evening with S, and said to her that when people die, they lay down the things they have loved and other people take them up and carry them and care for them. S, thinking about Sue, said, "like she loved music, and I love music."

Jane Austen's friendships with women were part of how she came to her literary understanding, and how she expressed her understanding. Mrs. Lefroy, her dear friend and literary patron, had first taken an interest in her when she was a girl writing. The fact that this friend was killed, at fifty-five, in a horseback riding accident on December 16, 1804, on Jane Austen's twenty-ninth birthday, made her birthday ever after sorrowful. She wrote a poem in memory:

> The day returns again, my natal day;
> What mix'd emotions in my mind arise!
> Beloved Friend; four years have passed away
> Since thou were snatched for ever from our eyes.

Paula Byrne begins one chapter of her observant book with the ivory miniature taken of Mrs. Lefroy. It was, as Byrne notices, "a little bit, two inches high . . . intended to hold the image of a beloved person in the memory during their absence." It could then, at the time of death, become "a piece of mourning jewellery." With the phrase "two inches high," Byrne is connecting this portrait to Jane Austen's well-known description of her own work, in a letter to a nephew who had aspirations to write fiction. Austen laughed that she had not been the one to steal his missing chapters:

> I do not think however that any theft of that sort would be really very useful to me. What should I do with your strong, manly, spirited Sketches, full of Variety & Glow?—How could I possibly join them on to the little bit (two Inches wide) of Ivory on which I work with so fine a Brush, as produces little effect after much labour?

The littleness and delicacy of ivory do not separate it from huge animals, violent conquest, or from music, and the keys of the piano. I felt a slight shiver when I noticed that the letter was written on her own birthday, December 16, 1816, that natal day when the ivory miniature of her dead friend would have had a special power. It was also only seven months before her own death, and she knew she was ill, though not how ill. Jane Austen's ivory miniatures are aware of how very much life and labor it may take to produce those little effects that never lose their meaning, and may last like the companionship of mourning jewelery.

Sir Walter Scott went back to reread *Pride and Prejudice* in 1826. He noted:

> Read again and for the third time at least Miss Austen's very finely written novel of *Pride and Prejudice*. That young lady had a talent for describing the involvement and feelings and characters of ordinary life which is to me the most wonderful I ever met with. The Big Bow-wow strain I can do myself like any now going, but the exquisite touch which renders ordinary commonplace things and characters interesting from the truth of the description and the sentiment is denied to me. What a pity such a gifted creature died so early!

Walter Scott wrote the most important critical recognition of Jane Austen's work to appear in her lifetime, after the publication of *Emma*. The review was anonymous, but it had been Austen's publisher who suggested the idea to Scott, and even if the publisher didn't tell her, she might well have recognized the prose style. The review goes carefully over the events and characters not only of *Emma* but also of *Pride and Prejudice* and *Sense and Sensibility*, with a just and rereaderly sense of proportions and significance. After reading it, Austen wrote to her publisher in April 1816, using her authorial name, "The Authoress of *Emma* has no reason I think to complain of her treatment in it—except in the total omission of Mansfield Park.—I cannot but be sorry that so clever a Man as the Reviewer of *Emma*, should consider it as unworthy of being noticed."

It might have particularly frustrated her that her reviewer had not taken account of *Mansfield Park*, which not only tried out a range of emotion he seemed not to credit her with but was a profound rejoinder to his idea of a novel of history. Still, the review is something I am grateful happened—a real consideration by a serious literary mind that places Austen's work as new in the history of the novel. It concludes with a sincere reflection that I am not the only one to think would have affected her, or perhaps confirmed her in what was already her intention for *Persuasion*. The clever Man writes that he knows that in former times novelists wrote too much of sweeping romantic love, and he sees the justice of noting instead "calculating prudence," but there may still be something worthwhile in the early "romantic feelings" felt by young people. "Who is it, that in his youth has felt a virtuous attachment, however romantic or however unfortunate, but can trace back to its influence much that his character may possess of what is honourable, dignified, and disinterested?" Perhaps the young person worked hard to attain "that distinction necessary to raise him to an equality with her."

One may grow by loving backward. Anne Elliot and Fanny Price, Austen's two rememberers, would hardly know what to make of Elizabeth's command "Think only of the past as its remembrance gives you pleasure." They would perhaps admire Elizabeth's freedom, but they would not give up their own greater discipline. Fanny and Anne do not have the same sense of the past, though. Both are readers, but one is more writerly; both are long confined to memories of their first families, but one ventures out, on the arm of a friend. The difference between Fanny and Anne, between one who waits, and one who waits and is heard? One answer might be: Mrs. Smith.

Austen's introduction of Mrs. Smith brings out compactly what matters most: kindness, a dead mother, fourteen years old, strong sensibility, good to her, remembered.

> Miss Hamilton, now Mrs. Smith, had shewn her kindness in one of those periods of her life when it had been most valuable. Anne had gone unhappy to school, grieving for the loss of a mother whom she had dearly loved, feeling her separation from home, and suffering as a girl of fourteen, of strong sensibility and not high spirits, must suffer at such a time; and Miss Hamilton, three years older than herself, but still from the want of near relations and a settled home, remaining another year at school, had been useful and good to her in a way which had considerably lessened her misery, and could never be remembered with indifference.

Now, some thirteen years later, although her snobbish father and sister disdain her old friend's lower-class address, her illness, debility, poverty, Anne goes to visit. The return of this friend is given in language like that which introduces the return of romance for Anne:

> The visit was paid, . . . their interest in each other more than re-kindled. The first ten minutes had its awkwardness and its emotion. Twelve years were gone since they had parted, and each presented a somewhat different person from what the other had imagined . . . But all that was uncomfortable in the meeting had soon passed away, and left only the interesting charm of remembering former partialities and talking over old times.

Life is quickened by her friend's good conversation and elasticity of spirits. Anne begins to go often, following a regular ritual, of being let in by the maid or the nurse, sitting together in chairs that have seen better days.

Just before the great scene at the White Hart, the two women have a long, intimate conversation, in which Anne learns more about what her friend's marriage was like, and also is given the proof and history of Mr. Elliot's scurrilous behavior. Anne has not been sure of him, and would not have married him, but now this different friend, one who knew her just at the time of her mother's death, has told her she need not listen to Lady Russell's persuasions, or be bewitched by the possibility of returning to her mother's place, and this is emboldening. Anne has not laughed once in the entire book, but in this scene she laughs, and then in the next scenes goes on laughing, as if she had got the knack of it again. I think without this conversation, which deepens the place of friendship for Anne, she would not have the spirits to give the declaration that follows in the next major scene, at the White Hart Inn.

A number of critics do not much like Mrs. Smith as a character, and find the friendly conversation in her room goes on a long time to unravel plot points that do not really affect the course of the novel. (This is not the only thing a bit akimbo in the last part of *Persuasion*. Ellen Moody, from a meticulous chronology of time both determinate and indeterminate in *Persuasion*, is one of several who believe there was a planned third volume of *Persuasion*, in which a whole inverting plot would have been revealed, as happens in *Emma*, but that Austen instead hurried it to conclusion, deciding it was ready enough, and leaving these threads suggestively dangling.) In any case, Mrs. Smith mattered to Austen. She gave Mrs. Smith that place in the book's last sentences that it was her habit to reserve for what a reader might otherwise be tempted to overlook. We are told that Captain Wentworth exerted himself on Mrs. Smith's behalf, getting back the property in the West Indies that would give her status and security again (suggesting to me that, although so much freer, the characters in *Persuasion* also cannot get out of Mansfield Park). Her poverty diminished, Mrs. Smith was the Wentworths' "earliest visitor" and remained their close friend. The friendship, and the qualities of its shared character, are the center of the last paragraph: "[Mrs. Smith's] spring of felicity was in the glow of her spirits, as her friend Anne's was in the warmth of her heart."

It is, and will be, good to have someone to talk things over with. Anne is the only Austen heroine who has a friend named in her last paragraphs who is not a family member, not a sister or an aunt, not one of a "small band of true friends," but just an actual friend whom you can imagine her laying out the sheets for and sitting up late with, crying and laughing together with.

Perhaps the friendship not only leads to the declaration but is, in turn, opened by the declaration, and, later, will do something to mitigate the fate we cannot help fearing will be Anne's; perhaps Mrs. Smith's resilience in widowhood will be of further help by and by. For the day that Anne and Captain Wentworth are united, Jane Austen chose in the calendar Sunday, February 25, 1815; Napoleon escaped from Elba on Monday, February 26. "His profession," Austen cautioned her reader about Captain Wentworth, "was all that could ever make her friends wish that tenderness less; the dread of a future war all that could dim her sunshine. She gloried in being a sailor's wife, but she must pay the tax of quick alarm for belonging to that profession which is, if possible, more distinguished in its domestic virtues than in its national importance."

Anne Sharp is the friend of Austen's who interests me most, whom I try to catch glimpses of in biographies and the letters. Miss Sharp was the governess, employed in the household of Jane Austen's brother Edward Knight, who took the masculine parts in the playacting that niece Fanny described in the summer of 1805. Anne Sharp was witty, a reader, a woman who always worked and eventually ran a school. Austen trusted her literary judgment.

Later in that summer of 1805, the women had been temporarily scattered and staying in different nearby places, and there was a brief encounter at Canterbury. Jane Austen wrote to Cassandra, "Pray say everything kind for us to Miss Sharpe, who could not regret the shortness of our meeting in Canterbury more than we did. I hope she returned to God-mersham as much pleased with Mrs. Knight's beauty and Miss Milles's judicious remarks as those ladies respectively were with hers." I seem to join Austen in finding Anne Sharp very attractive as she dashes in and out of the pages. Sharp left the Knight household in 1806, and the two friends went on with their correspondence until Austen's death. Eventually, in Austen's letters she was "my dearest Anne."

Austen carefully noted Anne Sharp's reaction to *Emma*, in the record she titled "Opinions" that she kept of the criticism she received for *Mansfield Park* and *Emma*. Miss Sharp liked *Emma*: "better than MP.—but not so well as P. & P.—pleased with the Heroine for her Originality, delighted with Mr. K—& called Mrs. Elton beyond praise.—dissatisfied with Jane Fairfax." Perhaps Austen recognized a coincidence of opinion between Anne Sharp and Walter Scott. The unsatisfactory Jane Fairfax falls pas-sionately in love with Frank Churchill, but there is something about what such love would be, something Austen knew from her own experiences and those of her friends, that she had not let come through in Jane Fairfax. Anne Elliot says one cannot always speak or write from the knowledge of what has "occurred within our own circle; many of which circumstances (perhaps those very cases which strike us the most) may be precisely such as cannot be brought forward without betraying a confidence."

That experience would be there in Anne Elliot: "She had been forced into prudence in her youth, she learned romance as she grew older—the natural sequel of an unnatural beginning." In her own copy of *Persuasion*, Cassandra, now alone, wrote in the margin next to these lines, "Dear dear Jane! This deserves to be written in letters of gold." I can imagine Austen laughingly recording this in her next list of "Opinions," near whatever Miss Sharp would have said.

Her friendship with Miss Sharp became one of the most enduring relationships of Jane Austen's life. In the correspondence, there are glim-mers of possible visits and encounters in various places and seasons; Aus-ten definitely arranged for Miss Sharp to come to Hampshire on a visit in

1815; and she wrote one of her last letters to her, a letter Sharp saved and carefully left in good hands at her own death. As a remembrance, Cassandra sent Sharp a lock of her sister's hair. I cannot help but think, as Claire Tomalin does, that for Austen, *Persuasion*, with its own Anne, was a kind of "present to herself, to Miss Sharp, to Cassandra."

Two years after Jessica and I had walked in the Connecticut woods and I had dreamt of us trying to write the books of our old neighborhood, we were walking in Connecticut again. She had been reading drafts of essays I was writing about Austen. I was standing a little behind her on the path, and she turned toward me. She said that I was holding back.

I began to tell her about a memory I had, another memory of first reading Austen, not the color of light in my late-afternoon room but a specific actual memory. I was in high school, and I had read all the Austen novels I could find, and I went to the public library to see if there were any more. I stood in the aisle, the books whose authors' names began with "Au" were on a high shelf. I saw among the familiar titles one I did not know, and reached up, high, to take it down. I remember that the title began with a large and perhaps slightly ornate capital *S*. I turned to the back to see what the story was about and found that Jane Austen herself had completed only about sixty pages of it before her death; the rest had been written by a later writer. What I remember was deciding against it, and reluctantly sliding the hardback in between the others in its high place on the shelf. I knew it would not be an Austen novel; I thought it might mar the books I had been reading.

I said to Jessica, I have been thinking that I have tried and tried to write my father's book, and it cannot be done.

Nine

IMAGINING

SEPTEMBER 2012

The last time I walked with my father around Fresh Pond, it was September. S, in the stroller, was about four months old. She could not yet sit up by herself but looked around with interest. The trees would have been mostly green, but drier, preparing for color. I think I remember a few leaves underfoot. My father had come to Cambridge for an academic conference, and to visit us. He had been having a lot of pain, which he couldn't get his doctors to pay attention to. He felt frustrated, and though he said he was confident that it could be fixed, I think he was wary. He was pleased that he could breathe well enough to take the walk, but he had to go quite carefully; each step anticipated shortness of breath and the pain he might feel in his back.

Fall in our family had always been the beginning of the new year, of classes and new learning. On that walk, about halfway around, as we came to the smaller pond where the dogs swim, my father urged me to return to teaching. My first feeling was aggravation: I had a small baby, I was trying to finish writing a biography, what did he want from me? I told him, sharply, that I was lucky to have time to be with S and to write, that perhaps he didn't realize how I had struggled to find time to write while I was teaching. I myself worried that leaving teaching was a repetition of how my mother had been forced out of her university career, and I was angry with him for seeming to raise that possibility. I think he may have wondered whether I had lost my way in what I was writing; that was not something I could bear to think of then.

We walked slowly on and spoke of other things. It might have been before the disagreement, but I think it was after, in another effort of care, that my father said he was glad I had done analysis. It had been five months since I had left analysis, and I felt I had scarcely had time to think of it since. It mattered to me that my father had noticed. He said I had become much less anxious, and, this I remember very particularly, that it had changed the way I sat in a chair. Now I think of having a daughter, and watching her be anxious for thirty-nine years, and then one day noticing that the way she sat in a chair had changed.

I remember rounding the last curve to complete the circle, and his relief that he had been able to walk the whole way. It had not occurred to me that he might not be able to, nor had I formed any plan of how we would have gotten back if he could not. We had argued about the future; and we had had different points of view.

It turned out that this was the last real walk we were to take together. We managed one other, that Christmas, around a few blocks of my childhood neighborhood on streets that had some fine snow and enough ice that we were careful about falling. But that September was the last real walk, and something about it failed. It can still be a pained, impacted memory, one I wince away from. It doesn't seem quite like him, somehow, and my mind catches on details, and things I wish had gone differently.

EMMA

Emma begins with a marriage and a possible crime. The marriage is of Emma's governess: her much-loved companion Miss Taylor becomes her near neighbor Mrs. Weston. Emma flatters herself that the marriage has been of her arranging, though their other close family friend, Mr. Knightley, tells her this is nonsense—Miss Taylor and Mr. Weston found each other in their own way. But now that the taste for matchmaking is upon her, and perhaps avoiding her own anxiety about whether she wants to find a match for herself and what will become of her if she doesn't, Emma begins to manage the fate of her new friend Harriet. Herein lies what seems to be a crime, on the scale of Highbury. Emma dissuades the young and impressionable Harriet from agreeing to marry a gentleman farmer whom Harriet has told us in her own words she likes and trusts very much. Again Mr. Knightley plays the counterpoint—by his lights, the proposal is a chance at a cheerful life among kind people, which, he thinks, for a young woman of uncertain origins, no means, and modest education, is unlikely to come again. Emma is arguing that Harriet, and perhaps young women more generally, deserve possibilities, but she does not seem to have thought these possibilities through well. The narrator seems to be siding with Mr. Knightley, who wants marriage and the social order to be more fixed and for Emma to accept finitude. It is a hard set of scenes to read—like it or not, you are Emma and are near her, and you feel things are going wrong, quite wrong. I skip these pages or read them averting my eyes.

Everyone lives together in Highbury, and often the book has a beautiful spaciousness, like the turning of the spheres in musical harmony. The new arrivals in town are barely new arrivals, they are known already—one is Mr. Frank Churchill, the son of Mr. Weston by a previous marriage. Frank Churchill has been raised by a wealthy uncle and aunt and now returns to spend some time with his father. The other is Jane Fairfax, likewise a child of Highbury, whose mother died, who was raised elsewhere by wealthy connections, and who now returns to stay with her aunt and grandmother, respectable and kindhearted, but living very frugally, the elderly Mrs. Bates and the garrulous and right-minded Miss Bates. Miss Bates is a spinster, not old, though often treated as irrelevant. She talks all the time, sees much that no one else notices, and her talk is revealing.

In Highbury, news is carried about by Miss Bates and openhearted Mr. Weston, and it seems that everyone knows about everyone. And yet, despite all the news, and despite Austen's tone of translucence, important aspects of the story are hidden from the characters, the reader, and even the narrator of the novel. Information always comes late. Emma is constantly astonished by how things turn out, and almost from the first lines, the other characters are casting their thoughts back to try to see why they had made the mistakes they did. "I was so astonished," cries Miss Bates, and Mrs. Weston says to herself that "she had herself been the stupidest of beings in not having thought of it, and wished it long ago.—" All of Austen is built to be read again, but it seems as if you actually cannot read *Emma* for the first time. To read *Emma*, William Galperin thinks, is but to take the first steps in rereading *Emma*. A rereader, Galperin says, will find that in *Emma*, a thing becomes "seeable and fathomable only after it has already been seen."

I have read *Emma* in varying degrees of thickness; some scenes of Emma's education I have probably read a hundred times—I can see Emma dancing with Mr. Knightley at the country ball like a vision—other scenes I have forced myself through on only a handful of occasions. I go on trying it, though.

In writing about *Emma*, people often mention that Jane Austen's family remembered her having said, when she began the project, "I am going to take a heroine whom no one but myself will much like." This is interesting. Of all the Austen heroines, Emma and Elizabeth are the two with the closest kinship, and Elizabeth was intended as the most delightful creature ever to appear in print: "How I shall be able to tolerate those who do not like *her* at least, I do not know." Both Emma and Elizabeth are handsome and clever, one is rich, the other is not, both are indulged by their fathers, yet one is so easy to like, and the other blunders continually, and the reader, at least this reader, does not want to be like her at all.

It is my idea of Jane Austen that when she picked up a word, felt its heft and looked into it, its meanings and history shone clearly to their depths. Her words never jar against one another, there are no overlooked sonic or metaphoric or etymological interferences or sentimentalities forming and clashing below the surface. "No one but myself will much like."

About "like." Originally the sense of pleasingness and the sense of sameness may have gone together. The derivation of "like" may follow from the sense that we feel liking because things of similar form suit well.

To begin with, "like" and "dislike" in English were impersonal. The On-line Etymology Dictionary (etymonline.com) points out that at first, "the liking flowed the other way," as in "the music likes you not" (which is from *The Two Gentlemen of Verona*).

Under the surface of "no one but myself will much like," there is a thought of seeking and resisting similarity of form. Liking Elizabeth, without friction or resistance, I may or may not notice the larger form in which she lives, or the one in which I do—disliking Emma, or being made to admit that I like her and am like her, despite her evident wrongheadedness, feeling this, I see form after form, hers, mine, that of the idyll and of the infinite.

I may have read *Emma* in the first year after my father died, but I don't have impressions of it. That year we lived at the Red House, and S was learning to stand and to walk. I don't remember it from staying up those nights in the square bed that nearly filled the square room with the windows facing the driveway, not the way I remember *Sense and Sensibility*, and *Persuasion*, and bits of *Mansfield Park*. I began to really read *Emma* later, as the children grew, and I can trace the progression through which I grew more ready for it.

My father died in February, and I know that on March 22, his birthday, there was still snow on the ground. Pictures remind me that just then I found a snowsuit that a friend had handed down, and that S could have been wearing all winter, and that I took her outside in it and she lay not mobile but alert in the snow. Four days later, the snow had melted, and S noticed the glossy rhododendron leaves that suddenly caught the light. In the new weather, she could stand outside. Little by little, during the summer, S was learning to walk, and to go down the front steps by herself, carrying one of the animals—a pig, a tiger, a turtle—that she always brought with on her investigations. By fall, M and I could take a walk with her, and she would wrap all her fingers around one of ours as we made our way around the shady block.

Fifteen months after my father died, when I was pregnant with T, and

S was two years old, and could walk and run, and we pulled her on a small purple bicycle by a length of string, we moved to a different house. That house we called the purple door house, because by then S loved purple, found in it a way of organizing her world, and the fortunate purple door was a talisman of rightness. At that house, I had a study on the second floor—it faced the street, there was a balcony in front of it from which I could look down the block to the park where the girls and boys practiced hitting with the satisfying metal thonk of bats. There was the winter of T's birth, and the spring of new beginnings. There was summer, he began to stand, and then, in the fall, to walk holding on to our hands. I began to work at *Emma*.

With time, I saw that imagination is central to *Emma*—variations on the word "imagine" appear ninety-nine times in the novel. I tried to think about the novel and about my father's last letter, the letter my father had told his colleague he anticipated he and I would talk about together: "It appears that a conversation about Coleridge-Shakespeare-imagination-fancy will soon ensue."

I went to my study and tried to write of my father, and how we might yet have that conversation:

I sit at my desk by the window in Cambridge—there is, immediately before me, a small tree making efforts and, across the street, a range of more massive ones behind the houses on the block beyond. If the ages of a person are in any way like the rings of a tree, then the concentric patterns, always of the same wood cells of elm, the same grain of oak, bear out a knowledge first evident in the core of the tree, making itself again and again with a like understanding, a like conviction.

I hoped that I would be able to read backward, through what I knew of him, to find what I had missed, and that he had been able to imagine forward, from what he knew of me, to what our life had become. In this mood, in the evenings, I went up to the bedroom we had, on the third floor, with a skylight that looked up into the branches of a large tree, and in the joy of what the children had done that day, in the sorrow of what I was working on, and in the greater spaciousness of our life then, I read *Emma*.

GUIDED

The first scenes I read when I began to attempt *Emma*, or at least parts of *Emma*, were a pair close to the end—the famous scene at Box Hill, that small masterpiece of Emma's education, and the turn in the shrubbery with Mr. Knightley where at last love is declared. At Box Hill, Emma insults the good, talkative Miss Bates, and Mr. Knightley reprimands her. Mr. Knightley says Emma has been unfeeling, insolent, thoughtless, proud, and that she has led wrongly, speaking to Miss Bates in front of others who "would be entirely guided by *your* treatment of her." Emma's transformations are at hand, and their form is both like and unlike Elizabeth's: "Never had she felt so agitated, mortified, grieved, at any circumstance in her life. She was most forcibly struck. The truth of his representation there was no denying. She felt it at her heart. How could she have been so brutal, so cruel to Miss Bates!"

It is a moment of realization, like Elizabeth's, but it is only the first in a series. That instantaneity that belongs to Elizabeth has more texture and delay in *Emma*. Austen tells us of Emma that "time did not compose her." Emma cries almost the whole way home in the carriage, tears running down her cheeks, without her "being at any trouble to check them, extraordinary as they were." There is going to be more effort, more mistakes, and more rough ground. Reversals have a subtle progression in Emma. Only at the very end of her novel, after several more revelations, does she see the whole series, and then she is in a still worse way:

> The blunders, the blindness of her own head and heart!—she sat still, she walked about, she tried her own room, she tried the shrubbery—in every place, every posture, she perceived that she had acted most weakly; that she had been imposed on by others in a most mortifying degree; that she

had been imposing on herself in a degree yet more mortifying; that she was wretched, and should probably find this day but the beginning of wretchedness.

A little after this, Mr. Knightley comes to find Emma in the shrubbery. They walk together. She relieves him of his fear that she loves elsewhere. He begins to tell her of his feelings, but she thinks he loves another and stops him. He is mortified, and she does not wish to give him pain. He asks whether she is done walking and intends to go inside. She gathers her courage and says, "I should like to take another turn." They walk around the shrubbery again. This time, they get in the track. He tells her he loves her. And there comes a sentence, fine, light, and indestructible: "While he spoke, Emma's mind was most busy, and, with all the wonderful velocity of thought, had been able—and yet without losing a word—to catch and comprehend the exact truth of the whole."

I would go out and walk near our house, around the Fresh Pond reservoir, summer and with a walking child, summer again and with a baby, summer with two children whose steps my father had not seen, and the phrase I loved best in *Emma* would come into my mind: "with all the wonderful velocity of thought." It seemed to me that those seven words were as beautiful as anything I had ever read.

In the beginning, Emma and Harriet often go out for a walk. They talk of Emma's plan for Harriet, which centers on the obsequious and self-important Mr. Elton, their vicar, who is popular with the young women of the village and who, though Emma does not realize this, fancies himself in love with Emma. For herself, Emma does not know what she thinks about marriage, but she rather suspects she would not like it, and perhaps resents that it is almost the only way forward for a woman in her situation. Once, as they are walking in Vicarage Lane, Harriet says to her, "I do so wonder, Miss Woodhouse, that you should not be married, or going to be married!" And Emma says a flurry of revealing things—she tries out Mr. Elton for

216

herself, then quickly recollects that that is not the project, she hazards that she could only marry a very superior person, or only for love, she says she already has consequence, could never hope to be "half as much mistress" of a "husband's house, as I am of Hartfield." She does not say that she feels bound to her ailing father, but she is certainly completely tied to his fortune, which is the only thing that saves her from having to marry. "It is poverty only which makes celibacy contemptible to a generous public" is one of her pronouncements. Meanwhile, Harriet's refrain is as consistent as the one that must have been familiar to Austen: "But then, to be an old maid at last, like Miss Bates!" "But still, you will be an old maid! and that's so dreadful!"

It is not entirely an accident that their thoughts have turned to Miss Bates, who was the daughter of an earlier vicar and must have lived in the vicarage then, before he died. (In Jane Austen, it is always a fact worth remembering that the earnings of a clergyman did not remain to support the women of his family.) This comparison to Miss Bates Emma wants to put a stop to. She says, "A single woman, of good fortune, is always respectable." I get a feeling of vertigo when I think of this together with the opening of *Pride and Prejudice*, and all the interest and attention pressed upon a single man of good fortune. No, no, says Emma of Miss Bates, "between *us*, I am convinced, there never can be any likeness." No likeness at all, Emma and Miss Bates are not much like. Miss Bates was introduced to us as exactly Emma's opposite, "neither young, handsome, rich, nor married." "Except in being unmarried," Emma admits, perhaps also except in sometimes giving rein to their imaginations, sometimes facing what it is to lose a father, and though we don't know yet—the possibilities are still to play out—in knowing what it is to love "when existence or when hope is gone."

In the scene immediately before this conversation, just a few pages before, Emma has said to Harriet that she thinks by spending time together at Emma's house, Hartfield, Harriet and Mr. Elton will soon have found their way. Really, she says, "there does seem to be a something in the air of Hartfield which gives love exactly the right direction, and sends it into the very channel where it ought to flow." Emma is often at once wrong and right—she has thoroughly misunderstood Mr. Elton, but

Emma, the book, does believe that love is a river moving in time over the ground, that, as liking does, it has a flow.

Emma goes on, instructing Harriet about how well her own game of love is proceeding, and she blithely quotes Lysander from the beginning of *A Midsummer Night's Dream*: "The course of true love never did run smooth." It seems obviously Emma's ignorance, her arrogance, that she then goes the poet one better, adding, "A Hartfield edition of Shakespeare would have a long note on that passage." At Hartfield, apparently, the course of love is ever smooth.

When I had heard Lysander say this, in my mother's production of *A Midsummer Night's Dream*, I took it to mean that love faces obstacles, which it eventually overcomes. But it is harder than that. The lovers themselves feel "sympathy in choice," but the world undermines them, either by not seeing their suitability or with the ravages of "war, death, or sickness." There isn't enough time: "And, ere a man hath power to say 'Behold!', / The jaws of darkness do devour it up. / So quick bright things come to confusion." Lysander's idea of time comes to one kind of culmination in what Hermia says next, for they make the meaning together. She says, "Then let us teach our trial patience, / Because it is a customary cross, / As due to love as thoughts and dreams and sighs, / Wishes and tears, poor fancy's followers." Leading and following, they have come to it. Love finds its form over time: "A good persuasion," Lysander pronounces it.

I, who am holding *Emma* in my hands—the faded green edition with the Trilling introduction, or the Dover paperback with the eighteenth-century botanical wallpaper on its cover—I am holding a Hartfield edition of Shakespeare, a book that is a long note on that old passage. Perhaps a book about the idea Emma comes to have, a deepened Hartfield idea, of the course of love, and how it runs.

Jane Austen is watching Emma and Mr. Knightley and Harriet and Frank Churchill and Jane Fairfax, Miss Bates and the Eltons all wandering about on Box Hill. Austen laughs at Mrs. Elton, who has wanted them to have pastoral experiences—"the thing would be for us all to come on donkeys"—and watches with interest as they all get tangled in one another's plans and errors.

If these are all the lovers in the woods, then who are the king and queen who give right, or nearly right, order when the lovers stumble back out of the woods? Critics notice how the parts are doubled—perhaps Emma plays both Hermia, who wants to run away from the tyranny of her father, and Hippolyta, who hesitates to cede her Amazonian powers in marriage.

It was so long after I began rereading my father's letter that I went back to see where, exactly, those lines were from:

> And, as imagination bodies forth
> The forms of things unknown, the poet's pen
> Turns them to shapes and gives to airy nothing
> A local habitation and a name.

The speech is a part of Theseus's argument to Hippolyta, about why the theater is meaningful. The four lovers, now reassorted, have stumbled out of the woods, encountered the two rulers, and told their adventures. Afterward, the rulers of Athens talk this over together, how one may know the truth of what has happened after the depths of the dream. Hippolyta says, "'Tis strange," the account the lovers have given, and Theseus says, "More strange than true." And then he explains what the difference is between strange and true. He says, "The lunatic, the lover, and the poet, / Are of imagination all compact." The sense of "compact" here is not a contract, but "composed of, given consistency by," as, in other cases, Shakespeare writes, "Love is a spirit all compact of fire," and "My heart is not compact of flint." The lunatic, the lover, and the poet are each held together by the faculty of imagination.

Imagination is more strange than true for the lunatic and the lover who have "seething brains," with private, estranged meanings. The poet is also compacted of imagination, but the poet's imagination is true, not strange. The poet's eye "Doth glance from heaven to earth, from earth to heaven," and these two realms, the green hedgerows, as in heaven they would be and as on earth they are, keep the poet's imagination true, and allow the poet to make of airy nothing a local habitation.

In *Will in the World*, Stephen Greenblatt describes a public festival that happened near Shakespeare's boyhood home when he was about eleven. The festivities honored Queen Elizabeth, who was in attendance, and included a traditional Hock Tuesday play presented by local artisans that certain religious reformers had been trying to shut down, but to which it was thought the queen might be sympathetic. The outdoor theater, the vulnerability of the players, the fact that theater itself was at the mercy of royal attention, the presence of the queen, these might have been among the young man's summer impressions. Decades later, Shakespeare's own company of players was to present a romantic comedy on the occasion of a noble wedding, and his queen was to be in attendance. He wrote *A Midsummer Night's Dream* and included a play within his play.

Theseus and Hippolyta go to the theater. The play they attend is a classical one, but rewritten with a modern eye. The actors are not especially good, but they are sufficient for their parts. In the play within the play, the lovers run away, the Wall announces, "Thus have I, Wall, my part dischargèd so; / And being done, thus Wall away doth go." Hippolyta protests, "This is the silliest stuff that ever I heard." And Theseus replies, "The best in this kind are but shadows, and the worst are no worse, if imagination amend them." Hippolyta says, "It must be your imagination then, and not theirs." But it seems it must be theirs, too. Theseus rejoins: "If we imagine no worse of them than they of themselves, they may pass for excellent men."

Bottom, striking poses, gives a pathetic and ridiculous speech. Suddenly, the queen says, "Beshrew my heart, but I pity the man." We join together with another character—we see from their point of view, enter their actions, grasp how their character hangs together—the Wall away doth go. Shakespeare's queen sat where we do, watching another queen watch a play. His queen was a clever woman.

"I'll be an auditor— / An actor, too, perhaps, if I see cause," Puck said of his vantage point attending the mechanicals' rehearsal in the woods. I thought, long ago, watching them, that Puck was right: at a rehearsal, once an auditor, one was easily an actor. It is such a thin, permeable membrane—you are a remote watcher, and then, you know not how, you are a part of the story, and you feel it as if it were happening to you.

My father had said in his letter that it was from my mother's work as a director that he had seen certain things about what holds character together, "how playwrights imagine great characters" and "how actors develop the characters they inhabit on the stage." In his letter to his colleague, he did not say that he knew those lines from our play, the one we had made for months and months, but he may have half remembered. Perhaps, when he had sat watching us in the play, he thought how we had made it without him, but that he could imagine us, imagining ourselves. His colleague quoted the lines, years later. Years more passed, and it still lived there for him, in the rhythm of those lines.

SMALL FORMS

My father and I always liked to take a long ramble, at home in Ann Arbor at Gallup Park, or around the neighborhoods of a city we happened to be in. He was a moderately tall man, a little over six feet. He had a long torso, and his back was upright. This straightness might have seemed at odds with his gait. Even at a quick pace he strolled, and his legs made his manner easy and patient. The effect of the whole, of the combination of uprightness and leisure, was of a readiness almost lilting; he anticipated pleasant discoveries. My father believed that small things—a little group of people acting together, a way of walking, a dream—could be shot through with all the forces of the larger world and time that contain them. He thought you could see in our steps and stumbles what the world meant to us, what we were trying to mean in the world.

My father's last research project was studying hospitals. He was interested in the ways that hospitals can have a character and individual atmospheres. Hospitals have institutional memory and forgetfulness, they have intentions about the future, they are actors on a larger stage. And, at the same time, they are themselves small societies, in which people are interacting, and taking different roles. The hospital is a small form—like the society of Highbury—in which individual and communal activity may be considered very completely.

His first book, written together with James March, was called *Leadership and Ambiguity*, and it was about the effects that presidents of universities may have. One of its points was that the presidents, although they seemed to lead their organizations, were often following a culture already in place. Sometimes, I reread the book's second chapter, in which he and Jim March named eight "metaphors of leadership" around which universities tend to organize their governance, and considered the roles that might follow. The university president might seem like a political candidate facing election, a bureaucrat attempting smooth administration, a mediator of collective bargaining, an entrepreneur in a business, a builder of consensus, a catalyst within anarchy, a judge, or an autocrat with some accountability. Depending on the kind of story the organization uses to explain itself, the president will have a different way of keeping step with the organization. There will be many possible combinations. And the whole thing will shift, subtly and rapidly, as reciprocal effects emerge among the different people playing different roles. Sometimes the chapter makes me cry. He had a flexible sense of people, and he made maps of possibilities and overlaps, ideals and practicalities.

LEADING

According to Cassandra Austen's notes, her sister began *Emma* in January 1814 and completed it a little over a year later, on March 29, 1815. This was an eventful year in the news. In the same month that the first lines of *Emma* took shape, the members of the Sixth Coalition to fight against the Napoleonic armies assembled in France. At the end of March, after nearly twenty years of war, Napoleon was defeated and the Allies entered Paris. In early April, Napoleon abdicated and reluctantly signed the treaty that exiled him to Elba, where he took up residence in May. The Congress of Vienna began negotiations over the re-creation of Europe in the fall of 1814, and these went on into 1815. At the very end of February 1815, when Austen was drawing the threads of *Emma* together, Napoleon and some of his loyal troops escaped from Elba; they made landfall in France on March 1. Further troops and commanders, even some who had loudly declared their opposition, still, in the presence of Napoleon's unparalleled personal charisma, converted to his cause. On March 20, the interim king having fled, Napoleon made his grand reentry at the Tuileries Palace. British newspapers and naval papers were, naturally, interested in this progress of events. The Allied powers officially formed the Seventh Coalition on March 25 and began their march on Napoleon April 1, three days after Austen felt she had finished *Emma*. It seems unlikely that she would have written her book while giving these events no thought whatsoever.

At first, after the 2016 election, I was puzzled that *Emma* was the only book I wanted. Later, it seemed obvious that I would want to go over and over the experience of being misled and of being misleading. I had assumed an idyll, had planned a future for our children, and other people's children, that was not going to come to pass. "In every place, every posture, she perceived that she had acted most weakly; that she had been imposed on by others in a most mortifying degree; that she had been imposing on herself in a degree yet more mortifying; that she was wretched, and should probably find this day but the beginning of wretchedness."

Emma, unlike every other one of Austen's novels, has no generals, admirals, or colonels, no army or navy, no mention of military exercises or the naval news or the spoils of war. For a part of the time she was writing *Emma*, Jane Austen might have thought the wars were over. If she did, she would, later in the writing, have reconsidered that the wars are never over. *Emma* makes the war powerful in not mentioning it. It may be that the fact that no actual, separate, existing Napoleon is named makes the possibility of Napoleon run clearly through and among all the characters of the novel. Or it may be the author thought it valuable to picture a world without Napoleon, to see what such a world would be compacted of. Perhaps Austen assumed her reader would notice that Emma was like Napoleon, or anyway susceptible to "insufferable vanity," to the grandiosity and "unpardonable arrogance" of attempting "to arrange everybody's destiny."

We are inclined now, I think, simply to marvel that Napoleon could induce so much of our world to follow him so quickly. We take his career abstractly, even lightly, perhaps we find it a touch humorous that he was so short. The fact of his power seems to justify his existence, as we now feel about the wealthiest capitalists. Napoleon's campaigns may appear to us as chess matches, brilliant tactical maneuvers that bore no moral responsibilities, as if the men and women he directed in their suffering and to their deaths were not themselves having a moral life and moral questions. The figures—so many millions of them—have become immaterial; no one we know was widowed. But how easy it was to follow Napoleon, or to fancy oneself a leader and not realize one was in fact misled; for Austen and her family, these were mortal questions.

In his essay on *Emma*, Lionel Trilling says something about leadership, and the words he uses are a little old-fashioned and help me to remember how Austen herself thought of the ideas:

> We understand self-love to be part of the moral life of all men; in men of genius we expect it to appear in unusual intensity and we take it to be an essential element of their power. The extraordinary thing about Emma is that she has a moral life as a man has a moral life. And she doesn't have it

as a special instance, as an example of a new kind of woman, which is the way George Eliot's Dorothea Brooke has her moral life, but quite as a matter of course, as a given quality of her nature.

Emma might have been a queen or a presidential candidate, had she been born to that scope. Trilling, thinking over the self-love of Emma's moral life, wonders whether "perhaps that is what Jane Austen meant when she said that no one would like her heroine." Leadership is compact of error. When you are Emma, you will lead yourself and others astray; when you follow her, you will often be misled.

The Austen family were not revolutionaries. They faulted the revolution for its violence, and for what followed it, the Terror. They thought the subsequent power vacuum had, as the French came to say, opened the boulevard for Napoleon. But they were no great admirers of royalty and the aristocracy either. The Austens thought, together with Rousseau and others of the eighteenth-century Enlightenment philosophers, that right governance ought not to be entirely a matter of class but also of education and self-education. I suspect they thought every form of government might corrupt.

The prince regent admired Austen's books, and when Austen was nearly done writing *Emma*, she was summoned by the prince's librarian and subsequently informed, in a tone that brooked no opposition, that she was at liberty to dedicate her next novel to the prince. She at first resisted the idea but acquiesced to the ostentatiously proper terms her publisher advised, perhaps hearing how they satirized themselves: "To His Royal Highness, the Prince Regent, this work is, by His Royal Highness's permission, most respectfully dedicated, by his Royal Highness's Dutiful and Obedient Humble Servant, The Author."

Her own domain may seem such a small form, but Jane Austen led well, and now there are many millions following her view of the prince and hardly any to notice his view of her. The scholar Colleen Sheehan has patiently traced out a hidden message in a charade that Emma and Harriet figure out, of a poem written by Mr. Elton. Read within the lines is a lampoon depicting the prince as a blubbery and contemptible prince of whales. We don't have the documents to determine whether Austen had already written this laughing condemnation, or whether she added it as a revision after the dedication was demanded, but its inclusion is entirely in keeping with the clever clue-bestrewn way *Emma* is made.

Emma's last crime is to attack Miss Bates. Emma and Frank have decided on a game, where one is to say one witty thing, or three dull ones. Miss Bates chatters good-humoredly:

> "Oh! very well," exclaimed Miss Bates, "then I need not be uneasy. 'Three things very dull indeed.' That will just do for me, you know. I shall be sure to say three dull things as soon as ever I open my mouth, shan't I? (looking round with the most good-humoured dependence on every body's assent)—Do not you all think I shall?"
>
> Emma could not resist.
>
> "Ah! ma'am, but there may be a difficulty. Pardon me—but you will be limited as to number—only three at once."
>
> Miss Bates, deceived by the mock ceremony of her manner, did not immediately catch her meaning; but, when it burst on her, it could not anger, though a slight blush shewed that it could pain her.
>
> "Ah!—well—to be sure. Yes, I see what she means, (turning to Mr. Knightley,) and I will try to hold my tongue. I must make myself very disagreeable, or she would not have said such a thing to an old friend."

Highbury finds its way, as Austen tells us midway through the book, because it is "not in the habit of judging," but rather in that of "following the lead of Miss Bates's good-will." A goodwill that Austen describes as "universal." Miss Bates is a single woman, not of good fortune, and deserves respect from Emma, but it is also because Miss Bates promulgates the town's news, and does not limit herself, but speaks of everyone at once and all together, that Emma's attack on her free tongue is so reprehensible. Miss Bates's principled optimism helps everyone to act according to what is best in one another.

"I see what she means," Miss Bates says, "(turning to Mr. Knightley.)" It was William Galperin's book that first alerted me to a relation I then felt surprised I had not seen, in all my hundreds of readings of *Emma*. There is a special intimacy between Mr. Knightley and Miss Bates. He is often bringing her the last of his store of apples, or arranging his carriage to take her to a dance; when he thinks her niece has sung enough, he touches Miss Bates—why is he so familiar—and tells her to take her charge home; when she is wounded by Emma, she immediately turns to him. Miss Bates is probably about the same age as Mr. Knightley. She was the daughter of the vicar, and only sank in the world when he died. Was there a time when Mr. Knightley might have married Miss Bates? But they didn't. A man with money has second chances that rarely come to a woman. Emma will take Miss Bates's second chance. Perhaps Mr. Knightley's harshness—Emma should be kind to Miss Bates, Emma should not prevent Harriet from marrying—comes partly from a wish to repress his own guilt, and his own fear of being dragged down like these vulnerable women. Mr. Knightley remembers very well that Miss Bates had known Emma from an infant, from the time of her mother's now indistinct caresses. At that time, he reminds Emma, "her notice was an honour."

Mr. Knightley is the governor of Highbury, he is literally its magistrate, informally its counselor. He also knows that Miss Bates leading people to think well of one another is necessary to their small kingdom. He protects her speech, not only on the grounds of past injustice, or present freedom, but also on the grounds of virtue. Good governance of one's polis and oneself was no more an idle question in Highbury than it is for us.

"In every respect," Austen wrote of her heroine, "it suited Emma best to lead." Emma finds insufferable the woman Mr. Elton eventually marries,

the magnificently irritating Mrs. Elton, in part because this latter is forever assuming that she is best suited to lead. "Must I go first?" Mrs. Elton
exclaims in false protest. "I really am ashamed of always leading the way."
Mrs. Elton extends her mistaken conviction of leadership to her husband:
"One is apt to speak only of those who lead.—I fancy Mr. E. and Knightley have every thing their own way." Emma is a much more thoughtful
person than Mrs. Elton, but they have in common that they are frequently
mistaken about when they are leading, when following, when misled.

Emma never gives it much thought, but she takes it for granted that a
quite different structure of leadership obtains in Highbury: "Mr. Knightley was a sort of general friend and adviser, and she knew Mr. Elton looked
up to him." Before Emma has met Frank Churchill, when she is still only
imagining what he will be like, she says to Mr. Knightley that her idea of
Frank Churchill is that, "being universally agreeable," he will adapt to
everyone's taste, be able to talk to anyone on any subject, and will know
when "to follow the lead, or take the lead, just as propriety may require."
Mr. Knightley says this would make him unbearable: "What! at three-
and-twenty to be the king of his company—the great man—the practised
politician, who is to read every body's character, and make every body's
talents conduce to the display of his own superiority." Frank Churchill
will turn out to be more like Puck, his mischievous pranks necessary to
reveal to the other characters how they actually feel. Even in this conversation, before they have seen Frank, Mr. Knightley suddenly recognizes
his own feelings for Emma, and Emma senses rightly that he is somehow "prejudiced" against Frank Churchill. Some see *Emma* as a battle
for who will be king of the company: will it be the generative, unreliable Frank, or the measured but oh-so-establishment Mr. Knightley. It is
possible to see the conclusion of *Emma* as putting down, or at least se-
dately incorporating, whatever rebellion has been introduced. But trying
to fathom afterward what has happened, you may see that no ending is
ever complete, there is only circling through experience. One might also
say that *Emma* comes to one kind of culmination in its middle, at the

dance that Frank has been the architect of, in which he makes the setting with as much dexterity and force as Puck arranges the lovers in the woods.

A dance was one of Jane Austen's favorite settings, in life and in literature, because of its rhythm and its sense of community, its variety and pattern, the way, within it, power might be swallowed or turned upside down. "She was fond of dancing," her brother wrote, "and excelled in it." Stuart Tave begins his book *Some Words of Jane Austen* by reflecting on the appropriateness of this—"that enjoyment and ability in moving with significant grace in good time in a restricted space."

Emma takes an important turn at the country dance Frank instigates, which is revelatory, though no very glamorous affair. Emma watches Mr. Knightley, and "she was more disturbed by Mr. Knightley's not dancing than by any thing else." She continues to watch him; he moves "a few steps nearer, and those few steps were enough to prove in how gentleman-like a manner, with what natural grace, he must have danced." Mr. Elton, puffed with the pride of his new marriage, makes a point of disdaining, and shaming, Harriet by not dancing with her. In Austen's day, it was an understood principle that every young woman without a partner was to be asked. Emma is angry, and upset for her friend, but then she looks up and sees "Mr. Knightley leading Harriet to the set!" Emma feels "all pleasure and gratitude, both for Harriet and herself." Watching them, she sees that "his dancing proved to be just what she had believed it, extremely good; and Harriet would have seemed almost too lucky" had she not just been slighted. A little later, Mr. Knightley asks Emma whom she will be dancing the next dance with, and she hesitates and then says, "With you, if you will ask me."

This reply is the basis of a famous remark by Virginia Woolf, in an essay where she, too, compares the way George Eliot writes Dorothea Brooke (who becomes Mrs. Casaubon) and the way Jane Austen writes Emma. Eliot, Woolf says, "lacks the unerring taste which chooses one sentence and compresses the heart of the scene within that. 'Whom are you going to dance with?' asked Mr. Knightley, at the Westons' ball,

'With you, if you will ask me,' said Emma; and she has said enough. Mrs. Casaubon would have talked for an hour and we should have looked out the window."

"With you, if you will ask me," Emma both leads and follows, which may be why it is always only the second time that one gets a right rhythm with her. Just before these words, Emma and Mr. Knightley have had a "little explanation." They have looked back together. He has "been warm in his reprobation of Mr. Elton's conduct," and she has admitted that she had completely misunderstood Mr. Elton, "it was through a series of strange blunders!" He says he will not scold her, but leave her "to your own reflections." "Can you trust me," she says, "with such flatterers?—Does my vain spirit ever tell me I am wrong?" "Not your vain spirit," he replies, "but your serious spirit.—If one leads you wrong, I am sure the other tells you of it." And then, I think quite crucially, he admits that he has been wrong, too, that Emma had chosen better for Mr. Elton than Mr. Elton had for himself. In fact, dancing with Harriet, Mr. Knightley has discovered that she is "infinitely to be preferred by any man of sense and taste to such a woman as Mrs. Elton."

Just then, Mr. Weston interrupts that the dancing must begin again: "Come Emma, set your companions the example." Emma says she is ready, "whenever I am wanted." Mr. Knightley wants to know whom she will dance with.

"The first thing you should do to test your compatibility," says Nassrin to Sanaz, in the room where they read together, in Tehran, "is dance with him." At first Azar Nafisi can't think what she might mean, then she remembers that the young women had formed, very briefly, only for a moment, a group they called "the Dear Jane Society." In class one day, Nafisi had "compared the structure of *Pride and Prejudice* to an eighteenth-century dance." Some of the women students had stayed after class, and she had tried to explain by "going over the motions of the dance with them." It is a moving moment in the book: "I took Nassrin's reluctant hands and started to dance with her, one-two and one-two. Then I asked the others to form a

230

line, and pretty soon we were all dancing, our long black robes twirling as we bumped into one another and into the chairs." This is the thing, the teacher says, "you have to harmonize your steps with the rest in the set, that's the whole point; you are mainly concerned with yourself and your partner but also with all the others—you can't be out of step with them." After their Austen dance, Sanaz dances in a Persian style, and the others gather watching. It matters that there was room for both kinds of dancing.

This episode of dancing began them, "a secret pact" that "planted the seed" for their reading group. When she writes the scene, and lives it again, Azar Nafisi sees it so clearly, and with such sadness: "I see it now as if through the large window of a house in the middle of an empty garden. I've pressed my face to the window, and here they come: five women, all in black robes and head scarves. As each passes by the window, I can begin to differentiate their faces; one is standing and watching the other four."

The women laugh, though, when they read Austen, because, of all their authors, she is the one with whom "we became childish and teasing and just plain enjoyed ourselves." "We need a Mr. Collins. Come on Mahshid, won't you enjoy stepping on my toes?" The worst dancer in Austen is Elizabeth Bennet's insufferable cousin Mr. Collins, who, at a ball, inflicts on her "dances of mortification. Mr. Collins, awkward and solemn, apologising without attending, and often moving wrong without being aware of it, gave her all the shame and misery which a disagreeable partner for a couple of dances can give." Of course this is so—Mr. Collins is a terrible prig, impossibly self-absorbed, humorless. Mr. Darcy, though he has first spurned Elizabeth, is almost as good a dancer as Mr. Knightley. To dance well with others, you have to be observant and self-disciplined, and able to respond to someone else's rhythm, their characteristic movement in time. Dancing together expands and harmonizes taking a walk together—the steps that are a part of the lines of a community may be undertaken with strangers, or old friends one is learning to love. Dancing, one may keep memories and hopes at once.

LEARNING

My father worked on a particular moment in the routine of hospital life, what's called a handoff, when one doctor hands off the care of a patient to another doctor. This is a particularly fraught moment, and it is responsible for a large proportion of the fatalities in hospitals. At this critical juncture, something often gets lost—that a doctor has already tried something for a fever, or that the patient has an allergy—and the patient dies.

My father, and the team of colleagues with whom he worked, video-taped thousands of hours of these handoffs and analyzed everything about the interactions—they had ways of coding hand gestures, tilts of the body, eye contact, dialogue. Many hospitals, genuinely sorry for the deaths that occur after handoffs, and also concerned about lawsuits, are computerizing their handoff processes in the hopes that mechanization will avoid human error. But, perhaps not surprisingly, no mechanical checklist can carry the expressive depth, and nuance of understanding and information, created between two people who know each other, talking and gesturing together for a minute or two. Handoffs are moments in a dance that everyone in the community knows.

My father and his colleagues found that there was one most important factor in producing clear communication, and the secure handoff of the patient's care. He told us, marveling at the simplicity of it, that what mattered was whether the receiving doctor or nurse asked a question. Just a question. A question changes the imagined point of view. Answering the question, the doctor handing off would, naturally, as people do, put herself in the place of the receiving doctor, would stop running through what she had done and justifying her own conduct and would think, "What does this doctor need to know?"

"Hospital" is part of a group of words that also includes "hospitable" and "host," words that have to do with obligations to other people. A lot of what defines the life within an organization is kinds of reciprocity. My father did not finish his work on handoffs; he encouraged the other people on the research team to go on with it after his death, and they have. I think one reason he was excited about it was that in the act of the handoff, he had seen a moment in which two people, together, learn.

In the last century or so, we have separated out the verbs "to teach" and "to learn," but people used to use "learn" for both aspects of the activity. From 1200 until the early nineteenth century, it was common, and correct, to say "he learned me to read." I think this older usage had more of the mutuality of learning in it, the necessary, shared quality it has. The word "learn" itself is full of what is beyond the self. Unlike "teach," which comes from a root (*deik-*) that means "show, demonstrate, instruct," our word "learn" comes from the root *leis-*, which means a track, or a furrow. Learning is to get in the track of something, a common path. This root also gave us the Old English word "laest," which is a track, or a footprint, from which we have the shoemaker's "last" that holds the place of a foot, and also the verb "to last," to endure, to go on following the track. The word "learn" carries the idea of walking after, and in front of, someone else through the world, and coming to know.

S still trips over her own feet quite often. Sometimes she is standing in the kitchen, and then with no warning she is lying tangled on the ground. This used to happen to me as a child. My father would recognize so much of how she moves.

INFINITE FORMS

The center of the house I grew up in is the stairwell. When you walk in the front door, it is the first thing you see, the plain wooden stairs, ten of them, the wooden banister on the right, the landing past which the stairs reverse, five more. It is the auricles and ventricles of the house, the channel through which public life and private life rise and descend. As a child, like many children, I used to sit on the stairs to think things over—it is a comfort and a clarification to sit on one step, place one's feet solidly on the step below.

Our stairwell was also where all the family pictures were hung, the memory and the family history are all here. At the top, a few black-and-white portraits of my sister and me, taken by a studio photographer; hers, at four, so beautiful that the photographer asked to use it in his advertisements, mine with the big teeth and awkward body I had at seven. There is my father's adoptive mother with a horse she felt proud to ride; there a blurry picture from the seventies of us behind the Hanukkah candles. Now, around the corner on the lower wall, there are pictures both more recent and earlier—ones of all of us from the day when M and I were married, and also older ones of grandparents, inherited when they died. When we are home now, there is often someone lingering on the stairs, looking at the pictures, or explaining them to one of the children.

I remember two explanations my father offered me on the stairwell—one I think may have been relocated in my memory to the stairwell but actually took place elsewhere, the other was certainly there. The relocated memory, which I think of sometimes as I go up and down the stairs, was of being a fairly young child, perhaps ten, and having encountered the Holocaust, and flailing. I was talking with my father about it, and he said that such a thing could happen because people didn't remember that other people were people. This was comforting, in a stark way, because it seemed to be something you could do something about. You could remember, insist on everyone remembering, that a person was a person. I suppose I think of this on the stairwell because for a long time we have had a picture up there, a picture of the Polish side of our family taken in Warsaw in the thirties—many adults, two children in front, one of whom was my cousin Sophie, at about twelve, the only one of the figures who survived the war and an important person in our lives. Her younger brother was shot in the ghetto. All those adults died in the camps or committed suicide—but there they are, with their clothes and features and stances.

In the second memory, I had asked my father what infinity was. Perhaps I had read the word in a book. He said, Imagine that you came to a wall, and you punched your way through it, and then you came to another wall and punched your way through that, and that you never came to the end of the walls, there was always another wall, that's infinity.

In the memory, I was at the top of the stairs, leaning over the banister, and he was standing on the stairs below, going down. The image he thought of to explain infinity was so vivid. I couldn't help but feel it physically, and I think I even resented a little that he made me experience space as something to punch my way through in endless repetition.

At night, when M and I slump down on the brown couch, we watch basketball, every night of the season. Each player, at times leading, at others follows, the five and more together with their shared character. M and I watch, and talk over the day. We review the particulars, wonderful and disheartening, surprising and tangible, but when we try to think of how we should act tomorrow, how better to raise these little children, we turn to the general, we try to find an idea of how to act that seems trustworthy. Raising children, you are immersed in particulars again, almost as you were when you were a child, but with the greater responsibility for determining in each instance when to step first, when to hang back.

Jane Austen is often lauded for her attention to the quotidian, and serious readers of Austen come away with the impression that she is deft in her handling of "the small things" of life. But, in Jane Austen, there are actually few particulars, not many adjectives or textures or facial features. It is not that Austen herself was not delighted by particulars. "You know," she wrote to Cassandra in 1808, partly laughing at her own sweet tooth, "how interesting the purchase of a sponge-cake is to me." But, when she comes to write fiction, as Ta-Nehisi Coates notices, she puts a hand over the particulars, "that interruption is an appeal to, a place-holder for, our imagination." The empty place into which we step, eager not to lose the flow of the dance. When Elizabeth Bennet goes to the ball where she is shunned by Mr. Darcy, we are told only that "she had dressed with more than usual care." Most of us have not got ourselves into a sprigged muslin, but we have all dressed with more than usual care.

This kind of interruption, one that demands you figure out how to step in and join, fills the days of children, who are engaged in the general inquiry: *how to act*. At six months, S and T dimly understood "be gentle"; at three, distinguished between "for real" and "pretend." From earliest childhood, there is action in the deep sense, shot through with understanding and the old virtues, and there is acting parts, becoming oneself by impersonation and comparison.

It is in the third sentence of *Emma* that we are told that Emma's mother died when she was so little that she has but "an indistinct remembrance of her caresses." As we are in a hurry to find out about our clever heroine who has nothing to vex her, we may pass by this rather quickly. Jane Austen wrote this sentence sitting in Chawton Cottage, where many motherless children came to visit. By this point, three of her sisters-in-law had died; Austen had written of one set of nieces, "One's heart aches for a dejected Mind of eight years old." When Austen came to the griefs that are a little beyond the edges of her novels, she tended to err on the side of caustic wit, as some sensitive people will do. Emma, with her indistinct remembrance of caresses, is not to be pitied.

Emma has been left with her father, Mr. Woodhouse, the kindhearted worrier, whose "talents could not have recommended him at any time," and who in fact severely limits Emma's range. She cannot leave the house without first preparing and persuading him, cannot take a walk by herself even as far as their own shrubbery if she does not provide him with a companion. He has always depended on Emma, never thought to guide her. But Emma also does have the fond attention of almost everyone in her community, people who dote on her and believe in her, and, in particular, she is held in mind by the two people who have acted as her adoptive parents. Mrs. Weston, who used to be her Miss Taylor, has cared about every smallest particular in Emma's life. Her marriage, the departure of this woman "little short of a mother in affection," is very disorienting for Emma. It is in part this second loss of a mother that brings her to turn to Mr. Knightley, who has acted the part of a guardian, too.

In a beautiful essay on *Emma*, Frances Ferguson says that the way we know that we can like Emma, even when she behaves badly, is by watching the community around her. It is their belief in her—Mrs. Weston's and Mr. Knightley's and Miss Bates's—that allows us to "recognize Emma as good even when she is not." Her community allows us "to say of Emma, from the very outset, that she will have come out right by the end." In a true idyll, Highbury must be both Emma's past and Emma's future. As much as her actions will eventually work to conserve the past of Highbury, Highbury will shape who she becomes. Ferguson writes of this in terms of grammar, and there may be no way of expressing it that is closer to Austen's own precisely syntactical understanding of time: the novel "assimilates the narrative present of an individual to the future perfect tense."

Although, in the present, all our own steps are stumbles, we keep our balance by the idea of the future toward which we walk. We offer this to our children, as our parents and the people alive with us have offered it to us. Held for us in the rhythm of other walkers, the future perfect.

In the months after the 2016 election, I missed my father acutely. There came the February after the election, the fourth anniversary of my father's death, and my sister's annual letter to our father's closest companions arrived, as if on wings. She said she was torn in the way she missed our dad, because she couldn't really "wish him back to see what is happening in the world right now." She said that, if he were here, she thought his optimism would be strong. "He'd be reading everything there is to read—perhaps about human nature and how people transform, perhaps about the building blocks of social movements, perhaps about some obscure corner of neuroscience that I cannot even imagine."

In the letter, she told a story. It went like this:

Many years ago, he sent an image to me by email that has been in my head the last few days. I think it was from an anti-war event in Ann Arbor, so probably in the early 2000s, though I can't find it anywhere now. It was a peace sign made out of people, an aerial shot—not one he took himself, but he put an arrow on it to show approximately where he was standing. Marching and rallying is more my thing than his, but he felt strongly in the moment, whatever it was. And it was a beautiful photo. I think of the photo now as one of those critical markers, pointing out humanity's better angels.

When a person dies, they leave behind a kind of reverberation, their rhythm in time that those used to walking next to them may be able to recall sometimes. It is not exactly a memory, though we learned it in the past. We all walk with our eyes on the future, and the rhythm holds within it a kind of ideal, a possible perfection of moving with other people, as all the neighbors gather for a dance or to make a sign of peace. This is what I am trying to make again, walking with our children. My sister and I live far apart. We are both carrying on.

RAISING CHILDREN

Emma's sister is married to Mr. Knightley's brother. "What a comfort it is," Emma says to Mr. Knightley, "that we think alike about our nephews and nieces. As to men and women, our opinions are very different; but with regard to these children, I observe we never disagree." Mr. Knightley takes his usual mode of correction, but only to admit to already agreeing: "If you were as much guided by nature in your opinions of men and women, and as little under the power of fancy and whim in your dealings with them, as you are where these children are concerned, we might always think alike." He has to agree again a bit later, when the Knightley brothers suggest that Emma is gadding about and perhaps the nephews should instead stay at Donwell, and she puts him irrefutably in his place: "As to my dear little boys, I must say, that if aunt Emma has not time for them, I do not think they would fare much better with uncle Knightley, who is absent from home about five hours where she is absent one—and who, when he is at home, is either reading to himself or settling his accounts." In forming the children and attending to them, time and habitation are on her side, and he knows she is right. "Mr. Knightley seemed to be trying not to smile; and succeeded without difficulty, upon Mrs. Elton's beginning to talk to him."

In her draft of *The Watsons*, Jane Austen had made a beautiful scene for another character named Emma who dances at a ball with a disappointed child, and the child is happy and loves her. Our Emma, too, is lovely with children. After a party of gypsies are seen in the neighborhood, gypsies who will turn out to matter in many dimensions, they are sent away by what the novel calls, drily, "the operations of justice." Emma makes a story of them that the children adore. "Henry and John were still asking every day for the story of Harriet and the gipsies, and still tenaciously setting her right if she varied in the slightest particular from the original recital."

Do not vary in the slightest particular, so little children demand of us. We can feel with Emma the slight despair of hearing a child say, "Again! You be . . . and I'll be . . ." Here we are again, obliged to pretend the same scenario, in just the same way. Children know, instinctively, that for them exact repetition is not just important but essential, not only because the details matter, but also because the repetition does. Repeating, the particular takes a general form; this is one of their first ideas of generality. They ask for the same foods; they want to go trick-or-treating on precisely the same route as last year. "More again," T would say for any song or action that he wanted to go on with. I imagine that Emma's nephews take all the parts: adventure and freedom, impoverishment, fear, bravery, and also exclusion, and the so-called operations of justice. As they go over the story, theater becomes the self, acting out a scene is incorporated into a way of being.

Everything in *Emma* reaches in several directions at once. In the third and last volume of the book, the raising of children, ideas and errors of imagination, how to resolve the difficult problem of Mr. Knightley and

Mr. Woodhouse changing their households—all of these considerations point to and take their lead from the seemingly odd moment of the gypsies camping on the green a bit beyond Highbury.

The day after the turning ball, Harriet goes for a walk with another friend, and the two young women see "a party of gipsies." In Jane Austen's time, certain writers recommended getting an effect of "the picturesque" by including gypsies on the green, as Gainsborough sometimes did in his paintings. It was thought that this would affirm the natural order (and the structure of power) that obtained within the village. The gypsies outside Highbury are neither so decorative nor so affirming. When their camp comes into view, and a single child comes toward Harriet and her friend to beg, the friend gives "a great scream" and hightails it, but Harriet has "suffered very much from cramp after dancing" and cannot move. The narrator mocks the overreaction of the young women. More children come, and how these "trampers might have behaved, had the young ladies been more courageous, must be doubtful; but such an invitation for attack, could not be resisted." This is the very language with which Austen will later describe Emma's attack on Miss Bates, whose vulnerability "Emma could not resist." The children are joined by "a stout woman and a great boy." And it is these two whom Frank Churchill, when he happens by, leaves "completely frightened," an accomplishment that perhaps casts a bit of doubt on the actual bravery of a grown man, of good fortune. It does not seem that the gypsies act differently from the people who think themselves privileged to live in Highbury, and who are also concerned with having enough to eat and providing food for one another.

Frank Churchill brings Harriet back to Hartfield and tells Emma to let Mr. Knightley know about it, but "the gypsies did not wait for the operations of justice; they took themselves off in a hurry." With this exclusion, Highbury tries to cut itself off from the world and, I think, may sever a connection with itself, for it is only at this point in the book that things threaten to go badly wrong for the young women whose futures we most care about—Harriet, Jane Fairfax, and Emma most of all.

AS IMAGINATION

Jane Austen's words are as well placed and purposeful as any in literature. She needed all of English, and English sufficed for her. Extremely rarely in her life as a novelist did she have need of a new word and coin it. We can assume the needs were important ones. In describing what happens to Emma's imagination after Harriet and Frank Churchill encounter the gypsies, Austen chose to call her "an imaginist."

Emma begins to think that Harriet and Frank Churchill may be destined for each other:

> Could a linguist, could a grammarian, could even a mathematician have seen what she did, have witnessed their appearance together, and heard their history of it, without feeling that circumstances had been at work to make them peculiarly interesting to each other?—How much more must an imaginist, like herself, be on fire with speculation and foresight!—especially with such a groundwork of anticipation as her mind had already made.

Right away, we see something of what this must mean—that Emma lets her imagination run away with her, that she indulges her imaginings, that she creates imaginary worlds and prefers them to the real one. Imagination is the true faculty; imaginism the distortion. "Imagination" would have been the right word if Emma had been using it to better understand herself and the people around her. An "imaginist" would be out of balance, out of contact with the world. She has allowed her powers of reason and observation to be absorbed into her fancy. As with other coinages from this same period—"self-important," "self-absorbed," "self-approbation"—the point is surely that in "imaginism" the imagination turns inward on itself, loses the continuous readjustment of self and the world.

When the story of the gypsies first circulates, of course, everyone can talk of little else: "the last night's ball seemed lost in the gipsies." This loss of the ball, and its clearer understandings, is consequential for Emma. Harriet has paid good attention to what transpired there, and she has begun to think of Mr. Knightley for herself, the gypsies do not muddle Harriet, but Emma gets distracted by the possibility of a romantic story at the edge of Highbury and does not go on working at the clarity she was just coming to with Mr. Knightley. Instead she persists, even at Box Hill, going on flirting with Frank Churchill, in a kind of willful haze of repeating an old behavior, a peripheral romance that no longer fits her actual desires. To grow up is to give up certain repetitions right for children. Emma is acting out a story more like something that would happen in a romantic novel by one of Austen's contemporaries, and has mistaken her ground.

In one of few places in the book where we are without Emma, Mr. Knightley is wondering over Frank Churchill's character and private understandings, but he hesitates. He wants, as we follow his thought, "to escape any of Emma's errors of imagination." He and the narrator think of a line of Cowper's. The poet is sitting by the fire at twilight, seeing images in the flames, "myself creating what I saw." Mr. Knightley does not want to create what he thinks he sees from his own desires. But to find the medium of imagination and observing the world is not to eliminate imagination.

Austen probably read the *Lyrical Ballads* during the years when she was writing less. I do hope Wordsworth's poems ran companionably in her thoughts, as they seem to have done for Fanny Price, and for Mr. Knightley. I first saw the link reading William Deresiewicz: that Jane Austen was probably thinking not only of what Cowper said but of what Wordsworth thought of what Cowper said. For in "Tintern Abbey," Wordsworth reworked Cowper's line to assert that imagination does, in fact, play an important part in true understanding: "Of eye, and ear,— both what they half create, / And what perceive." Making a good persuasion from Emma's errors of imagination, and Mr. Knightley's resistance to them, *Emma* thinks there is no real seeing without imagining, the thing is to keep imagination and observation harnessed together.

The opposite of imaginism is not, in Jane Austen, some external, error-less reality. There is not a reality, like some sort of bath, that we can set ourselves down in to correct our mistakes. The opposite of imaginism, which is an interior self-distortion, would be a self-clarification.

My father reread all of Wordsworth in the last few years of his life. He loved those poems, and it is a comfort to me that they were with him in the nights when he lay awake, trying to guess at the state of his own body. The phrase "both what they half create, and what perceive" comes from a long sentence in "Tintern Abbey." In it, I find an idea of how we may, eyes up, hold ourselves in the learning track:

> Therefore am I still
> A lover of the meadows and the woods,
> And mountains; and of all that we behold
> From this green earth; of all the mighty world
> Of eye, and ear,—both what they half create,
> And what perceive; well pleased to recognise
> In nature and the language of the sense
> The anchor of my purest thoughts, the nurse
> The guide, the guardian of my heart, and soul
> Of all my moral being.

FRESH POND

To get to Fresh Pond from our old neighborhood in Cambridge, you walk up Concord Avenue or up Vassal Lane, cross the parkway, enter by one of the thin paths, join the wayward circle. The band of woods has been care-fully cultivated so that one feels quite far from the surrounding parkway; the brick water-treatment facility seems quiet and civic, the golf course along one side bucolic. On weekdays, there are people and dogs getting exercise, sometimes a few bird-watchers, telescope trained on a knothole favored by a small owl, sometimes a fleet of high school boys running cross-country. S was two months old when we moved to that neighborhood; walking at Fresh Pond was the other thing I did with the most regularity, with many kinds of attention, in the years when I was reading Austen. It was a place that held specific griefs and joys, and general ones. Sometimes M and I walked there together, or I walked with one of two close friends; more often I walked by myself, or with a stroller and one or both of the children. Along the bumpy wooded path around the wide reservoir, I would have a momentary feeling of both seclusion and expanse.

I knew Fresh Pond in its different seasons, and knew those seasonal changes repeatedly. I didn't have to notice the places where the cracks impeded a stroller's progress, or to remember to put on my hat for the part where there was a strong glare between the larger pond and the smaller one. My circlings around seemed to contain or tread over and through one another.

Sometimes I would pass a flat rock, one that we had come to on a walk with my parents and S, the first real walk we had taken her on, when my father still walked easily, before we even moved to the neighborhood, when she was a few weeks old, lying in the buggy, and we had changed her diaper on it, a large, flat rock, and she had looked up and seen a tall, old tree and had been startled. I could see her thinking clarify on her face. I knew she was seeing the tree. On some later walks, I would pause and remark it, her first tree, other times I would just go by. I never did learn what kind of tree it was, though I took pictures of it in different shades of foliage with the idea of finding out.

The winter walks were harder, and on cold days, I thought of harder times, of the first winter after T was born, and it had taken all my effort to get to the stand of pines overlooking the pond, a great strain of body to arrive at that preliminary point. Snow on the etched branches reminded me of the winter right after my father died when, walking, what I had felt most distinctly was that I could feel none of what I usually felt. The flow of intimate particulars had ceased, and my estrangement was perceptible in the way I seemed in a kind of exile from my usual walking here.

Over time, even the memories of this winter walking got blended into the round. The hardest memory, the one that refused obstinately to become a part of the circle, that if I thought of it would always catch me and tear me away, was the one of my last walk there with my father, in the autumn, when he told me to teach, which I thought meant to stop doing the writing in which I was getting lost. One thing I think now is that my disquiet on that walk was from a misunderstanding that went even deeper. As we went, up and down the slopes, over the graveled part and the paved, I was worried in a molecular way that I'd never experienced before: there was a strange faltering in the pace of walking next to my father. I knew I was angry with myself for not quite being able to love a walk together, one I could not say to myself might be among the last we would have. I didn't know that my body was registering a truth—we had already lost walking next to each other.

Of all the heroines in Austen, Emma is the one who would do what Jane Austen did when Austen's sister-in-law Elizabeth died, and Austen had charge of her nephews in their first grief and shock. Jane Austen took her nephews out on the river. She reported to Cassandra, in a letter of the twenty-fourth and twenty-fifth of October 1808, that they crossed by the Itchen ferry and were rowed upriver—"both the boys rowed great part of the way, and their questions and remarks, as well as their enjoyment, were very amusing"—and all together, the excursion had been "so much enjoyed that I had intended to take them to Netley today; the tide is just right for going immediately after noonshine, but I am afraid there will be rain; if we cannot get so far, however, we may perhaps go round from the ferry to the quay."

Earlier in her letter, their aunt had written with satisfaction that the boys were in a good state of feeling: "George is most industriously making and naming paper ships, at which he afterwards shoots with horse-chestnuts . . . and Edward equally intent over the 'Lake of Killarney,' twisting himself about in one of our great chairs." Let them be in nature, in playing, and in books—that is where they may feel some freedom around their grief, and learn to live after their mother is gone.

The children in Jane Austen's novels and letters live in their bodies, their joy bursts within them; they run and dance; in sorrow they droop; their solace is rivers, streams, sticks, trees. Sometimes the children are acting naturally, as adults only remember doing, sometimes they are learning to act as society expects, and sometimes they are learning how to act like themselves, an act of repeated imagination, one that demands someone else be imagining with them. Now that their mother is becoming an indistinct remembrance of caresses, who will do this imagining with them—the natural world will, and other people.

ROUGH GROUND

Learning is a process in time that can, eventually, enter a realm that we might call timeless, or that seems to inhabit a different kind of time. A child is practicing steps. He goes up and down the room, pushing a walker; he does this day after day. He drags his parents around, determinedly grasping a finger, step, step, fall, step, step, twist to the ground. He is pushing himself every minute, is aware of each step and the second it takes to complete or to fail at it. Then he learns to walk, and he is just walking. He sees a spoon across the room and walks to it. Now the walking does not have the same time quality for him; it seems almost no time at all between thinking of wanting the spoon and grasping it in his hand. Walking is a part of his being, and will be so until it is hampered again.

Here is another version of this, for adult walkers. The first time we walk to a new place, the way is long. We look at each house, each street name. Do we turn left here, or wait another block; the unfamiliar block seems interminable. Have I gotten turned around, these look like the same buildings I just passed. The second time we walk it, already the way is less difficult, but there are many interruptions—is this where I made the wrong turn? By the third time, or the fourth, it is surprisingly fast. But this is no distance at all, we say to ourselves, are we here already? It's just a couple of blocks, it's quite a pleasant walk. The way has been incorporated into our way—it's not a series of individual steps and choices anymore, it's a habit of our being. And when it's a habit, we experience it not in pieces but as integrated into our whole consciousness. As I was walking, I was thinking about different things—the fight I had with my husband, my anxiety about my mother's visit, whether that tree is suffering from the construction in the neighborhood, the rain boots the children will be needing, the difficulty of writing about *Emma*—the particular walk has merged into the activity of walking, it's part of a state of being, integrated with thinking and observing and worrying. And the way that I feel the difference is as a different experience of time—not second-by-second time but time fluent, in and out of time, that is myself not aware of learning but in character.

The one thing every parent says to every other parent of young children—it has been said to me in the last seven years hundreds, if not thousands, of times, by hospital nurses and taxicab drivers and my parents and M's parents and people delivering takeout and dear old friends and parents at the day care; it was said to me once by a businessman at an airport and another time by a father who was homeless, and who caught up with me at a street corner because it was important to say—this one thing is: "It goes so fast." I say it to other people, too, we agree to it together on playgrounds and in line for ice creams and taking out the trash. There is nothing like the unrememberability of an ordinary year in which you love and are loved. It goes by faster than a familiar walk—it's winter already? you think to yourself, where did the time go? Nothing is swifter than habitual time formed in love.

We make, day by day, the continual atmosphere that we will remember deeply but not distinctly. We will not be able to recall how our children looked to us when they were eighteen months old. Even if we take a thousand pictures, when we look at them it will be hard to get back the feeling we had day after day in that time. Nevertheless, we and they are making a habit of life together, our way of living, which will be ingrained in our characters and in theirs. Emma is good at this. When she is trying to make something unusual, a grand romantic story, she blunders and has much still to learn, but, with her nephews, she has a good regular practice of days. She always has a hearty meal ready for her neighbors, she visits people who are poor and brings them good cheer and sympathy without condescension, she sends the Bateses the hindquarter of a pig. Hers are what Wordsworth in "Tintern Abbey" calls "that best portion of a good man's life, / His little, nameless, unremembered, acts / Of kindness and of love." To live in a family is a small form of civic life; unremembering, we are working on keeping together in time.

As they pass, the hours are slow and ragged. One is fatigued, impatient, how will we get through the half hour until your father comes home, I cannot stack those blocks for him and run with her to the bathroom at the same time. Ordinariness is a jarring, jolting effort. Making a habit is intensely hard work. In love, we struggle bitterly in the hours and float across the years—the way we love is us at our most miraculously habitual, but when we blunder, which we do continually, how we stagger and fall down.

I think Jane Austen may be arguing that these experiences are not opposed. Lysander and Hermia are even more right than we may realize—it is not just that true love faces obstacles, or even that it proves itself in being able to surmount roughness, but that love just is learning a general way of going, patiently, over rough ground.

Emma and her neighbors and the children are walking forward together. When Emma's mind moves with "all the wonderful velocity of thought," the whole book, all that has happened and is happening in that moment, takes definitive shape and makes sense. The wonder, to me, is that every time I read these lines, I feel in my own mind the tumbling kaleidoscope of impressions and misimpressions, everything sorted and rearranged in an instant, the wonderful velocity is mine, Emma's, and Austen's, all on the page at once. Wretchedness comes to comedy again. We know that Mr. Knightley loves her, that she has, just the moment before, again acted out of misunderstanding, to her detriment and other people's; she and her friend Harriet have blundered, again; still, in this great expansion, she can think of what is right by her friend, and what is right for the man she loves, and right for herself, all together and at once. Austen is so deliberate: "her way was clear, though not quite smooth."

A FATHER DYING

Emma does not quite come to conclusion with the turn in the shrubbery. Mr. Knightley's great revelation, the solution to one fundamental problem of the book, is that he will leave his own house and come to hers, joining the household that she has made. Perhaps I am too optimistic, but I see this as a quite radical step. They will form their household together on Emma's ground. The characters in the novel see this as a large matter. When she learns of it, Mrs. Weston thinks of the match this way:

> In one respect, one point of the highest importance, [it was] so peculiarly eligible, so singularly fortunate, that now it seemed as if Emma could not safely have attached herself to any other creature, and that she had herself been the stupidest of beings in not having thought of it, and wished it long ago.—How very few of those men in a rank of life to address Emma would have renounced their own home for Hartfield! And who but Mr. Knightley could know and bear with Mr. Woodhouse, so as to make such an arrangement desirable!

Here, as Mrs. Weston thinks of it, the ideal hovers hopefully above the present: "But here there was nothing to be shifted off in a wild speculation on the future. It was all right, all open, all equal. No sacrifice on any side worth the name. It was a union of the highest promise of felicity in itself." Not quite all open, probably, for it does not seem that Emma will tell Mr. Knightley that Harriet loved him, and it does not seem that Mr. Knightley will tell Emma whether Miss Bates did. Still, "all equal" bodes well.

However, Mr. Woodhouse will not agree to having Mr. Knightley move in with them. A few fowls are stolen in the neighborhood. This is "arguably the work of the gypsies," William Galperin writes, "(for there are no other suspects in the novel so far as I can tell)." The gypsies reaffirm an order in *Emma* but in a much more complicated way than they do in Gainsborough; Emma would not have gotten married when she did without them. Mr. Woodhouse, nervous about his property, decides he would like to have a son-in-law in the house.

Emma's is the most gently mocked wedding in Austen. Mrs. Elton, learning "the particulars" from her vicar husband, deplores its lacks: "'Very little white satin, very few lace veils; a most pitiful business!'" But, unlike Austen's other heroines, whose happiness is left more than a little precariously, dependently leaning on other things—a sister, an extended family, a place, the navy, the peace, a friend—Emma is to find happiness in marriage itself, in her own household, and this is understood by her community, as we learn from the novel's last line: "In spite of these deficiencies, the wishes, the hopes, the confidence, the predictions of the small band of true friends who witnessed the ceremony, were fully answered in the perfect happiness of the union."

This happy continuance was not deathless. About the time that Emma and George Knightley's first child would have been learning to walk, her father was to die. This we know by word of mouth, from the members of Austen's family. At the very end of his memoir, Jane Austen's nephew reports of his aunt, "She would, if asked, tell us many little particulars about the subsequent career of some of her people. In this traditionary way we learned that . . . Mr. Woodhouse survived his daughter's marriage, and kept her and Mr. Knightley from settling at Donwell, about two years." He will be a part of the pattern of their family life, but mostly he will not be there.

HELD TOGETHER

The Christmas before he died, my father mounted a baby gate at the bottom of the stairwell. My sister's little girl was more than a year old and was crawling and walking; S was beginning to show signs that she might soon crawl, too. They thought we would be visiting often enough that it made sense to have a gate. I think my parents liked having the gate there, even though it was only an impediment most of the time. Perhaps it held us all there, their beloved children and grandchildren, on the stairwell, as much as it kept the babies from accident.

When my parents made the decision to call the paramedics and my father was taken to the hospital for the last time, they brought him down the stairs, and they had to take the gate off, to fit him and the stretcher through. He went out through the front door. I remember the paramedics offering to help remount the gate, but I don't remember now whether they did it, or whether my sister did, or M, but it went back up, and it has stayed up, six years now, through the next pregnancies, and as the second babies came, and learned to crawl and then to walk. They are fine on the stairs, but my mother says it should stay for a little cousin who visits. I suppose eventually there will be no argument for keeping it any longer, and the last barrier, the one it did turn out you could punch your way through into infinity, will be gone.

My father died in one of the hospitals he had studied, the University of Michigan Hospital. Some of the people who came to visit in those last days were doctors and nurses and staff with whom he had worked as a researcher. He was graceful with them, still a colleague, still seeing the hospital as a place to be understood. He was also visited by other nurses he did not know, in the regular round of their duties, and then he took the role of a patient. As one of the protocols of the hospital, patients were regularly asked a series of irritating questions about their "goals for the day" and so on. I remember him, then waiting through the day before he died, patiently, though with discernible reproof, answering that his goal was to stay alive to see my sister and her family, who were to arrive that evening. They came, and he saw them.

On the morning of his last day, my father woke with the feeling that he was soon to die. We had planned to be at the hospital in shifts, and I was to stay at the house, but he asked my mother and sister to call me to come. Not long after I arrived, he said that he had had a dream the night before. The dream had been about the Internet. In the dream, he told us, the Internet had been organized so that it required him to repeatedly give his date of birth. My father was an early computer scientist; he loved and understood the beautiful possibilities of the web's shared space long before most people I knew had email; his dream was prescient, I think, and it was of a cruelly inverted and flattened future. My father said—and there was consternation, and although he knew there was wit in the dream, it was hollow for him, even a little appalling—that in the dream he thought, "If this is the way the Internet is organized, I must already be dead."

Later, though, doctors and other people from the hospital came in again. He was again constant, full of wit, completely in character. A chaplain asked him whether he was spiritually at peace. M remembers that my father replied, "Just spiritual." When the doctors, on that last day, had to acknowledge, though they tried not to, that they had not saved him, and had not even really understood what was killing him, he said with good humor that he would like there to be an autopsy. "Write me up," he said, and there was laughter in his voice. "I'll be curious."

Some years ago, a few weeks before I finished an early draft of this book (I wrote down the date, so I know it was September 14, 2015), I went for a walk at Fresh Pond. I left my desk to take the walk, and felt the walk to be a part of the thinking I was trying to do, and wrote notes with more than usual care when I came back:

> Finished writing for the day, at work now on Wordsworth, on the transition to childhood. Went to Fresh Pond. Day after Rosh Hashanah. We

all had apples last night, and, except T, honey. A sweet new year. Thinking on the way to Fresh Pond that if we ever lost the year, the sense of a round year, we'd really be screwed.

Walked through the cut through, at speed, having walked fast to get there and see it before going to pick up the children. Had gone because it was a beautiful day, a fresh fall day, a day for a walk. But came out from the trees and saw the pond and was stunned. A glorious day. Wind up and the usually placid reservoir covered in choppy waves, enough clouds in the sky for the water to seem gray and the sunlight breaking through a white-silver. Sudden uplift. And I thought without thinking, "We got lucky, my Dad and me, to see this." His favorite kind of day, windy, senses quickened, joy. And I really meant that we both saw it, him and me, not that we were each lucky to have been alive on the earth, or that we had been lucky to have walked there once, years ago, but that we saw that very thing together today, the choppy water, the white-silver sunlight, the leaves racing in the wind. I thought that I'm some ways away from the end of this book, but that maybe this is the end of this book.

Years have passed, and it hasn't happened again to me that I looked out at the world with my father. We have left the last places that I actually walked with him, and that we knew together. I thought that I would often have my father with me in that way, and that this would mean I had at last escaped from grief into mourning. I thought I was writing something of an end. But I didn't feel it again. It was just a slight tipping of the universe, just a place where a deeper continuity was sufficiently raised to become perceptible.

On the last walk I took with my father at Fresh Pond, he must have been making every effort to go on walking next to me as he always had. He would have worried that as I lost walking next to him, I was also in danger of losing my confidence in being able to make myself understood. That was why, I think, he wanted to remind me that I had been a good teacher, and was careful to say that he was glad that analysis had changed me, and glad that, in being better known to other people, it had become easier to be myself. He might have been trying to tell me how he imagined it, how I would err and learn again.

I think, though it was never my favorite, that I will read *Emma* again years from now, and that it will give this back to me. Emma and I are not done with each other yet.

Now that the dust that was my father—first stardust, then my father, now dust again—now that this dust is flung into the air and traveling through wall after wall into the infinite reaches, I think I can say we made some kind of meaning together on our stumbling walk. Perhaps neither he nor I was as alone as we feared. If he could see me now, he would see that my body has changed again, the way I walk, the way I sit in a chair. He would know when he saw me that he is nowhere in the world, and yet he would know that he had been here, that other people he would have loved are here now.

On the last day, shortly before the morphine began to take effect, I asked my father whether he had any messages for people. He said that he had tried to write to some of his closest friends but had found it impossible. I said I would tell people that he had always hated goodbyes. And I added, tentatively, that I thought he would say to them that he would be satisfied to feel—and I tried to get the words he would use, and I knew to say—that life was going on. He made a sign that indicated that this was a right expression. Then I said to my father that people would be acting in his honor and thinking of his memory. He shook his head. He said: "It all going on is miracle enough."

Ten

LATE PERSUASIONS

It was a rainy June. We were returning to Venice six years after we had scattered my father's ashes there. I had looked forward to the trip and thought I might have a minute, alone on the canals, and that there might come a moment of closeness. On the plane I sat between T, now four, and S, seven. T and I were looking out the window of the plane as it descended and I saw the lagoon. I saw the lagoon and before I could think, I thought, "He is there." In my mind, below the plane and over us rose a tall wave of greenish-gray water that was my father. Severity and regret, love, and fierce longing—he had been waiting. For me, and for me to bring them.

I looked down and T was studying my face, his eyes thoughtful. Not quite concerned. Attending to an unusual force. He had seen it go across my face.

I have brought myself to read the final fragment of *Sanditon* only a few times. It was not Austen who called it *Sanditon*, that name was chosen by the devoted and sympathetic scholar R. W. Chapman. She had called it *The Brothers*. It grows in the same Austen pattern and would have been comic, would have had an intricate plot revealed to cast all in new light. The heroine, Charlotte, has something of Elinor's self-sufficiency, something of Anne's firmness about literary matters. The book breaks off just as the brother arrives, who "often makes me laugh at them all inspite of myself." To me, the novel seems slight, but I have learned from other people's accounts that it holds wit and promise, monologues that might lead from *Emma* to Dickens, apparitions that suggest the modernists. I have not reached that equanimity yet. The first time, I hurried through the pages, crying. I missed the writer. Perhaps I had had the intimation of not wanting to come to the end, even in high school, when I refused to read this last work. I still fear the loss. What will it be when I finally acknowledge that there is no more Austen? I think it might be like seeing my own death from nearer by.

"If a sound can be preserved in the same manner as a leaf or a butterfly," Azar Nafisi wrote, "I would say that within the pages of my *Pride and Prejudice* . . . is hidden like an autumn leaf the sound of the red siren." When I put petals and leaves into books, it is for my future self to find them later dried, but I often think that it will not be me who opens the book, it will be someone else.

When Anne makes her declaration and changes the form of her life, it is possible that it is a change like having children, and she will not really remember her life as it used to be. I wonder if, in writing memoirs, we may also be gradually, necessarily, unavoidably, liberatingly, terrifyingly declaring ourselves in a way that weakens the old ties that both confined us to narrow places and bound us to people we love.

On darker days, I think the fact that Anne has to make a declaration—that she has loved, long, when hope and existence are gone—is also a sign that we will never inhabit Highbury. If our experiences are so separate that only by writing memoirs can we join them together, then perhaps that village is gone even from our shared imagination. *Emma* thinks it is still there, difficult, but still there; *Persuasion*, I worry, does not. This must have been hard for Austen to contend with. She was ill, the world kept moving on. She had tried balancing factors—a critique of Walter Scott, an essay on writing, a history of Bonaparte—and still her form, her beautiful form, the novel, was tearing at the edges, had to be torn.

Perhaps this is why I can find within myself the wish that Austen had stopped after *Emma*, when it seemed that it could be got whole. But I never would have understood what I could of *Emma* if she had stopped.

I think if there had not been *Persuasion*, I probably never would have read Austen at all.

The last two years of Jane Austen's life were quiet and eventful. In 1815, she finished *Emma* as winter gave way to spring, and Anne Sharp came to visit in June. Cassandra wrote that her sister began *Persuasion* on August 8 of that year. Austen's new publisher brought out *Emma* in the last days of 1815. *Emma* brought her Anne Sharp's happy approval, and the important consideration in the *Quarterly Review* that Austen may have realized was written by Walter Scott. Most touching, her brother Charles wrote from a ship far away—a year now since his beloved Fanny had died and still his dreams were of her, their children—that, comfortless, he had received *Emma*, which "arrived in time to a moment." He read it three times in succession, turning from the last page back to the first. "I am delighted with her, more so I think than even with my favourite Pride and Prejudice."

At the beginning of 1816, she began to feel more ill, although it seems she had been ailing, perhaps for three years or more. There are many uncertain retrospective diagnoses: Addison's disease, Hodgkin's lymphoma, some kind of tuberculosis, even, recently, an idea of accidental arsenic poisoning. It was a chronic and worsening condition. In February, Charles was shipwrecked off the coast of Turkey; he and all the crew survived. In March, the bank belonging to her brother Henry, her delightful and not entirely dependable brother Henry, failed. With it went all his money and a fair amount of his brothers' and the contributions he and his brothers had been making for the support of their mother and Jane and Cassandra. In this situation, when she might again lose all she had worked to establish, Jane Austen became very sick. Paula Byrne suggests this supports a diagnosis of Addison's, a disease that makes the sufferer extremely sensitive to stress. *Emma* sold well. But *Mansfield Park* had also been moved to the new publisher and reprinted; it hardly sold at all, and its losses canceled out whatever *Emma* profited.

By the summer, Jane Austen was really declining, and she had great exertion to gather the energy to write. In the summer, she finished *Persuasion* and rewrote its two late chapters, creating the scene at the White Hart. In the beginning of 1817, she began the new novel that she thought of as *The Brothers*, in which brothers set out on a precarious financial speculation. By March of that year, she had written what would be about sixty pages of a printed book, and then became too ill to work. She was extremely ill for several weeks. She died on July 18, 1817.

Her sister, Cassandra, wrote to their niece Fanny Knight a beautiful and often quoted letter about the last hours:

> Her looks altered & she fell away, but I perceived no material diminution of strength & tho' I was then hopeless of a recovery I had no suspicion how rapidly my loss was approaching.—I *have* lost a treasure, such a Sister, such a friend as never can have been surpassed,—She was the sun of my life, the gilder of every pleasure, the soother of every sorrow, I had not a thought concealed from her, & it is as if I had lost a part of myself.

As Jane Austen had gone through the rigors of death, her body had bent so that she could not lie on her pillow. Her head lay, off the bed, in her sister's lap, on a pillow, for six hours. Cassandra allowed herself to be relieved by another for two hours, then returned to take the head again. An hour later, Jane Austen died.

We scattered his ashes in Venice. When my father had talked about it with my mother before his death, he said that he wanted to be cremated and that for the scattering she should choose between two places, one was a remote island, the other Venice, both were far from most of the people with whom he had lived his everyday life. After his death, my mother chose Venice, thinking that, while still expensive and far, it was a little more visitable for herself and us. Not only a place in which he had himself felt leisure and beauty and love, but also a place where he had worked and made his contribution, and that might hold the whole of life and of his life. It was important to all of us that in Venice lives Massimo, the colleague with whom my father worked most closely in the last ten years, a friend for thirty years. If any friend is capable of watching out for my father, watching over him, and watching for signs of him, it is Massimo.

Nonetheless, and even though we all have some fragments of his ashes, and in the strange, modern way can place him on the surface of any place in the world we choose, it was, especially in those first dragging winter months, strange to me that my father was not to be in Ann Arbor, his place for almost exactly forty years. Because he had wished it, no other decision was possible, but it felt so far away. For six years I was not able to go back to Venice, and I sometimes said to myself that Ann Arbor is of the world, too. I wished, as perhaps the families of people who write memoirs do, too, that he had chosen to be a little less of the world, a little more with me.

My father loved Ann Arbor, and especially its trees. He used to tell us about the woman who had left her fortune to the trees of Ann Arbor. He would sometimes say that it was an inspired legacy. One of the things he did in those late working days, when he was trying to think about habits and imagination, was to walk and walk in Ann Arbor. He would walk out to Gallup Park, and he would skirt the river and walk through the protected land and up to the Arboretum—he walked for hours along the edges of the Huron River, in the different parks and over the bridges. In the week after he died, when I tried to think what to say at his memorial, it made sense to go out to Gallup Park in the snow, as it did to go there with my mother and S on the first anniversary of his death. I still go to Gallup Park to think about him. Mostly, he is not there. Once in a great while, in other places, through the water and the air, he has come again.

It was hard to decide whether to go. The weather report was uncertain and weather in Venice changes rapidly. There were many crossed messages between the boat captain and our friends Massimo and Anna and us—we had Skype, but no working cell phones—there was a lot of crackling and dissonance and then it seemed we would go. The first boat came for us, which would take us through the canals and across to the lagoon, and in it were Massimo and Anna, who had not been able to come to the memorial service, and so this was the first time they were meeting the babies— our niece, who was then a year and seven months old, and S, whose first birthday would be the next day. And so there was something joyful, the little girls were pleased about the boat, were watching out the windows, and there was a bewildering incongruity.

We went across the lagoon. We came to the boathouse where we were met by the captain who was to take us in the open boat. He, too, was uncertain about the weather. There were further discussions. It was decided that we would go ahead to the water. We readied ourselves, clambered in. A motorboat like a skiff, with ledges around the edge on which to perch, shallow; we held close to the girls. It began to rain. Large drops. We were out on the water.

Of what we read, and tried to say, and how we cried and how the ashes and rain fell on us and in the water, I think I will just say that it had its own absurdity and solemnity. It was raining quite hard, and we were all very wet. The captain quietly circled around until we were done, and then offered to take us back to the apartment where we were staying, as perhaps being somewhat quicker by that point than going back to the boathouse and finding another boat to return us. The waters of Venice were running very high that spring, unusually high; certain canals were impassable to larger boats. We made our way across the lagoon in the open skiff in a driving rain. We were soaking. Instructed by the captain, my sister and I sat in the bottom of the boat, deep in a large puddle, each of us holding a little girl tightly. I had brought a couple of rolls of bread and fed the girls small pieces under their hoods. It rained torrentially. We came to Venice.

On the canals, the water was so high that the boat could barely pass beneath the bridges, and we all, even the captain, had to lie down as we passed under them. The canals were empty; everyone had gotten themselves inside. The city, darkened, was stormily, rigorously beautiful. When we got home, our clothes were as wet as they had ever been in our lives. We laughed. And we changed, and lent ill-fitting garments to Massimo and to Anna. We drank together, and to my father, in the kitchen of the apartment where we were staying, and that was what happened.

When it came time to leave Venice, I experienced a strange paralysis. I went from room to room picking things up and putting them down. S, feeling my terror, clung to my legs and cried, so that I became immobilized. The others shuttled everything around us; we did at last get into the boat that would take us away.

Jane Austen did not forget that her books would be read in rooms where babies had just been born, and where parents had breathed their last. In this rare period of my life, drawing to a close now, where I lived only in rooms of the recently born and the recently dead, she was a companion in thought. At last I read her less. The children are growing, my father is years dead, and I turn toward other things.

Austen's niece Anna wrote a remembrance long after her aunt's death. When she thought of going to the library, bringing home the ridiculous stories that she would laugh over with her aunt, this was mingled together with the acuteness of her absence: "It comes back to me now how strangely I missed her. It had become so much a habit with me to put by things in my mind with a reference to her, and to say to myself, I shall keep this for aunt Jane." To me, she is not an aunt or Jane, she is Austen and a writer. But in the vicinity of her novels, as, apparently, in the company of their author, one does work to make habits of reading and imagination that one can hope will endure.

These Austen years have been beautiful. I knew them to be beautiful, and there was not time to trust that I would understand them or even know how to remember them without help of a wise order. Reading and reading Austen, and writing of it, has been a way to put them by.

APPENDIX

A Letter Presented to Karl Weick on the Occasion of His ICOS Celebration, Written in April 2012

Dear Karl,

It was nearly a decade ago that you lectured at the ICOS Seminar on the role of imagination in building theories of organizing. Somewhat in passing, you mentioned a distinction Coleridge and the Romantics had, but that we have mostly abandoned, between fancy and imagination. You said that in his usage the terms distinguished two mental processes, one (fancy) that produces new ideas by combining elements from memory rather mechanically. Your example, I think, was Pegasus, the winged horse. The other (imagination) was a more fully harmonized combining, a characterization of a whole that organically integrates its parts. You developed the concept of imagination, as Coleridge did, by invoking that radiant passage from *A Midsummer Night's Dream*:

> And, as imagination bodies forth
> The forms of things unknown, the poet's pen
> Turns them to shapes, and gives to airy nothing
> A local habitation and a name.

You didn't make the fancy/imagination distinction your central point that day, and colleagues of ours who were there mostly don't seem to recall it now, but it took hold of me. I've been returning to it often through all the years since. This letter is a grateful report on what I've found along the way.

"Habitation" and "name" both seemed importantly connected somehow to my efforts to understand routine in organization. "Habitation" because I was increasingly convinced, as I suspect you may have been, by the central role given to habit as a fundamental human faculty by the American Pragmatists—Mead, James, Dewey, and Peirce—whom we both find so inspiring. Since their time, the idea of habit has diminished in our society's way of thinking about action, while our reliance on notions of choice and decision has greatly increased. But our reading Dewey together convinced me that there is something deep and very worth recovering in the Pragmatist idea that repeated action patterns take on properties of habit, and this makes them different from actions undertaken through conscious reflection on circumstances that are more novel or unprecedented.

"Name" because so many organizational routines, or practices, or customary procedures have names, most commonly everyday verbs, such as "purchase," or "assemble," or "balance," or "shut down." They are the capabilities we create by organizing. (It has helped me so much to follow your advice of thinking of the verb [or gerund], and to remember that it means creating capabilities [organs].) Of course, in a particular context of organizational action such everyday labels take on highly specialized meanings very unlike what they might mean around the house. Indeed, they are even unlike what the same terms might mean in another organization that does the same work. So it's become clearer to me how mergers of banks, say, may fail surprisingly often, when the parties can't reconcile the different meanings each organization has for «purchasing» assets or «balancing» accounts.

The conveners of the ICOS celebration asked us to write notes that recalled favorite moments with you. I have many, but that moment where you brought Shakespeare and Coleridge into the study of organizing seems to me a most beautiful example of how much your way of reading and thinking has enlarged the perspectives available to the rest of us. It was perhaps just an intriguing detail for you, but it has catalyzed my efforts to make sense of what had been a disorderly pile of vaguely related fascinations. What you began in an effort to shape better theories has spilled over into my view of how people better shape their actions. Hence this letter, sketching some ideas that have started to come together for me in the light of your remark. I hope you'll find it a fitting tribute to your way of thinking about organizing, which I so much admire.

One of the forces that kept returning me to your observation was Hilary's work as a theater director. She has a deep interest in how playwrights imagine great characters like Shakespeare's Falstaff or Hamlet and in how actors develop the characters they inhabit on the stage. From her, I've learned that there are two basic approaches actors use—with lots of variations, of course. One might be labeled inside out, and examples would come from Stanislavsky or the Actors Studio. It involves finding in one's own life emotional experiences that can be mapped onto the situation faced by the character. The other, outside in, was exemplified by Sir Laurence Olivier, who said he worked first on how a character moved. It might take a week to get the walk, but once he had it, he knew how to say the lines.

Though they are very different methods, each of these involves completing an integrated whole from fragments, very like one of the definitions of imagination that you've cited. When Jeremy Birnholtz convinced me there was a deep puzzle in the way his summer camp re-created itself each year despite high turnover and nine months of closure, we saw that it was also a kind of re-creation from fragments, and we came back to this idea of character. For a detail to be characteristic, it has to be revealing or suggestive of the larger whole in which it participates. We ended up proposing that organizations may have character, just as people do, so that doing a few tasks «the way we do things around here» may provide a guide to how many other tasks should be approached. (Later, I discovered that Peirce already had this idea of organizational character, which he called organizational "personality.")

Something I have to admit is that for all the many times I've come back to your idea, it took me until just recently to finally come to Owen Barfield's commentary on Coleridge's distinction, and that was when the pieces began to align more strongly and the idea for this letter arose.

If I'd been a more thorough scholar, I might have followed your citation of Holmes and worked back through him to Barfield much sooner. But my guess is that, in the strange way these things grow, I wouldn't have been able to learn from Coleridge, Holmes, or Barfield if I'd gone to them directly. In particular, Barfield's scholastic realism would have put me off a decade ago. I was still too much the uncritical nominalist. Time spent in the interim struggling to understand Peirce was probably a requisite.

As it happened, I got to Barfield just recently, through his visibility among linguists interested in metaphor. It's striking to me how the effort to counter Chomsky has rallied around concepts like imagination and metaphor, and hence around linguists like Lakoff, while the effort to go beyond organizational rationality—bounded or unbounded—has been sustained by your work with the same concepts. And both of these parallel the way the Romantics rallied around imagination and metaphor in their reaction to the Age of Reason that preceded them. I doubt this is an accident. I hope, in fact, the most recent cycles are a portent.

In any event, Barfield has now helped me to see further into what you were getting at. In his work *Poetic Diction* and *History in English Words* he focuses on metaphor as a main way poets—and all of us in our creative moments—exercise imagination, stretching existing meaning to capture a situation that doesn't quite fit within the established scope of available terms. He describes this as meaning something by saying something else. (It's not identical, but it has a nice resonance with your exposition of "until I see what I say.") Barfield argues there is a fundamental tension—maybe it's even a contradiction—between two requirements of language. In the shorter run, words need to mean pretty much the same thing on successive occasions of their use. Otherwise, they become useless for communication or coordination, and you get the absurdity of Humpty Dumpty telling Alice that words can mean whatever he wants them to mean. But in the longer run, the meanings we've established, that we've made customary or collectively habitual, can't possibly be adequate to all the circumstances that can arise, or all the changes that time engenders. So meanings have to be plastic as well as fixed.

Mulling this over, I began to get a feeling for how "purchasing" might mean something so different when I am acting as an employee of our university or shopping at the farmer's market, for how the name for some everyday activity can be stretched into an elaborate new meaning in a community of jointly acting organizational participants, into a kind of local-dialect sense for the name.

This has helped me to a fuller appreciation of what has been at stake in the debate over "mindlessness" that you and Kathie have had with Dan and Claus. I see better how contrasting mechanical fancy with organic, characterful imagination has aligned for you with a contrast of mindless and mindful action. And I'm struck by the further parallel to Dewey's distinction of "dead habit" from the livelier form he regards as normal.

I still haven't found the set terms in this area that I think will work well without sometimes being misleading. "Routine" has engendered a large literature, but it remains burdened by the connotations of rigidity that led both you and Dewey to consign it to a largely pejorative role. On the other hand, "mindful" seems to suffer from the opposite malady: implying more conscious deliberation than may be present in many organizational situations where recurring action is quite effective, in part because its demands on conscious reflection are low. I'm holding out some hope for a revival of the older, richer meaning of "habit." That was actually Dewey's strategy, though since his time "habit" has been increasingly confined to designating failures of choice and will, as in "bad habit." But "inarticulate" need not imply rote or inflexible, as we all can observe when a gifted athlete or jazz musician struggles to put into words what they can perform with such evident grace in the ever-shifting context of their skill.

My hopes for a terminology centered on "habit," like my hopes that the interest in metaphor and imagination may be a portent, are buoyed by what seems to be going on in psychology these days. Habit seems to be recovering a bit from the collapse of the Skinner–Watson caricature of Dewey and James. There are now many studies elucidating processes like procedural memory and dorsal perception that seem to provide foundations for the skillful yet inarticulate recurring action patterns we call habits. And there is good work showing the fundamental, rather than derivative, role of emotion in shaping action.

Don Tucker's *Mind from Body* is a nice example I encountered recently. He traces out the architecture of the brain, with an outer cortex connected to distinct objects of perception and action and innermost layers closely connected to the integrative actions of emotions and viscera. Reentrant connections allow these layers to affect and reshape each other, as might happen in imaginative action. Dampening those interconnections seems to foster action driven by memory without that creative interplay. The differing modes look a lot like Coleridge's imagination and fancy.

Revisiting *Art as Experience*, I've found that Dewey actually takes up Coleridge's distinction and builds on it to describe the inner experience of genuine imagining, the creative back and forth between inner vision and outer object, in terms that resonate closely with Tucker's neuropsychology. This would have made sense to Dewey as part of his larger view that "consciousness . . . marks the place where the formed disposition and the immediate situation touch and interact. It is the continuous readjustment of self and the world in experience."

The whole emerging argument is still a bit of a ramble, of course. That's why it has been set out as a letter to an admired and generous reader, rather than published as an article with attendant claims of being complete and conclusive. Still, it feels like it's going somewhere. And if there turns out to be some worth in it for you, or for our colleagues who study organizing, the story will trace back to your invocation of the way imagination can give "to airy nothing a local habitation and a name."

In warm anticipation of conversations yet to come,
Michael D. Cohen

NOTES

A NOTE ON READING

Certain sources are consistently important throughout this book. My father's letters, diary, and books, and especially his letter to Karl Weick, published here in an appendix with grateful acknowledgment to Karl Weick, were my guides to his thinking. For biographical information about Jane Austen, I drew on Paula Byrne's biography, *The Real Jane Austen: A Life of Small Things*, and, for a psychological sense of Austen's inner life, on Claire Tomalin's *Jane Austen: A Life*. For the Austen family's understanding of Jane Austen, James Edward Austen-Leigh's memoir of his aunt is essential, as are the remembrances by her nieces Caroline Austen and Anna Lefroy. For the chronology of Jane Austen's life, and the record left by the Austen family, all writers on Austen are deeply indebted to the work of Deirdre Le Faye, in both *Jane Austen: A Family Record* and *A Chronology of Jane Austen and Her Family, 1600–2000*. For the movements of time within the novels, I used the meticulous timelines established by Ellen Moody in her online resources at http://www.jimandellen.org. I spent a lot of time wandering Austen byways on the Internet, and I want to note my gratitude to the Jane Austen Societies of North America, Britain, Canada, and Australia, to the many institutions that curate Austen resources in Britain, and to all the individuals working on Austen and posting their thoughts and discoveries online. I learned much from these sources.

When I have quoted Jane Austen in the text, I have indicated which novel is quoted, or the date of the letter quoted, but have not provided the locations of quotations again in these notes. These references, with variations in punctuation, are easily found by searching in the online Gutenberg editions of the novels, and in the various full-text editions of her letters. For quotations from Austen's writing, I have used, as detailed in the bibliography, the Oxford editions of her novels, except the Cambridge edition of *Emma*, and the Deirdre Le Faye edition of her letters. For quotations from Shakespeare, I have used the Oxford modern critical edition, 2016.

Within the text of my book, I have written of the influence different thinkers had on my own writing. Below I have noted important background sources for each chapter and given the page numbers for quotations from secondary sources.

1: BEGINNING

For the sense of the breadth of Jane Austen's world and interests, Paula Byrne's *The Real Jane Austen*, Brian Southam's *Jane Austen and the Navy*, and Margaret Doody's *Jane Austen's Names* were all extremely helpful. I first began to grasp the significance of Jane Austen's move away from the family home in Steventon by reading Claire Tomalin's *Jane Austen: A Life*.

On the topic of memoir, I read with interest Mary Karr's *The Art of Memoir*, Ben Yagoda's *Memoir: A History*, and, among other compendia, *Truth in Nonfiction*, edited by David Lazar.

   7 *"beginning to put into their proper places"*: Es'kia Mphahlele, *Down Second Avenue*, 133.

  12 *"the tyranny of time and politics"*: Azar Nafisi, *Reading Lolita in Tehran*, 6.

  12 *"Every great book we read"*: Nafisi, *Reading Lolita in Tehran*, 289.

  12 *"If a sound can be preserved"*: Nafisi, *Reading Lolita in Tehran*, 187–88.

  17 *"that radiant passage"*: Michael D. Cohen, "A Letter Presented to Karl Weick," in Appendix. Passage of Shakespeare is from *A Midsummer Night's Dream*, V.i.14–17.

  23 *"two words at a time"*: Virginia Woolf, February 2, 1925, *The Letters of Virginia Woolf: Volume III, 1923–1928*, 162.

  23 *"My* Pride and Prejudice . . . *is"*: Ta-Nehisi Coates, "Snobbery."

  23 *"we have lives enough of Jane Austen"*: Virginia Woolf, *A Room of One's Own*, 45.

  24 *"For books continue each other"*: Woolf, *A Room of One's Own*, 80.

  27 *"As soon as she was fixed in her second home"*: James Edward Austen-Leigh, *A Memoir of Jane Austen and Other Family Recollections*, 81.

2: A WRITER

Some critics whose readings of *Persuasion* affected my own throughout are Virginia Woolf; Jocelyn Harris; Stuart Tave; Deidre Shauna Lynch, in her introduction to the Oxford edition; and D. A. Miller, through the whole of *Jane Austen, or The Secret of Style*, but also particularly the second section, "Broken Art," pages 68–76.

  36 *"saying* I*"* and *"saying* you*"* and *"impersonality"*: D. A. Miller, *Jane Austen, or The Secret of Style*, 1.

  37 *"consumed all impediments"*: Woolf, *A Room of One's Own*, 68.

  37 *"the great sentimental favorite"*: Miller, *Secret of Style*, 68.

  37 *"retraction"*: Miller, *Secret of Style*, 75.

  37 *"a peculiar beauty"*: Virginia Woolf, *The Common Reader*, 143–45.

3: MEMORIALS

For ideas about "sense" and "sensibility," about the meanings of the words and their proportions, see Gilbert Ryle's essay "Jane Austen and the Moralists," in *Critical Essays on Jane Austen*, edited by B. C. Southam, and for "sensibility" and "exertion," see

Stuart Tave, *Some Words of Jane Austen*, chapter two, "The Sensibility of Marianne and the Exertion of Elinor Dashwood." I thank Amy Cohen for permission to quote from her memorial remarks.

54 *"Being not only a profound scholar"*: Henry Austen, "Biographical Notice of the Author," in Austen-Leigh, *A Memoir*, 135.

55 *"was considered to read aloud remarkably well"*: Caroline Austen, "My Aunt Jane Austen," in Austen-Leigh, *A Memoir*, 174.

56 *"The loss of their first home"*: Austen-Leigh, *A Memoir*, 50.

56 *"My Aunt was very sorry"*: Caroline Austen to James Edward Austen-Leigh, April 1 [1869?], in Austen-Leigh, *A Memoir*, 185.

64 *"I couldn't bend my knees inside the box"*: Amy Cohen, memorial remarks, February 9, 2013, quoted by permission of the author.

66 *"A local habitation and a name"*: Shakespeare, *A Midsummer Night's Dream*, V.i.17.

66 *"continuous readjustment of self and the world"*: Quoted in Michael Cohen, "A Letter," in Appendix, from John Dewey, "Mind and Consciousness," in *Intelligence in the Modern World*, ed. J. Ratner (New York: Random House, 1939).

67 *"in an uncharacteristically capitalist moment"* and *"I remember very clearly his answer"*: Amy Cohen, memorial remarks, February 9, 2013.

69 *"old habits of composition"*: Austen-Leigh, *A Memoir*, 81.

69 *"saying nothing for a good while"*: Marianne Knight, quoted in Deirdre Le Faye, *Jane Austen: A Family Record*, 206.

69 *"returning to . . . often"*: Michael Cohen, "A Letter," in Appendix.

70 *"You developed the concept"*: Michael Cohen, "A Letter," in Appendix. Passage from Shakespeare is from *A Midsummer Night's Dream*, V.i.14–17. (I think my dad was mistaken; although Coleridge wrote so much about both the imagination and Shakespeare, I have not been able to locate Coleridge referring to this passage in either his essays on Shakespeare or his work on imagination.)

71 *"shape and empower"*: Michael D. Cohen, "Reading Dewey," May 1, 2007, 775.

71 *"the way the Romantics"* and *"I doubt this"*: Michael Cohen, "A Letter," in Appendix.

75 *"if I cannot take a walk"*: Elizabeth Alexander, *The Light of the World*, 134.

76 *"Poverty; my mother's resignation; Aunt Dora's toughness"*: Mphahlele, *Down Second Avenue*, 133.

4: REVISION

For a discussion of the two versions of the late chapters of *Persuasion*, Jocelyn Harris's *A Revolution Almost Beyond Expression* is particularly helpful; it reprints large sections of the drafts so that a reader can witness the process of revision. I have quoted from Virginia Woolf's essay "Jane Austen," in *The Common Reader*; the long passage on pages 137–39 is extremely insightful about the gathering life that came in revision. It was Mary Lascelles who decided to include Austen's earlier draft as an appendix in the Oxford editions of the novel. James Edward Austen-Leigh included the draft chapter as an appendix after his *Memoir*.

88 *"sat like Patience on a monument"*: Shakespeare, *Twelfth Night*, Viola speaking to Orsino, II.iv.113–17.

88 *"women and fiction"* and *"the room and the money"*: Woolf, *A Room of One's Own*, 4.

90 *"had been the gradual performances"*: Henry Austen, "Biographical Notice of the Author," in Austen-Leigh, *A Memoir*, 138.

91 *"it is the one novel of the six"*: Gilbert Ryle, "Jane Austen and the Moralists," in *Critical Essays on Jane Austen*, ed. B. C. Southam, 113.

91 *"The stiffness and the bareness"*: Woolf, *Common Reader*, 137–38.

5: READING AGAIN

For discussion of Virginia Woolf's sense of Jane Austen, I learned from Emily Auerbach and Janet Todd, though most of course from Woolf herself. For illuminating discussion of the relationship between Jane Austen and Walter Scott, see Jocelyn Harris's "A Critique on Walter Scott," chapter six in *A Revolution Almost Beyond Expression*. For details on Jane Austen's books and influences, see also Jane Stabler, "Literary Influences," in *Jane Austen in Context*, ed. Janet Todd. For ideas of self-knowledge, my understanding is influenced by Matthew Boyle and what I have absorbed from papers of his, including "Transparent Self-Knowledge."

99 *"feral"* and *"a man's panic fear"*: Lionel Trilling, "Mansfield Park," in *The Opposing Self*, 209.

102 *"without hate, without bitterness"*: Woolf, *A Room of One's Own*, 68.

103 *"gorge on Jane Austen"*: Woolf, August 12, 1928, *The Diary of Virginia Woolf: Volume III, 1925–1930*, 190.

103 *"the niminy piminy spinster"*: Virginia Woolf to R. W. Chapman, November 20, 1936, *The Letters of Virginia Woolf: Volume VI, 1936–1941*, 87.

103 *"You cannot break off a scene"*: Virginia Woolf, "her greatness as an artist," unsigned review, *Times Literary Supplement*, May 8, 1913, in *The Critical Heritage, Volume II*, ed. B. C. Southam, 244.

103 *"two words at a time"*: Woolf, February 2, 1925, *Letters of Virginia Woolf: Volume III, 1923–1928*, 162.

104 *"At this moment, as so often happens in London"*: Woolf, *A Room of One's Own*, 96.

110 *"How she was able to effect all this"* and *"She wrote upon small sheets"*: Austen-Leigh, *A Memoir*, 81.

110 *"There was, between the front door and the offices"*: Austen-Leigh, *A Memoir*, 81–82.

112 *"ten thousand a-year"*: Walter Scott, *Waverley, or 'Tis Sixty Years Since* [1814], cited in Jocelyn Harris, *A Revolution Almost Beyond Expression*, 110.

123 *Johnson had written*: Samuel Johnson, "The New Realistic Novel," in *The Major Works*, 175–78.

124 *"is not attained"*: Stuart Tave, *Some Words of Jane Austen*, 30.

125 *"because he had behaved"*: George and Edward Lefroy, cited in Le Faye, *A Family Record*, 93.

126 *"At Ashe also"*: Austen-Leigh, *A Memoir*, 48.

126–27 *"met at some watering place"* and *"perhaps regretted"*: Catherine Hubback to James Edward Austen-Leigh, March 1, 1870, in Austen-Leigh, *A Memoir*, 191.

127 *"all the military furor"*: Lady Craven, quoted in Le Faye, *A Family Record*, 91.

127 *"wedded to each other"*: Fanny C. Lefroy, comment of her grandmother's in the unpublished manuscript "Family History," cited in Park Honan, *Jane Austen: Her Life*, 186.

127 *"always said her books were"*: Hubback to Austen-Leigh, March 1, 1870, in Austen-Leigh, *A Memoir*, 191.

6: MOURNFUL WORLD

For an account of Jane Austen's letter to Cassandra about *Pride and Prejudice* and the emergence of *Mansfield Park*, see Paula Byrne, *The Real Jane Austen*, page 207. Various ideas of the novel's emergence are also in Jocelyn Harris, *Satire, Celebrity, and Politics in Jane Austen*, and in the work of John Wiltshire.

141 *"vocation"*: Lionel Trilling, "Why We Read Jane Austen," in *The Moral Obligation to Be Intelligent*, 520–22.

7: FORGETTING

The history and biography surrounding *Mansfield Park* are particularly complex. For an account of the influence of Lord Mansfield on *Mansfield Park*, and the biographical intersections that took place at Godmersham in 1805, I am most indebted to Paula Byrne, *The Real Jane Austen*, and to Deirdre Le Faye's *Chronology*. For an understanding of the role of the navy in Jane Austen's life and work, and for detailing the experiences of her sailor brothers, Brian Southam's *Jane Austen and the Navy* is indispensable. For the brothers' experiences of slave ships, see Margaret Doody, *Jane Austen's Names*, page 313; Southam, page 51; and Byrne, pages 219–20. As noted in the text, numbers of enslaved persons exported from the British empire are from Slave Voyages (https://www.slavevoyages.org). Edward Said's *Culture and Imperialism* started many people on new considerations of *Mansfield Park*. As mentioned, I also caught a very helpful atmosphere from watching Patricia Rozema's 1999 film *Mansfield Park*. For the calendar of time within *Mansfield Park*, see Ellen Moody, http://www.jimandellen.org/austen/mp.calendar.html. For thinking about Jane Austen's reading and the ways it influenced her writing, I was very much helped by the works of Jocelyn Harris, and, for *Mansfield Park*, her *Jane Austen's Art of Memory*. Some particular considerations of Jane Austen's use of Shakespeare came to my attention in reading John Wiltshire, and especially through Jocelyn Harris's work. I first wrote about Austen and the theater out of my own preoccupations, and later was interested in Paula Byrne's *Jane Austen and the Theatre*.

153 *"Ye fallen avenues'"*: William Cowper, *The Task*, Book I, 1785.

161 *"Now I am reading the divine Jane"*: Samuel Beckett to Thomas McGreevy, February 14, 1935, in *The Letters of Samuel Beckett: Volume I, 1929–1940*, 250.

164 *"Grandmama, Aunts Cassandra & Jane"*: Fanny Knight, diary, as quoted in Deirdre Le Faye, *A Chronology of Jane Austen and Her Family*, 311.

165 *"knowledge of Richardson's works"*: Austen-Leigh, *A Memoir*, 71.

166 *"taken more entire possession of"*: Anna Lefroy, *Lefroy MS*, cited in Le Faye, *A Family Record*, 44.

167 *"No authority can be found for it"*: Somersett v Stewart, King's Bench, June 22, 1772, cited in Paula Byrne, *The Real Jane Austen: A Life in Small Things*, 215.

168 *"they themselves, once ferried"*: Cowper, *The Task*, Book II, 1785, quoted in Byrne, *Real Jane Austen*, 216.

168 *"her favorite moral writers"*: Henry Austen, "Biographical Notice of the Author," in Austen-Leigh, *A Memoir*, 141.

170 *"cruel proslavery delegate"*: Margaret Doody, *Jane Austen's Names: Riddles, Persons, Places*, 129.

171 *"a Black"*: Thomas Hutchinson, *The Diary and Letters of His Excellency Thomas Hutchinson* (1884–86), vol. 2, 277, entry for August 1779, cited in Byrne, *Real Jane Austen*, 214.

174 *"there simply is no common language"*: Edward Said, *Culture and Imperialism*, 96.

174 *"Time, and many perusals"*: Henry Austen's description of his sister's method, "Biographical Notice of the Author," in Austen-Leigh, *A Memoir*, 138.

175 *"Chaced a ship"*: Francis Austen, unpublished manuscript addition intended for second edition of John H. and Edith C. Hubback, *Jane Austen's Sailor Brothers* (1906), cited in Brian Southam, *Jane Austen and the Navy*, 189.

176 *"her own liberty"*: Francis Austen, "Remarks on the Island of St. Helena," written in April 1808, cited in Doody, *Jane Austen's Names*, 313.

178 *"the age of reason"*: Claire Tomalin, *Jane Austen: A Life*, 6.

178 *"Who has not seen these banished children"*: William Cobbett, from *Advice to Young Men* (1829), quoted in Tomalin, *Jane Austen*, 6.

179 *"It was her own doing"*: Anna Lefroy, "Recollections of Aunt Jane," written as a letter to James Edward Austen-Leigh, December 1864, included in Austen-Leigh, *A Memoir*, 160.

179 *"sat busily stitching"*: Anna Lefroy, "Recollections of Aunt Jane," in Austen-Leigh, *A Memoir*, 159.

185 *"larger and better administered spaces"*: Said, *Culture and Imperialism*, 88.

185–86 *"To earn the right to Mansfield Park"*: Said, *Culture and Imperialism*, 88.

186 *"taken more entire possession of"*: Anna Lefroy, *Lefroy MS*, cited in Le Faye, *A Family Record*, 44.

187 *"'With what intense desire'"*: William Cowper, *The Tirocinium, or a Review of Schools*, printed as part of *The Task*, 1785, cited in Byrne, *Real Jane Austen*, 26.

188 *"life for a moment"*: Trilling, "Why We Read Jane Austen," 521.

189 *"extremely tenacious"*: Henry Austen, "Biographical Notice of the Author," in Austen-Leigh, *A Memoir*, 141.

8: A FRIEND

As mentioned, for discussion of the relationship between the works of Jane Austen and Walter Scott, see Jocelyn Harris's "A Critique on Walter Scott," chapter six in *A Revolution Almost Beyond Expression*. For their permission to quote from their memorial texts for Susan Kister, I thank Hilary Cohen and Jessica Francis Kane.

199 *"a little bit"*: Byrne, *Real Jane Austen*, 193.

200 *"Read again and for the third time at least"*: Walter Scott, "Scott on Austen," in *Jane Austen: The Critical Heritage*, ed. B. C. Southam, 106.

201 *"calculating prudence"*: Walter Scott, "An Unsigned Review of *Emma*, *Quarterly Review*," in B. C. Southam, *Critical Heritage*, 68–69.

205 *"better than MP"*: Anne Sharp, in "Opinions of *Emma*: Collected and Transcribed by Jane Austen," probably 1816, in B. C. Southam, *Critical Heritage*, 55.

205 *"Dear dear Jane!"*: Cassandra Austen, quoted in Le Faye, *A Family Record*, 267.

9: IMAGINING

William Galperin has been of great importance in my long struggle with *Emma*. For Galperin's thoughts on Miss Bates and Mr. Knightley, see *The Historical Austen*, pages 189–96; for his thoughts on the presence of the gypsies, 44–66. I am also much indebted to the work of Frances Ferguson and to conversations with her. Lionel Trilling has been a recurring point of reference. My thoughts on dancing in Jane Austen began with Stuart Tave's lovely account in *Some Words of Jane Austen*, and this thinking was echoed and amplified when I encountered Azar Nafisi's experiences of dancing Austen in *Reading Lolita in Tehran*. For the lampoon of the prince regent, see Colleen Sheehan's two-part article in *Persuasions On-Line*. The links between Jane Austen and the Romantic poets have been considered by many; I first encountered a persuasive sense of Austen's relationship to Wordsworth through William Deresiewicz's *Jane Austen and the Romantic Poets*. I thank Amy Cohen for permission to quote her memorial letter of February 2017.

212 *"seeable and fathomable"*: William Galperin, *The Historical Austen*, 184.

212 *"I am going to take"*: Austen-Leigh, *A Memoir*, 119.

213 *"the liking flowed the other way"*: Etymonline, https://www.etymonline.com /word/like.

222 *"metaphors of leadership"*: Michael D. Cohen and James G. March, *Leadership and Ambiguity*, chapter two, 29–40.

224 *"We understand self-love"*: Lionel Trilling, introduction to *Emma*, x.

225 *"perhaps that is what Jane Austen meant"*: Trilling, introduction to *Emma*, xi.

229 *"She was fond of dancing"*: Henry Austen, "Biographical Notice of the Author," in Austen-Leigh, *A Memoir*, 139.

229 *"that enjoyment and ability"*: Tave, *Some Words of Jane Austen*, 1.

229 *"lacks the unerring taste"*: Woolf, "George Eliot," in *Common Reader*, 170.

230 *"The first thing you should do"*: Nafisi, *Reading Lolita in Tehran*, 258–66.

235 *"that interruption is an appeal"*: Coates, "Snobbery."

237 *"recognize Emma as good"*: Frances Ferguson, "Jane Austen, *Emma*, and the Impact of Form," 164–65.

237 *"Many years ago"*: Amy Cohen, unpublished letter, February 2017.

242 *"myself creating"*: Cowper, *The Task*, Book IV, 1785.

242 *"Of eye, and ear"*: Wordsworth, "Lines Composed a Few Miles Above Tintern Abbey," in *Selected Poetry of William Wordsworth*, ed. Mark Van Doren, 101–102.

248 *"little, nameless, unremembered, acts"*: Wordsworth, "Tintern Abbey," 100.

250 *"arguably the work of"*: Galperin, *Historical Austen*, 51.

250 *"She would, if asked"*: Austen-Leigh, *A Memoir*, 119.

10: LATE PERSUASIONS

258 *"If a sound can be preserved"*: Nafisi, *Reading Lolita in Tehran*, 187–88.

259 *"arrived in time to a moment"* and *"I am delighted with her"*: Charles Austen, in "Opinions of *Emma*: Collected and Transcribed by Jane Austen," probably 1816, in B. C. Southam, *Critical Heritage*, 57.

260 *"Her looks altered"*: Cassandra Austen to Fanny Knight, Sunday, July 20, 1817, in Deirdre Le Faye, *Jane Austen's Letters*, 344.

263 *"It comes back to me now"*: Anna Lefroy, "Recollections of Aunt Jane," in Austen-Leigh, *A Memoir*, 159.

SELECTED BIBLIOGRAPHY

The works here influenced my thinking about memoir, criticism, Austen, and form. Austen scholarship and reflection are vast, and similar ideas often originate at multiple points; below are the chief works from which I built my own thinking.

BOOKS

Alexander, Elizabeth. *The Light of the World*. New York: Grand Central Publishing, 2015.

Austen, Jane. *Emma*. Edited by R. W. Chapman. With an introduction by Lionel Trilling. Cambridge, MA: Riverside Press / Houghton Mifflin, 1957.

————. *Emma*. Edited by Richard Cronin and Dorothy McMillan. Cambridge: Cambridge University Press, 2005.

————. *Jane Austen's Letters*. 3rd ed. Collected and edited by Deirdre Le Faye. Oxford: Oxford University Press, 1995.

————. *Jane Austen's Letters to Her Sister Cassandra and Others*. Collected and edited by R. W. Chapman. Oxford: Clarendon Press, 1932.

————. *Mansfield Park*. Edited by James Kinsley. With an introduction and notes by Jane Stabler. Oxford: Oxford University Press, 2003. Reissued 2008.

————. *Northanger Abbey, Lady Susan, The Watsons, and Sanditon*. Edited and with notes by John Davie. Oxford: Oxford University Press, 1971. Reissued with an introduction by Terry Castle, 1990.

————. *Persuasion*. Edited by James Kinsley. With an introduction and notes by Deidre Shauna Lynch and further bibliography, notes, and appendices by Vivien Jones. Oxford: Oxford University Press, 2004.

————. *Pride and Prejudice*. New York: Random House, Vintage Classics, 2007.

————. *Pride and Prejudice*. With an afterword by Joann Morse. New York: Signet Classic, New American Library Penguin, 1980.

————. *Sense and Sensibility*. Edited by James Kinglsey. With an introduction by Margaret Anne Doody and notes by Claire Lamont. Oxford: Oxford University Press, 1980. Rev. ed., 2004; reissued 2008.

Austen-Leigh, James Edward. *A Memoir of Jane Austen and Other Family Recollections*.

With an introduction and notes by Kathryn Sutherland. Oxford: Oxford University Press, 2002.

Axelrod, Robert, and Michael D. Cohen. *Harnessing Complexity: Organizational Implications of a Scientific Frontier.* New York: Free Press, 1999.

Baldwin, James. *The Fire Next Time.* New York: Vintage International, 1993. First published 1963 by Dial Press (New York).

Barfield, Owen. *A Barfield Reader: Selections from the Writings of Owen Barfield.* Edited and with an introduction by G. B. Tennyson. Middletown, CT: Wesleyan University Press, 1999.

Beckett, Samuel. *The Letters of Samuel Beckett: Volume I, 1929–1940.* Edited by George Craig, Martha Dow Fehsenfeld, Daniel Gunn, and Lois More Overbeck. Cambridge: Cambridge University Press, 2009.

Birkerts, Sven. *The Art of Time in Memoir: Then, Again.* Minneapolis: Graywolf Press, 2008.

Brodsky, Joseph. *Watermark.* New York: Farrar, Straus and Giroux, 1992.

Byrne, Paula. *Jane Austen and the Theatre.* London: Hambledon and London, 2002.

———. *The Real Jane Austen: A Life in Small Things.* London: William Collins, 2014.

Coates, Ta-Nehisi. *The Beautiful Struggle.* New York: Spiegel & Grau, 2008.

———. *Between the World and Me.* New York: Spiegel & Grau, 2015.

Cohen, Michael D., and James G. March. *Leadership and Ambiguity: The American College President.* 2nd ed. Boston: Harvard Business School Press, 1986.

Clarkson, Thomas. *An Essay on the Slavery and Commerce of the Human Species, particularly the African.* Translated from a Latin Dissertation, which was Honoured with the First Prize, in the University of Cambridge, for the Year 1785, with Additions. London: J. Phillips, 1786. Online Library of Liberty, https://oll .libertyfund.org/titles/clarkson-an-essay-on-the-slavery-and-commerce-of-the -human-species.

Coleridge, S. T. *Biographia Literaria.* 2 vols. Edited with his aesthetical essays by J. Shawcross. Oxford: Oxford University Press, 1907. Reprinted lithographically, with corrections, 1965.

———. *Coleridge's Literary Criticism.* With an introduction by J. W. Mackail. Oxford: Oxford University Press, 1908. Reprinted 1949.

———. *Lectures and Notes on Shakespeare and Other Dramatists.* Oxford: Oxford University Press, 1931.

Cowper, William. *The Task.* London: J. Johnson, 1785; Project Gutenberg, 2015.

Danticat, Edwidge. *Brother, I'm Dying.* New York: Vintage Books, 2007.

Deresiewicz, William. *Jane Austen and the Romantic Poets.* New York: Columbia University Press, 2004.

———. *A Jane Austen Education.* New York: Penguin Press, 2011.

Dewey, John. *Art as Experience.* New York: Perigree, 1980. First published 1934 by Penguin Putnam (New York).

Doody, Margaret. *Jane Austen's Names: Riddles, Persons, Places.* Chicago: University of Chicago Press, 2015.

Doty, Mark. *Heaven's Coast.* New York: HarperCollins, 1996.

Dyer, Geoff. *Out of Sheer Rage: Wrestling with D. H. Lawrence*. New York: Farrar, Straus and Giroux, 1997.

Equiano, Olaudah. *The Interesting Narrative of the Life of Olaudah Equiano, or Gustavus Vassa, The African. Written by Himself*. Edited by Joanna Brooks. Chicago: Lakeside Press; R. R. Donnelly & Sons, 2004. First published 1789 (London).

Galperin, William H. *The Historical Austen*. Philadelphia: University of Pennsylvania Press, 2003.

Gornick, Vivian. *The Situation and the Story*. New York: Farrar, Straus and Giroux, 2001.

Greenblatt, Stephen. *Will in the World: How Shakespeare Became Shakespeare*. New York: W. W. Norton, 2004.

Harris, Jocelyn. *Jane Austen's Art of Memory*. Cambridge: Cambridge University Press, 1989.

———. *A Revolution Almost Beyond Expression: Jane Austen's* Persuasion. Newark: University of Delaware Press, 2007.

———. *Satire, Celebrity, and Politics in Jane Austen*. Lewisburg, MD: Bucknell University Press, 2018.

Henchman, Anna. *The Starry Sky Within: Astronomy & the Reach of the Mind in Victorian Literature*. Oxford: Oxford University Press, 2014.

Honan, Park. *Jane Austen: Her Life*. New York: Fawcett Columbine, Ballantine Books, 1987.

House, Humphry. *Coleridge: The Clark Lectures, 1951–52*. London: Rupert Hart-Davis, 1969.

Jasanoff, Maya. *The Dawn Watch: Joseph Conrad in a Global World*. New York: Penguin Press, 2017.

Jay-Z. *Decoded*. New York: Spiegel & Grau, 2011.

Johnson, Samuel. "The New Realistic Novel," *The Rambler*, no. 4, March 31, 1750. In *The Major Works*. Edited and with an introduction and notes by Donald Greene. Oxford: Oxford University Press, 1984. Reissued 2008.

Karr, Mary. *The Art of Memoir*. New York: HarperCollins, 2015.

Lazar, David, ed. *Truth in Nonfiction: Essays*. Iowa City: University of Iowa Press, 2008.

Le Faye, Deirdre. *A Chronology of Jane Austen and Her Family, 1600–2000*. Rev. ed. Cambridge: Cambridge University Press, 2013.

———. *Jane Austen: A Family Record*. 2nd ed. Cambridge: Cambridge University Press, 2004.

Lynch, Deidre Shauna. *Loving Literature: A Cultural History*. Chicago: University of Chicago Press, 2015.

Macdonald, Helen. *H Is for Hawk*. New York: Grove Press, 2014.

McCracken, Elizabeth. *An Exact Replica of a Figment of My Imagination*. New York: Back Bay Books, Little, Brown, 2008.

Mead, Rebecca. *My Life in Middlemarch*. New York: Broadway Books, 2015.

Miller, D. A. *Jane Austen, or The Secret of Style*. Princeton, NJ: Princeton University Press, 2003.

Mphahlele, Es'kia. *Down Second Avenue*. With a foreword by Ngugi wa Thiong'o. New York: Penguin Group, 1959. Rev. ed., 2013.

Mullan, John. *What Matters in Jane Austen? Twenty Crucial Puzzles Solved*. New York: Bloomsbury Press, 2014.

Nafisi, Azar. *Reading Lolita in Tehran: A Memoir in Books*. New York: Random House, 2003. Pbk. ed., 2008.

Nelson, Maggie. *The Argonauts*. Minneapolis: Graywolf Press, 2015.

Nicholsen, Shierry Weber. *The Love of Nature and the End of the World: The Unspoken Dimensions of Environmental Concern*. Cambridge, MA: MIT Press, 2002.

O'Rourke, Meghan. *The Long Goodbye*. New York: Riverhead Books, 2011.

Page, Scott E. *The Model Thinker: What You Need to Know to Make Data Work for You*. New York: Basic Books, 2018.

Rose, Phyllis. "Whose Truth?" In *Truth in Nonfiction: Essays*, edited by David Lazar, 31–41. Iowa City: University of Iowa Press, 2008.

Rosenbaum, Ron. *The Shakespeare Wars*. New York: Random House, 2006.

Rothschild, Emma. *The Inner Life of Empire*. Princeton, NJ: Princeton University Press, 2011.

Ruefle, Mary. *My Private Property*. New York: Wave Books, 2016.

Ryle, Gilbert. "Jane Austen and the Moralists." In *Critical Essays on Jane Austen*, edited by B. C. Southam, 106–22. New York: Routledge Kegan & Paul, 1968.

Sacks, Oliver. *Awakenings*. New York: Vintage Books, 1990. First published 1973 by Summit Books, Simon & Schuster (New York).

Said, Edward W. *Culture and Imperialism*. New York: Vintage Books, 1994.

Scarry, Elaine. *Dreaming by the Book*. Princeton, NJ: Princeton University Press, 2001. First published 1999 by Farrar, Straus and Giroux (New York).

Scott, Walter. "An unsigned review of *Emma, Quarterly Review*," and "Scott on Jane Austen." In *Jane Austen: The Critical Heritage*, edited by B. C. Southam, 58–69 and 106. London: Routledge, 1968.

Shakespeare, William. *A Midsummer Night's Dream*. Edited by Horace Howard Furness. New Variorum Edition of Shakespeare, Vol. 10. New York: Dover, 1963. First published 1895 by J. B. Lippincott (Philadelphia).

———. *The New Oxford Shakespeare: Modern Critical Edition*. Edited by Gary Taylor, John Jowett, Terri Bourus, and Gabriel Egan. Oxford: Oxford University Press, 2016.

Sheridan, Richard Brinsley. *The School for Scandal and Other Plays*. Edited and with an introduction and notes by Eric Rump. London: Penguin Books, 1988.

Shields, David. *Reality Hunger: A Manifesto*. New York: Vintage Books, 2011.

Simons, Judy, ed. *New Casebooks: Mansfield Park and Persuasion*. New York: St. Martin's Press, 1997.

Southam, B. C., ed. *Critical Essays on Jane Austen*. New York: Routledge Kegan & Paul, 1968. Reprint, 1987.

———. ed. *Jane Austen: The Critical Heritage*, London: Routledge, 1968.

———. ed. *Jane Austen: The Critical Heritage, Volume II, 1870–1940*. New York: Routledge, 1987. Reprint, 2009.

Southam, Brian. *Jane Austen and the Navy*. London: Hambledon and London, 2000.

Tave, Stuart. *Some Words of Jane Austen*. Chicago: University of Chicago Press, 1973.

Thompson, B. L., ed. *Prose of Lakeland: An Anthology*. Illustrated by W. Heaton Cooper. London: Frederick Warner, 1954.

Thoreau, Henry David. *Collected Essays and Poems*. Edited by Elizabeth Hall Witherell. New York: Library of America, 2001.

Todd, Janet, ed. *Jane Austen in Context*. Cambridge: Cambridge University Press, 2005.

———. *Jane Austen: New Perspectives*. Women & Literature, Volume 3. New York: Holmes & Meier Publishers, 1983.

Tomalin, Claire. *Jane Austen: A Life*. London: Penguin Books, 1998.

Trilling, Lionel. "Why We Read Jane Austen." In *The Moral Obligation to Be Intelligent*. Edited and with an introduction by Leon Wieseltier. New York: Farrar, Straus and Giroux, 2000.

———. *The Opposing Self: Nine Essays in Criticism*. New York: Viking Press, 1959.

Turner, Katherine, ed. *Selected Poems of Thomas Gray, Charles Churchill and William Cowper*. London: Penguin Books, 1997.

Wang, Jack, and Holman Wang. *Cozy Classics: Jane Austen's Pride and Prejudice*. Board book. Vancouver: Simply Read Books, 2012.

Warner, Sylvia Townsend. *Jane Austen: 1775–1817*. London: Longmans, Green for The British Council and The National Book League, 1951. Reprint 1961.

Woolf, Virginia. *The Common Reader: First Series*. Edited and with an introduction and notes by Andrew McNeillie. New York: Harcourt, 1984. First published 1925.

———. *The Diary of Virginia Woolf: Volume III, 1925–1930*. Edited by Anne Olivier Bell. New York: Harcourt Brace Jovanovich, 1980.

———. *The Letters of Virginia Woolf: Volume III, 1923–1928*. Edited by Nigel Nicholson and Joanne Trautmann. New York: Harcourt Brace Jovanovich, 1975.

———. *The Letters of Virginia Woolf: Volume VI, 1936–1941*. Edited by Nigel Nicholson and Joanne Trautmann. New York: Harcourt Brace Jovanovich, 1980.

———. *The Moment and Other Essays*. Edited by Leonard Woolf. New York: Harcourt, Brace, 1948. Renewed 1975.

———. *Moments of Being*. 2nd ed. Edited and with an introduction and notes by Jeanne Schulkind. New York: Houghton Mifflin Harcourt, 1985.

———. *A Room of One's Own*. With a foreword by Mary Gordon. New York: Harcourt, Brace, 1929. Reissued with introduction, 1981.

———. *The Second Common Reader*. New York: Harcourt, Brace, 1932. Reissued 1960.

Wordsworth, Dorothy. *The Grasmere and Alfoxden Journals*. Edited and with an introduction and notes by Pamela Woof. Oxford: Oxford University Press, 2002.

———. *The Letters of Dorothy Wordsworth*. Edited by Alan G. Hill. Oxford: Oxford University Press, 1981.

Wordsworth, William. *The Prelude, 1799, 1805, 1850*. Edited by Jonathan Wordsworth, M. H. Abrams, and Stephen Gill. New York: Norton Critical Editions, 1979.

———. *Selected Poetry of William Wordsworth*. Edited by Mark Van Doren and with an introduction by David Bromwich and notes by Michele Turner Sharp. New York: Modern Library, Random House, 2002.

Yagoda, Ben. *Memoir: A History*. New York: Riverhead Books, 2009.

ARTICLES, FILMS, ONLINE PUBLICATIONS, DATABASES, AND ONLINE RESOURCES

Auerbach, Emily. "The Geese vs. the 'Niminy Piminy Spinster': Virginia Woolf Defends Jane Austen." *Persuasions On-Line* (Jane Austen Society of North America) 29, no. 1 (winter 2008): http://www.jasna.org/persuasions/on-line/vol29no1/auerbach .html.

Auerbach, Nina. "Jane Austen's Dangerous Charm: Feeling as One Ought About Fanny Price." *Persuasions On-Line* (Jane Austen Society of North America) no. 2 (1980): http://www.jasna.org/persuasions/printed/number2/auerbach.htm.

Boyle, Matthew. "Transparent Self-Knowledge." *Proceedings of the Aristotelian Society*, Supplementary Volume LXXXV (2011): http://homepages.wmich.edu/~rvr5407 /6000readings/transparent%20self%20knowledge.pdf.

Coates, Ta-Nehisi. "Her Love Made No Answer . . ." *The Atlantic*, March 14, 2011, https://www.theatlantic.com/personal/archive/2011/03/her-love-made-no -answer/72428/.

———. "Jane Austen Just Dissed You." *The Atlantic*, February 18, 2011, https://www .theatlantic.com/entertainment/archive/2011/02/jane-austen-just-dissed-you /71437/.

———. "She Eats Writers Like Part of a Complete Breakfast." *The Atlantic*, March 7, 2011, http://www.theatlantic.com/entertainment/archive/2011/03/she-eats-writers -like-part-of-a-complete-breakfast/72095/.

———. "Snobbery." *The Atlantic*, March 1, 2011, http://www.theatlantic.com /entertainment/archive/2011/03/snobbery/71862/.

Cohen, Michael D. "A Letter Presented to Karl Weick on the Occasion of His ICOS Celebration." Written in April 2012. Published here in an appendix by permission of Karl Weick.

———. "Reading Dewey: Reflections on the Study of Routine." *Organization Studies* 28, no. 5 (May 1, 2007): 773–86.

Coleman, Tyrese L. "Reading *Jane Eyre* While Black." *LitHub*, August 28, 2017.

Etymonline. https://www.etymonline.com/, Copyright 2001–2019, Douglas Harper.

Ferguson, Frances. "Jane Austen, *Emma*, and the Impact of Form." *MLQ: Modern Language Quarterly* 61, no. 1 (March 2000): 157–80.

Hemingway, Collins. "How the 'Long War' Affected Jane Austen's Family and Her Novels." *Persuasions On-Line* (Jane Austen Society of North America) 39, no. 1 (winter 2018): http://www.jasna.org/publications/persuasions-online/volume-39-no-1 /how-the-long-war-affected-jane-austens-family-and-her-novels.

Mansfield Park (film). Written and directed by Patricia Rozema, produced by Sarah Curtis. Miramax Films. Released November 19, 1999.

Moody, Ellen. Calendars for *Sense and Sensibility, Pride and Prejudice, Mansfield Park*,

Emma, and *Persuasion*. http://www.jimandellen.org/austen/s&s.calendar.html; http://www.jimandellen.org/austen/p&p.calendar.html; http://www.jimandellen .org/austen/mp.calendar.html; http://www.jimandellen.org/austen/emma.calendar .html; http://www.jimandellen.org/austen/persuasion.calendar.html.

Mullan, John. "Noticing and Not Noticing." *London Review of Books* 36, no. 22 (November 20, 2014).

Rankine, Claudia. "The Condition of Black Life Is One of Mourning." *New York Times Magazine*, June 22, 2015.

Sense and Sensibility (film). Written by Emma Thompson, directed by Ang Lee, produced by Lindsay Doran. Columbia Pictures Mirage Enterprises. Released December 13, 1995.

Shakespeare's Words. https://www.shakespeareswords.com/, Copyright 2018, David Crystal and Ben Crystal.

Sheehan, Colleen. "Jane Austen's 'Tribute' to the Prince Regent: A Gentleman Riddled with Difficulty." *Persuasions On-Line* (Jane Austen Society of North America) 27, no. 1 (winter 2006): http://www.jasna.org/persuasions/on-line/vol27no1/sheehan .htm.

———. "Lampooning the Prince: A Second Solution to the Second Charade in *Emma*." *Persuasions On-Line* (Jane Austen Society of North America) 27, no. 1 (winter 2006): http://www.jasna.org/persuasions/on-line/vol27no1/sheehan2.htm.

Slave Voyages. https://www.slavevoyages.org/v.2.2.3, Copyright 2019 Emory University.

Southam, Brian. "Jane Austen's Sailor Brothers: Francis and Charles in Life and Art." *Persuasions On-Line* (Jane Austen Society of North America), no. 25 (2003).

Wiltshire, John. "'The Hartfield Edition': Jane Austen and Shakespeare." *Persuasions On-Line* (Jane Austen Society of North America), no. 21 (1999): http://www.jasna .org/persuasions/printed/number21/wiltshire.pdf.

ACKNOWLEDGMENTS

In these years of reading closely, I have been both near to and far from people I love. Reading has been a part of different experiences of distance—sometimes a solitude, sometimes a place of companionship. I have been grateful to be able to share the books I was reading and the book I wrote with friends.

Jessica Francis Kane's friendship and her writing are a part of the fabric of this book. She read it at every stage, and she took many long walks with me. Benjamin Lytal read the whole book twice, early on and late; his literary understanding has been very valuable. Maya Jasanoff was incisive, lucid, and kind, about history and about family, reading first drafts of first chapters and the very last of the last. Anna Henchman suggested and encouraged, and walked with me, often, around Fresh Pond. Vijay Seshadri, with whom I have been talking about writing for eighteen years, read with characteristic generosity and exhortation some four versions of these chapters. Every section of this book was first worked out either sitting at the door Matt Boyle turned into a desk or talking with him on the brown couch in the evenings. I have been guided by both his sense and his sensibility.

In professional life, too, I have close readers to thank. Eric Simonoff, agent and friend of twenty years, read this book in two versions, and helped me see it again each time. It is my good fortune to have written and revised three books for the wonderful editorial hand of Ileene Smith. I am grateful to have had the chance to work with her again. I would also like to thank the whole organization of Farrar, Straus and Giroux, including Jackson Howard, Na Kim, Lottchen Shivers, Abby Kagan, Carrie Hsieh, Jane Elias, Debra Helfand, Tanya Heinrich, Janet Renard, Jeff Seroy, Peter Richardson, Maia Sacca-Schaeffer, and many others. I am extremely grateful to have been the recipient of a Guggenheim Fellowship during the years when I was writing this book.

Close reading runs through the working life I have had in universities. My thanks to my own students of the past fifteen years, who have done so much to shape my understanding. To my insightful colleagues in creative writing at Sarah Lawrence College and at the University of Chicago. To Maud Ellmann and Julie Orlemanski and their classes, thoughtful interlocutors on *Persuasion* and *Emma*. To Sarah Johnson and Tina Post, new colleagues whose work helped me to grasp something about

Mansfield Park. And, especially, to Frances Ferguson, for her work on Austen and for illuminating conversation about criticism and the novels.

This book also grew out of university communities in which I grew up. The friendship of these kind people, and watching them work, has helped me to understand my father's ideas, and my mother's. To Massimo Warglien and Anna Gerotto, Robert Axelrod and Amy Saldinger, Sandy Ryder and Attila Huth, the late James and Jayne March, George Furness and Maria Slowiaczek, Carl Simon, Marjorie and Barry Checkoway, Dan Levinthal, Scott Page, John Padgett, Sidney Winter, and Paul Courant and Marta Manildi, my thanks. I am grateful to Karl Weick, for his generosity in sharing both letters my father wrote to him and his own thoughts about my dad and his work.

Looking back and looking out, there are years of close conversation in three cities. In New York: Lucy LaFarge, Justin Richardson and Peter Parnell, Tara Geer, Beth Schachter, and Peter Helm. In Cambridge: Natalie Dykstra, Dick Moran and Borgna Brunner, Amelie Rorty, and Claire Messud. In Chicago: Rachel DeWoskin, Susan Augustine and Daniel Sutherland, Gabriel and Jonathan Lear, Megan O'Grady, Giuliana Chamedes and Farid Masrour, Matthias Haase, Ben Laurence and Julie Oppenheimer, and Anton Ford and Salomé Skvirsky.

I am grateful to my family for all we have shared in these years, for many acts of kindness, generosity, and love, and for the contributions they made to this book. I want to thank my mother, Hilary Cohen, and Amy Cohen, Laura Helton, Hazel Cohen, and Zinnia Cohen. And I am very glad to thank the extended family who helped with the making and the remembering, especially Latham Boyle, who read all of Austen because he was curious, and to keep me company, Elina Mer, Lillian Boyle, Ivy and James Boyle, Alex Boyle, Stephanie Arnold and Mark Prieto, Daniel Arnold and Ashley Laird, Sage Laird, Patricia Kelvin, Taylor and Melissa Leonard, and Avi Leonard.

I talked about ideas in this book with three wise friends: Susan Kister, William Louis-Dreyfus, and our cousin Sophie Degan. All three of them died in these years, and I miss them.

Last, I want to say one more word of gratitude to the book's abiding presences for joining me within its pages. To Michael Cohen, who shared with me the work of making this space of imagination. To Sylvia Boyle and Tobias Boyle, beautiful illuminators. And to Matt Boyle.

A Note About the Author

Rachel Cohen is the author of *A Chance Meeting: Intertwined Lives of American Writers and Artists*, which won the PEN/Jerard Fund Award and was a finalist for the Guardian First Book Award, and *Bernard Berenson: A Life in the Picture Trade*, which was long-listed for the Jewish Quarterly–Wingate Literary Prize. Her essays have appeared in *The New Yorker*, *The New York Times*, *The Guardian*, the *London Review of Books*, *The Believer*, and other publications, and have been anthologized in *The Best American Essays*. She is the recipient of fellowships from the Guggenheim Foundation, the MacDowell Colony, and the New York Foundation for the Arts. She is Professor of Practice in the Arts in the creative writing program at the University of Chicago.